The Unschooled Mind

HOWARD GARDNER

THE UNSCHOOLED MIND

How Children Think and How Schools Should Teach

BasicBooks
A Division of HarperCollins*Publishers*

Library of Congress Cataloging-in-Publication Data
Gardner, Howard.
    The unschooled mind: how children think and how
schools should teach/Howard Gardner.
        p.   cm.
    ISBN 0–465–08895–3
    1. Cognitive learning.   2. Education—Aims and ob-
jectives.   I. Includes bibliographical references (p.   ) and
index.   II. Title. LB1062.G36   1991
370.15′2—dc20   91–70058
                                                                              CIP

For Jerome S. Bruner
And in memory of Lawrence A. Cremin

Contents

II   UNDERSTANDING EDUCATIONAL INSTITUTIONS

Acknowledgments

Many friends and colleagues gave me valuable feedback on this book. I would like to thank Mihaly Csikszentmihaly, William Damon, Robert Glaser, Peter Kugel, Ricardo Nemirovsky, and David Perkins for their helpful comments. I am especially indebted to Robbie Case, Mindy Kornhaber, and my wife, Ellen Winner, for their extremely careful readings of the manuscript and for many useful suggestions. My thanks, too, to Karen Donner, who helped in numerous ways with the preparation of this book, and to Mindy Kornhaber, who capably prepared the indexes. My colleagues at Harvard Project Zero have given me many valuable insights over the years, and I wish to express my general indebtedness to each of them.

I am also greatly indebted to the several funding agencies that have supported work by my colleagues and me over the past several years: the William T. Grant Foundation, the Lilly Endowment, the John D. and Catherine T. MacArthur Foundation, the James S. McDonnell Foundation, the Markle Foundation, the Pew Charitable

Trusts, the Rockefeller Brothers Fund, the Rockefeller Foundation, the Spencer Foundation, and the Veterans Administration.

The Unschooled Mind is my sixth book with Basic Books. I consider myself fortunate to have had a sustained and rewarding relationship with this fine publisher. Special thanks to Susan Arellano and Martin Kessler for many valuable editorial suggestions, and to Nina Gunzenhauser, Ellen Levine, Bill Davis, and Susan Zurn for their help in other phases of the book's preparation.

When I think about the individuals who made it likely that I would write this book, two names stand out. At Harvard in 1965 Jerome Bruner first introduced me to the cognitive approach to education; he has remained a friend and inspiration for over a quarter of a century. Several years ago, Lawrence Cremin saw promise in some initial ideas about a pedagogy centered on understanding; in his position as president of the Spencer Foundation, he encouraged me and my colleagues to pursue our notions in a systematic way. It is a privilege to have the opportunity to dedicate this book to these two remarkable persons.

CHAPTER

1

Introduction:
The Central Puzzles
of Learning

Many a person who has tried to master a foreign language in school has thought back wistfully to his (or her*) own learning of his native tongue. Without the help of a grammar book or a trained language instructor, without the sanctions of a course grade, all normal children readily acquire the language spoken in their vicinity. More remarkably, children who are too young to sit at a school desk but who happen to grow up in a polyglot environment can master a number of languages; they even know under which circumstances to invoke each tongue. It is humbling to realize that language learning in early life has operated exquisitely over the millennia, yet linguists are still unable to describe the grammar of any naturally occurring language in a completely satisfactory way.

One can, of course, attempt to dismiss language as a special case. After all, we are linguistic creatures, and perhaps we have special dispensation to speak, just as warblers and chaffinches sing as part of their avian birthright. Or one can stress the immense importance

*For expositional ease, I vary the gender forms from now on.

of language in all human intercourse; perhaps therein lies the solution to the question of why all children successfully master language within a few years of their birth.

Upon examination, however, language turns out to be unexceptional among human capacities. It is simply the most dramatic instance of one puzzle in human learning—the facility with which young humans learn to carry out certain performances that scholars themselves have not yet come to understand. During the first years of life, youngsters all over the world master a breathtaking array of competences with little formal tutelage. They become proficient at singing songs, riding bikes, executing dances, keeping scrupulous track of dozens of objects in their home, on the road, or along the countryside. In addition, though less visibly, they develop powerful theories of how the world works and how their own minds work. They are able to anticipate which manipulations will keep a machine from functioning properly; they can propel and catch balls hurled under various conditions; they are able to deceive someone else in a game even as they can recognize when someone is trying to play a trick on them. They evolve clear senses of truth and falsity, good and evil, beautiful and ugly—senses that may not always be consistent with communal standards but that prove remarkably serviceable and robust.

INTUITIVE LEARNING AND SCHOLASTIC LEARNING

We are faced with another puzzle. The very young children who so readily master symbol systems like language and art forms like music, the same children who develop complex theories of the universe or intricate theories of the mind, often experience the greatest difficulties upon their entry in school. Speaking and understanding language have proved unproblematic, but reading and writing may pose severe challenges; counting and numerical games are fun, but learning mathematical operations can prove vexing, and the higher reaches of mathematics may remain forbidding. Somehow the natural, universal, or intuitive learning that takes place in one's home or immediate surroundings during the first years of life seems of an entirely different order from the school learning that is now required throughout the literate world.

So far, this puzzle is not unfamiliar and has been commented upon often. Indeed, one might go so far as to claim that schools were instituted precisely to inculcate those skills and conceptions that, while desirable, are not so readily and naturally learned as the intuitive capacities cited above. Accordingly, most of the recent raft of books and reports about the "educational crisis" perseverate on the difficulties students have in mastering the overt agenda of school.

Such a description of the failings of school may be accurate as far as it goes, but in my view it does not go nearly far enough. In this book I contend that even when school appears to be successful, even when it elicits the performances for which it has apparently been designed, it typically fails to achieve its most important missions.

Evidence for this startling claim comes from a by now overwhelming body of educational research that has been assembled over the last decades. These investigations document that even students who have been well trained and who exhibit all the overt signs of success— faithful attendance at good schools, high grades and high test scores, accolades from their teachers—typically do not display an adequate understanding of the materials and concepts with which they have been working.

Perhaps most stunning is the case of physics. Researchers at Johns Hopkins, M.I.T., and other well-regarded universities have documented that students who receive honor grades in college-level physics courses are frequently unable to solve basic problems and questions encountered in a form slightly different from that on which they have been formally instructed and tested.* In a typical example, college students were asked to indicate the forces acting on a coin that has been tossed straight up in the air and has reached the midway point of its upward trajectory. The correct answer is that once the coin is airborne, only gravitational pull toward the earth is present. Yet 70 percent of college students who had completed a course in mechanics gave the same naive answer as untrained students: they cited two forces, a downward one representing gravity and an upward one from "the original upward force of the hand." This response reflects the intuitive or common-sense but erroneous view that an object cannot move unless an active force has somehow been transmitted to it from an original impelling source (in this instance, the hand or arm of the coin tosser) and that such a force must gradually be spent.

---

*Sources for all quotations, research findings, and allied factual information will be found in the notes beginning on page 265.

Students with science training do not display a blind spot for coin tossing alone. When questioned about the phases of the moon, the reasons for the seasons, the trajectories of objects hurtling through space, or the motions of their own bodies, students fail to evince the understandings that science teaching is supposed to produce. Indeed, in dozens of studies of this sort, young adults trained in science continue to exhibit the very same misconceptions and misunderstandings that one encounters in primary school children—the same children whose intuitive facility in language or music or navigating a bicycle produces such awe.

The evidence in the venerable subject of physics is perhaps the "smoking gun" but, as I document in later chapters, essentially the same situation has been encountered in every scholastic domain in which inquiries have been conducted. In mathematics, college students fail even simple algebra problems when these are expressed in wording that differs slightly from the expected form. In biology, the most basic assumptions of evolutionary theory elude otherwise able students who insist that the process of evolution is guided by a striving toward perfection. College students who have studied economics offer explanations of market forces that are essentially identical to those proffered by college students who have never taken an economics course.

Equally severe biases and stereotypes pervade the humanistic segment of the curriculum, from history to art. Students who can discuss in detail the complex causes of the First World War turn right around and explain equally complex current events in terms of the simplest "good guy–bad guy" scenario. (This habit of mind is not absent from political leaders, who are fond of portraying the most complicated international situations along the lines of a Hollywood script.) Those who have studied the intricacies of modern poetry, learning to esteem T. S. Eliot and Ezra Pound, show little capacity to distinguish masterworks from amateurish drivel once the identity of the author has been hidden from view.

Perhaps, one might respond, these distressing results are simply a further indictment of the American educational system, which has certainly experienced (and perhaps merited) its share of drubbing in recent years. And in fact the majority of the research studies have been carried out with the proverbial American college sophomore. Yet the same kinds of misconceptualizations and lack of understanding that emerge in an American setting appear to recur in scholastic settings all over the world.

4

What is going on here? Why are students not mastering what they ought to be learning? It is my belief that, until recently, those of us involved in education have not appreciated the strength of the initial conceptions, stereotypes, and "scripts" that students bring to their school learning nor the difficulty of refashioning or eradicating them. We have failed to appreciate that *in nearly every student there is a five-year-old "unschooled" mind struggling to get out and express itself.* Nor have we realized how challenging it is to convey novel materials so that their implications will be appreciated by children who have long conceptualized materials of this sort in a fundamentally different and deeply entrenched way. Early in the century, the work of Freud and other psychoanalysts documented that the emotional life of the young child strongly affects the feeling and behavior of most adults. Now the research of cognitive scientists demonstrates the surprising power and persistence of the young child's conceptions of the world.

Consider examples from two quite different domains. The changing seasons of the year come about as a function of the angle of the earth on its axis in relation to the plane of its orbit around the sun. But such an explanation makes little sense to someone who cannot shake the deeply entrenched belief that temperature is strictly a function of distance from a heating source. In the domain of literature, the appeal of modern poetry resides in its powerful images, its often unsettling themes, and the way in which the poet plays with traditional formal features. Yet this appeal will remain obscure to someone who continues to feel, deep down, that all poetry worthy of the name must rhyme, have a regular meter, and portray lovely scenes and exemplary characters. We are dealing here not with deliberate failures of education but rather with unwitting ones.

Unwitting, perhaps, but not necessarily unnoticed. That some of us may be at least dimly aware of the fragility of our knowledge was brought home to me powerfully in a conversation with my daughter, then a sophomore in college. One day Kerith phoned me, quite distressed. She voiced her concern: "Dad, I don't understand my physics course." Ever eager to assume the role of the patient and sympathetic father, I replied in my most progressive tone, "Honey, I really respect you for studying physics in college. I would never have had the nerve to do that. I don't care what grade you get—it is not important. What's important is that you understand the material. So why don't you go to see your teacher and see if he can help?" "You don't get it, Dad," responded Kerith decisively. "I've never understood it."

Without wishing to burden these words with cosmic importance,

I have come to feel that Kerith's comment crystallizes the phenomenon I seek to elucidate in these pages. In schools—including "good" schools—all over the world, we have come to accept certain performances as signals of knowledge or understanding. If you answer questions on a multiple-choice test in a certain way, or carry out a problem set in a specified manner, you will be credited with understanding. No one ever asks the further question "But do you *really* understand?" because that would violate an unwritten agreement: A certain kind of performance shall be accepted as adequate for this particular instructional context. The gap between what passes for understanding and genuine understanding remains great; it is noticed only sometimes (as in Kerith's case), and even then, what to do about it remains far from clear.

In speaking of "genuine understanding" here, I intend no metaphysical point. What Kerith was saying, and what an extensive research literature now documents, is that even an ordinary degree of understanding is routinely missing in many, perhaps most students. It is reasonable to expect a college student to be able to apply in a new context a law of physics, or a proof in geometry, or the concept in history of which she has just exhibited "acceptable mastery" in her class. If, when the circumstances of testing are slightly altered, the sought-after competence can no longer be documented, then understanding—in any reasonable sense of the term—has simply not been achieved. This state of affairs has seldom been acknowledged publicly, but even successful students sense that their apparent knowledge is fragile at best. Perhaps this uneasiness contributes to the feeling that they—or even the entire educational system—are in some sense fraudulent.

THREE CHARACTERS IN SEARCH OF A FRAMEWORK

In these opening pages I have in effect introduced three characters who will accompany us throughout this book:

- First, there is the *intuitive learner* (sometimes known hereafter as the natural, naive, or universal learner), the young child who is superbly equipped to learn language and other symbolic systems and who evolves serviceable theories of the physical world and of the world of other people during the opening years of life.

- Second, there is the *traditional student* (or scholastic learner), the youngster from age seven to age twenty, roughly, who seeks to master the literacies, concepts, and disciplinary forms of the school. It is these students who, whether or not they can produce standard performances, respond in ways similar to preschool or primary school youngsters, once they have been removed from the context of the classroom.
- Third, there is the *disciplinary expert* (or skilled person), an individual of any age who has mastered the concepts and skills of a discipline or domain and can apply such knowledge appropriately in new situations. Included in the ranks of the disciplinary experts are those students who are able to use the knowledge of their physics class or their history class to illuminate new phenomena. Their knowledge is not limited to the usual text-and-test setting, and they are eligible to enter the ranks of those who "really" understand.

Throughout this introductory discussion, these three characters will be lurking in the background. In coming to know each of them more intimately, we should receive not only insights into the puzzles of learning but clues to the creation of an educational system that could yield genuine understandings. In what follows, I introduce a number of other terms and distinctions that help me to flesh out my argument.

As we examine the three characters more closely, we find that each of them operates in accordance with several constraints—intrinsic or extrinsic factors that limit his behavior in specific ways—and demonstrates his understanding in characteristic types of performances. We will look first at the various kinds of constraints and then at the performances.

The intuitive learner reflects *neurobiological* and *developmental* constraints—constraints owing to species membership and to principles of human development that operate predictably in physical and social environments encountered all around the world. Children learn language as readily as they do, and in the ways in which they do, because there are strong constraints built into their nervous systems; such constraints powerfully affect the ways in which they initially refer to the world, categorize objects, and interact with other individuals. By the same token, children the world over develop comparable theories about the world in which they live and the persons with whom they communicate; these reflect an interaction between biological inclinations and the children's own construction of the world into which

7

they are born. These constraints, the result of hundreds of thousands of years of evolution, are very powerful, and, as we will have occasion to see over and over again, they prove very difficult to dissolve.

The fact that children are considered ready for school at a certain age, and that they can be expected to master specific skills and concepts in scholastic settings, probably reflects these neurobiological and developmental constraints. But the more profound constraints that operate on traditional students are of an extrinsic sort: the *historical* and *institutional* constraints that are embedded in schools. Schools have evolved over the centuries to serve certain societal purposes in certain ways. From the need to teach literacy to large numbers of young students to the pressures for turning out citizens who embody certain attitudes and virtues, schools reflect these constraints. The relative absence in schools of a concern with deep understanding reflects the fact that, for the most part, the goal of engendering that kind of understanding has not been a high priority for educational bureaucracies.

In relation to the disciplinary expert, the term "constraints" may at first seem inappropriate. After all, in some ways, experts are empowered to overcome constraints, to stretch their skills and concepts in new and even unanticipated directions. This state of enablement, however, is possible only because of a mastery that has been obtained, often quite painstakingly, over a number of years. Each discipline (like physics or history) and each domain (like chess or sculpture or marketing) exhibits its own particular practices and approaches, which have developed over its lengthy if idiosyncratic history. One cannot begin to master a domain, or to understand it, unless one is willing to enter into its world and to accept the *disciplinary* and *epistemological* constraints that have come to operate within it over the years.

Taken together, these constraints place severe limitations on what students can learn in educational settings and how they can achieve understanding. Yet the constraints often harbor opportunities as well, and it is up to the ingenious educator to exploit constraints as well as to seek to circumvent them.

Just as each of three central characters exhibits predictable constraints on his understanding, so too has each come to be associated with performances that reflect that understanding. As the behavioral psychologists of days past were fond of insisting, we cannot peer directly into the mind or the brain. And so, for our index of understanding, we will focus on three varieties of performance.

The young child masters a great deal of information and appears highly competent in her circumscribed world. As we have seen, the child can use and comprehend symbol systems fluently and can also offer workaday theories and explanations of the worlds of mind, matter, life, and self. Because of the ease with which these performances are expressed, I shall term them *performances of intuitive (naive or natural) understanding.* It should be emphasized that these understandings are often immature, misleading, or fundamentally misconceived; this is certainly the case with many of the protoscientific understandings embraced by young children. Such intuitive understandings are powerful, however, and in many instances they prove serviceable enough.

In the school context, educators have ordinarily sought and accepted *rote, ritualistic,* or *conventional performances.* Such performances occur when students simply respond, in the desired symbol system, by spewing back the particular facts, concepts, or problem sets they have been taught. Of course, "correct" responses in these circumstances do not preclude genuine understanding; they just fail to guarantee that such genuine understanding has occurred.

To these rote performances, I contrast *performances of disciplinary (or genuine) understanding.* Such performances occur when students are able to take information and skills they have learned in school or other settings and apply them flexibly and appropriately in a new and at least somewhat unanticipated situation. Of course, most problems are presented in a form that is at least marginally different from their original incarnation, but a performance of disciplinary understanding is most reliably elicited when a significant stretch from familiar territory is required. Such desirable performances occur, for example, when physics students invoke the appropriate laws of mechanics in explaining why a newly encountered apparatus or game operates in a certain way; when literature students can provide a reasoned judgment concerning the respective merit of two poems whose authorship is unknown to them; when history students who have studied the French and Russian revolutions are able to discuss the factors that have precipitated a contemporary revolutionary movement and to offer grounded predictions of what is likely to occur during the coming months. Disciplinary understanding is always changing and never complete; expertise is manifest when an individual embodies his culture's current understanding of the domain.

Thus we have encountered three characters, each operating under a particular set of constraints, each exhibiting a characteristic performance. Now it is conceivable that the existence of this trio could prove unproblematic in an educational sense. Possibly each one might be smoothly replaced by the next, with the intuitive learner giving way gradually to the scholastic learner, who is in turn replaced by the master of the discipline. In that case, this book could be a short one; perhaps none would be needed at all.

It is my claim, however, that these three characters do not mesh smoothly with one another and that the resultant gaps among them pose tremendous educational problems, particularly because those gaps have not until now been widely appreciated. I call attention to three gaps:

1. *The gap between the intuitive learner and the traditional student.* Students who have perfectly adequate intuitive understandings often exhibit great difficulty in mastering the lessons of school. It is these students who exhibit "learning problems" or "learning disorders," and it is their difficulties that have fueled many of the indictments of our educational system. Yet even those who prove successful in school typically fail to appreciate the gaps between their intuitive understandings and those that are embodied in the notations and concepts of schools.

2. *The gap between the traditional student and the disciplinary expert.* This gap has been dramatically revealed by recent cognitively oriented research. Even esteemed students typically do not successfully transfer their knowledge to new settings, and, worse, they typically do not appreciate that they have fallen back on the powerful but naive understandings of early childhood. Hence the traditional student emerges as at least as remote from the disciplinary expert as the younger, intuitive learner.

3. *The gap between the intuitive learner and the disciplinary expert.* These two characters share the benign property that they can use their skills and knowledge in a fluent way: Their current comprehension seems to be less studied and more easily elicited than that exhibited by students attempting to invoke the knowledge obtained— often arduously—in school. Yet it is crucial to appreciate that the two understandings are of a fundamentally different order. In the intuitive case, one is encountering the natural but naive understandings that have evolved over the centuries to yield a reasonably serviceable first-order grasp of the world. In the case of the disciplinary expert, one is encountering understandings that have arisen on the part of scholars and artisans who have worked in a self-conscious

and cumulative fashion in their respective disciplinary preserves. These individuals have sought to establish concepts and practices that provide the best possible account of the world in which we live, even when that account flies in the face of long-standing intuitions, received wisdom, or unwitting but well-entrenched stupidity. Instead of accepting the earth as flat, they have—in the spirit of Christopher Columbus—amassed evidence that it is spherical in shape.

Why, one may ask, should we care about erasing these gaps? And, in particular, why is it important that natural or scholastic understandings give way to disciplinary understandings? To my mind, the answer is simple: The understandings of the disciplines represent the most important cognitive achievements of human beings. It is necessary to come to know these understandings if we are to be fully human, to live in our time, to be able to understand it to the best of our abilities, and to build upon it. The five-year-old knows many things, but he cannot know what disciplinary experts have discovered over the centuries. Perhaps our daily lives might not be that different if we continue to believe that the world is flat, but such a belief makes it impossible for us to appreciate in any rounded way the nature of time, travel, weather, or seasons; the behaviors of objects; and the personal and cultural options open to us. And it was because Christopher Columbus dared to entertain a contrasting belief that he embarked on a journey of fateful consequences.

THE SEVEN INTELLIGENCES

Up to this point, I have treated all students as if they learned in the same way and displayed the same kinds of conceptions or misconceptions, understandings or misunderstandings, rote performances or, more happily, performances of disciplinary (genuine) understanding. This ploy is defensible because certain features do characterize the learning of all students, or at least of the vast majority.

Another leitmotif emerging from recent cognitive research, however, documents the extent to which students possess different kinds of minds and therefore learn, remember, perform, and understand in different ways. There is ample evidence that some people take a primarily linguistic approach to learning, while others favor a spatial or a quantitative tack. By the same token, some students perform best when asked to manipulate symbols of various sorts, while others are better able to display their understanding through a hands-on demonstration or through interactions with other individuals.

I have posited that all human beings are capable of at least seven different ways of knowing the world—ways that I have elsewhere labeled the *seven human intelligences*. According to this analysis, we are all able to know the world through language, logical-mathematical analysis, spatial representation, musical thinking, the use of the body to solve problems or to make things, an understanding of other individuals, and an understanding of ourselves. Where individuals differ is in the strength of these intelligences—the so-called *profile of intelligences*—and in the ways in which such intelligences are invoked and combined to carry out different tasks, solve diverse problems, and progress in various domains.

The tenets of multiple intelligences (MI) theory are not a necessary part of the analysis undertaken here, but some acknowledgment that people do learn, represent, and utilize knowledge in many different ways is important to my argument. Such well-documented differences among individuals complicate an examination of human learning and understanding. To begin with, these differences challenge an educational system that assumes that everyone can learn the same materials in the same way and that a uniform, universal measure suffices to test student learning. Indeed, as currently constituted, our educational system is heavily biased toward linguistic modes of instruction and assessment and, to a somewhat lesser degree, toward logical-quantitative modes as well.

I argue that a contrasting set of assumptions is more likely to be educationally effective. Students learn in ways that are identifiably distinctive. The broad spectrum of students—and perhaps the society as a whole—would be better served if disciplines could be presented in a number of ways and learning could be assessed through a variety of means.

One consequence of the current situation is that many people unjustifiably deemed successes, as well as many needless casualties, emerge from contemporary educational systems. Those students who exhibit the canonical (in our terms "scholastic") mind are credited with understanding, even when real understanding is limited or absent; many people—including at times the author of this book and his daughter—can pass the test but fail other, perhaps more appropriate and more probing measures of understanding. Less happily, many who are capable of exhibiting significant understanding appear deficient, simply because they cannot readily traffic in the commonly accepted coin of the educational realm. For instance, there is a significant population that lacks facility with formal examinations but can display relevant understanding when problems arise in natural contexts. One aim of this book is to suggest educational interventions and assessments that might better serve such a population.

While the recognition of different ways of representing and acquiring knowledge complicates matters in certain ways, it is also a hopeful sign. Not only are chances of acquiring understanding enhanced if multiple entry points are recognized and utilized, but in addition, the way in which we conceptualize understanding is broadened. Genuine understanding is most likely to emerge, and be apparent to others, if people possess a number of ways of representing knowledge of a concept or skill and can move readily back and forth among these forms of knowing. No one person can be expected to have all modes available, but everyone ought to have available at least a few ways of representing the relevant concept or skill.

Excepting this last point, our discussion thus far has been rather devoid of cheer. There are three characters, each relatively secure in her own practices, each reflecting her own peculiar constraints and performances. But there are disturbing gaps among the characters and little sign that the desired goal of disciplinary understanding can be readily achieved.

I would not have undertaken this study merely to document the vexed difficulties of obtaining an education for understanding. Rather, it is my belief that a fuller understanding of each of these characters—their constraints as well as their potentials—contains within it clues crucial for the mounting of a more effective educational system. In the concluding chapters of this book, I review a number of efforts that show promise of bridging the gaps among the different characters, of yielding more potent educational approaches. Intriguingly, I find clues for these efforts in highly contrasting institutions: the ancient institution of the apprenticeship and the new institution of the children's museum.

THE FRAMEWORK FOUND

In the aggregate, then, we face intriguing puzzles. First, children come to master many apparently complex domains easily, but not those matters for which schools have been designed. Second, and perhaps more disturbingly, even those students who apparently succeed in school often have not understood in a deep sense the very concepts and principles around which their educational program has been designed.

Complicating this picture yet further, I have questioned the assumption that all children learn in the same way. Studies of cognition suggest that there exist many different ways of acquiring and representing knowledge; these individual differences need to be taken into account in our pedagogy as well as in our assessments. Sometimes students who cannot pass muster on the usual measures of competence reveal significant mastery and understanding when these have been elicited in a different, more appropriate way. One finds intimations everywhere of the familiar disjunction between the literate person who can read the instructions perfectly but cannot assemble the machine and the illiterate person who can determine at a glance just where every part fits. This differentiated view of the mind harbors hope. Different students may be reached in quite different ways, and the disciplinary expert emerges as one who can exhibit his mastery in multiple, flexible modes.

In an effort to clarify these various puzzles and complications, I have identified a set of characters, constraints, performances, gaps, and bridges. These factors are summarized in the accompanying table as a quick overview of what is to come.

Framework for Educational Understanding at a Glance

Characters			
	Intuitive learner (also natural, naive, or universal)	Scholastic learner (also traditional student)	Disciplinary expert (also skilled person)
Age	Up to age 7	School age	Any age
Constraints	Neurobiological, developmental	Institutional, historical	Disciplinary, epistemological
Performances	Intuitive understanding	Rote, ritualized, and conventional understanding	Disciplinary understanding

14

Other Factors		
Gaps	Intelligences	Bridges
Intuitive-scholastic	Linguistic	Traditional apprenticeships
Scholastic-disciplinary	Logical-mathematical	Contemporary children's museums
Intuitive-disciplinary	Spatial	
	Musical	
	Bodily-kinesthetic	
	Interpersonal	
	Intrapersonal	

Clearly the ensemble of circumstances captured in the framework should be of concern to anyone interested in education, whether in the troubled educational system in the United States or in apparently less disabled educational systems abroad. Both the gaps uncovered and the bridges discerned merit consideration. Yet I believe that the significance of this scheme extends beyond the walls of the school-house, touching on issues of human nature, human institutions, and human values.

HUMAN NATURE, INSTITUTIONS, AND VALUES: THE PLAN FOR THIS BOOK

The kinds of materials and skills that we master easily seem to be those to which the species is especially attuned. Potent evolutionary reasons allow certain realms (like language) to be mastered in a natural way; by the same token, otherwise adaptive factors may give rise to the misconceptions and stereotypes that emerge as so troublesome in a school setting. It is presumably no accident that five-year-olds have clear notions of what it means to be alive (that something is moving), that they tend to interpret events in terms of "good guys" versus "bad guys," and that they see themselves as capable of imparting force to objects or persons; these simplifying assumptions can help them survive and even triumph in their daily arena.

Addressing such issues, the savants of the eighteenth century wrote unembarrassedly about "human nature" and "human understanding." In this book, I favor the phrase "constraints on human knowledge." As we come to comprehend better the mind of the young child, its inclinations and its constraints, we may achieve some insights into our minds and, perhaps, into the human mind in general.

No less than human beings, human institutions exhibit constraints. Schools or factories or offices may be malleable, but they are not infinitely so. Economies of scale, vexations of human relations, bureaucratic histories, diverse and changing expectations, and pressures for accountability burden all significant human institutions. In the past, serving a smaller and less diverse clientele, schools faced certain problems; today, in a rapidly changing world, where the schools are expected to serve the multiple needs of every young individual, the limitations of this institution are sometimes overwhelming. If one wishes to bring about change in the schools, it is important to understand their modes of operation no less than one understands the operations of individuals within them. Accordingly, following the investigation of constraints on human knowing, I consider some limits governing educational institutions, most especially schools.

A focus on children and schools brings us face-to-face with a third dimension: the question of which knowledge and performances we value. If one considers school strictly as a place in which certain criteria are to be met (say, for the purposes of certification), it matters not what use one can subsequently make of the skills and knowledge acquired there. One could readily tolerate schools where understanding was considered irrelevant or even noxious. But if one wishes to argue that school should relate to a productive life in the community, or that certain kinds of understanding ought to be the desiderata of education, then the research results I have described are consequential.

In such a discussion it is important to indicate when one is being descriptive and when one has moved toward prescription. In this book, for the most part, I describe the value systems of individuals, institutions, and cultures as I have found them. In the final portions of the book, however, I move quite explicitly toward prescription. I take a stand in favor of a certain kind of education, one that yields "generative" or "deep" or "genuine" understandings.

This trio of concerns—human nature, human institutions, human values—forms the structure of this book as well as the backdrop against which our three characters are encountered and described. In Part I, I present my synthesis of current knowledge about how human beings develop and learn during the early years of life—the way that the powerful unschooled mind of the five-year-old comes into being and its major properties, conceptions, and limitations. The survey is deliberately broad, including a review of earlier efforts to conceptualize the developing mind. Only if we examine critically the ways in which scientists have approached issues of human development can we evaluate the significance of recent claims about the mind of the young child.

Throughout the survey of cognitive development in early childhood, I pay particular heed to those inclinations and constraints that are likely to play a prominent role in our schools and in other learning environments. I contrast the sensorimotor and symbolic forms of knowing available to every normal individual with the more rarefied notational, conceptual, and epistemic forms of knowing, which cause appreciable difficulty for many, perhaps most, children when they enter that sharply chiseled environment called school. Only in the light of detailed knowledge about the particular configurations of mind in the young child is it possible to appreciate their considerable distance from the agenda of school.

Most of the work described in the opening chapters is known to researchers in psychology, cognitive science, and education, but it is little known to the wider public, and its unsettling implications for education are only beginning to be understood even within the scholarly community. In Part I, I wear the hat of a cognitively oriented scientist, attempting to describe the human mind "as it is," but even without tackling the connotations of that ontologically loaded phrase, I must stress that the presentation of the developmental evidence is a personal and, at times, perhaps even a tendentious one.

The emphases in the second part of this book fall on a different set of focal points: the educational process in general, the particular institutions called schools, and the norms embedded in these cultural institutions. Education has been a principal goal of all cultures (Can one conceptualize a culture devoid of educational concerns?), and cultures have employed a multitude of approaches for the education of their young. During much of human history, some form of apprenticeship has been the educational mode of choice. Schools—quite specialized kinds of educational institutions—have evolved in human societies for a variety of reasons, and it is important to understand the nature and constraints of the processes that have led from the apprenticeships of earlier times to the schools of yesterday and today.

A concern with educational institutions seems to me inseparable from the goals they are designed to achieve and the values they embody. To be sure, many of these goals and values are not particularly cognitive in nature; to the extent that that is true, I shall note but not dwell on them. Just as surely, however, the leaders of a society have clear learning outcomes in mind when they create certain kinds of educational institutions, admit certain students, and assess their success or failure using certain kinds of tests. And even in instances where the educators' own thoughts about goals or values have been implicit or confused, it is important for analysts to attempt to get them straight.

On this issue my own assumptions are quite clear, and they ought to be reiterated here. Whatever their other cognitive and noncognitive facets, educational institutions—and preeminently schools—ought to seek to inculcate in their students the highest degree of understanding. I call into question the desirability of performances that are merely rote, ritualized, or conventional, and in so doing, I take issue with many traditional educators who call for "basic skills," "cultural literacy," or the mandating of standardized tests. By the same token, I embrace the position that educational institutions need to reach the broadest number of students and that they must therefore be responsive to different forms of learning, performance, and understanding.

In endorsing an education for understanding, I should stress once more that I have in mind here no esoteric meaning; I mean simply a sufficient grasp of concepts, principles, or skills so that one can bring them to bear on new problems and situations, deciding in which ways one's present competences can suffice and in which ways one may require new skills or knowledge. An important symptom of an emerging understanding is the capacity to represent a problem in a number of different ways and to approach its solution from varied vantage points; a single, rigid representation is unlikely to suffice. Nearly every teacher I know would claim to teach for understanding; certainly I would make that claim myself. But if pressed to demonstrate that our students understand—indeed, that we ourselves are able to display convincing understanding—we soon realize how slender is the reed of our confidence.

The heart of the problem is documented in chapters 8–9. There I lay out a portion of the overwhelming evidence documenting the limited nature of student understanding across the disciplines. I risk overkill in order to stress how pervasive this problem is and how little appreciated it has been until now. If we educators are to tackle this nexus of difficulties, it is essential that we confront it directly: Teacher, educate thyself!

In the third and concluding portion of the book I adopt, in a tentative vein, the mantle of the educational reformer, or perhaps more aptly the social engineer. While the difficulties en route to achieving understanding are significant, they are not insurmountable. I am convinced that an education for understanding is possible, that it can be extended to the vast majority of students, and that a society that strives to achieve understanding will be the better for it in humane as well as in economic terms. Part of my presentation is programmatic and speculative, but the larger portion builds upon the analysis of constraints in earlier chapters and upon experiments in which I and many other colleagues around the world have been engaged. This analysis allows me to recommend a number of specific interventions that can dissolve the powerful misconceptions and stereotypes entertained by the unschooled mind.

If we cannot today implement an education that yields full understanding, we can certainly do a much better job than we have done up to this point. The process of achieving such an education ought to be challenging and enriching, far more so than the implementation of the less ambitious education with which we have been saddled—even in places where students are required to work on their assignments until the wee hours of the morning. Important clues for the achievement of such an education come from venerable sources such as the traditional apprenticeship; equally important clues come from new sources of evidence, ranging from recently developed technologies like videodisks to newly evolving institutions such as children's museums. But to achieve such a goal we—especially we in the United States—may need to rethink many of our most cherished assumptions about how we set our educational goals and go about achieving them. For example, instead of cultural literacy, we may need to call for understandings shared by all students; and instead of local control of educational policy, we may need to embrace single, nationwide standards whereby these understandings can be authentically assessed.

The principal question addressed in this book can now be stated succinctly: Why do members of a species who master certain concepts and skills so readily exhibit so much difficulty in obtaining the skills and understandings that school at its best strives to provide? The question may appear an old one, but neither its proper formulation nor the evidence relevant to it has been fully appreciated until now. Only a mastery of scientific knowledge about human development and learning, considered in the light of institutional history and constraints, allows us to grasp the problem in its fullness.

An understanding of the constraints that govern children and schools is a necessary prerequisite for the improvement of education. In my view, the key to a better education lies in uncovering ways to connect our three characters: the intuitive five-year-old learner, featuring her conceptions and constraints; the traditional student working in an institution with its agenda and customary mode of operations; and the disciplinary expert, who can extend skills and understanding in new ways.

Once one has conceptualized the problem in this way, its value dimension becomes manifest, for what we choose to teach and how we choose to evaluate reflect what we deem important in our society and in human life. I argue that an education geared to understanding is the proper one to pursue and that our burgeoning knowledge about human development and institutional arrangements can and ought to be mobilized toward those ends. My own recommendations about how to achieve those ends form the concluding themes of this book.

PART

I

The "Natural" Learner

CHAPTER

2

Conceptualizing the Development of the Mind

I n 1840 Charles Darwin began to keep a diary on the activities of his first-born infant son, William. Darwin noted William's early reflexes, contrasting them with subsequently learned behaviors. He examined the child's sensory systems, noting for example that William gazed at a candle on his 9th day, attended to a brightly colored tassel on his 49th day, and attempted to seize objects on his 132d day. William's "higher senses," including memory, language, curiosity, and reasoning powers, were also surveyed. Countless parents had made such observations before, but Darwin was perhaps the first to publish his observations, as he did, thirty-seven years later in the second volume of the British journal *Mind*.

Darwin realized, as medieval painters apparently had not, that infants and young children are not just miniature versions of adults. While there is a continuity between the young child and the mature adult, just as there is between human beings and their primate antecedents, there exists a developmental or evolutionary process through which every human being must pass. Through his own example as an observant parent, and by dint of his seminal ideas about the evolution of the species, Darwin did more than any other figure to stimulate scientific study of the mind of the child.

EARLY STUDIES OF THE MIND

At first, observers of young children were content simply to chronicle what they had seen. Nor, in an embryonic science, is this an ill-chosen point of departure. Before one can tease out underlying laws, first principles, or causal models, it is well to have the facts laid out. As part of a communal effort to establish these basic facts, there began to emerge around 1900 a considerable number of "baby biographies," elaborate notebooks kept by doting parents, aunts, and uncles about the young children in their charge or within their purview. This period of scientific history is less remote than it may seem. In the 1940s and 1950s, while Dr. Benjamin Spock was prescribing the measures whereby children might maintain physical health, Dr. Arnold Gesell laid out the calendrical milestones that mark normal child development. Parents all over the United States, and in many other countries as well, flushed with pride when their five-year-old jumped higher than "the norms," even as they fretted nervously when their child grew fewer inches or remembered fewer numbers than others of her cohort.

At the same time that Gesell was sharing his pediatric research with the general public, a highly vocal school of psychology was dominating professional discussions of human growth. That branch, labeled "learning theory" or "behaviorism," also traced its origins to Darwin. But whereas the Gesellians were content to chronicle the orderly milestones of development, systematic thinkers like John B. Watson and B. F. Skinner were more ambitious; they wanted to *explain* development and to do so in as plain and decisive a fashion as possible. Not for them any qualitative differences between animal and human, or between child and adult; an older child was simply a more knowledgeable and more efficient toddler. Nor was there any need to consider the intricacies of the brain; behavior could be explained readily in a "black-box" fashion. Indeed, organisms of all stripes—be they Norwegian rats or college sophomores—simply did what they were rewarded or "reinforced" to do and quickly "extinguished" those behaviors that were not so prized. A human being could learn to do almost anything that his surroundings dictated and could as readily cease a line of behavior once the environment judged it to be dysfunctional. There was no need for legitimate scientists to invoke "idealistic" emotions like love or "fuzzy" concepts like ideas, ideals, or imagination. As for the brain, that was a matter for physiologists or surgeons, not psychologists. All that mattered were the overt behaviors that could be objectively observed and measured across the animal kingdom.

For a while the behaviorist approach held sway. In the research laboratory it gave rise to many laws of learning that seemed to hold reasonably well for rats or for pigeons, but that proved disturbingly remote when it came to organisms that reasoned, conversed, or composed. In the home it gave optimism to those whose children may have seemed modestly endowed ("anything is possible"). But it frustrated those ordinary souls who continued to experience proscribed emotions like "love" or to believe in proscribed concepts like "ideas."

Explicit theories about child development are not only of interest to scientists and to laypersons (not necessarily for the same reasons) but also highly relevant to educators. Whether consciously or not, all educators harbor conceptions of what the child's mind is like at birth or upon entry to school, what sorts of educational goals can be accomplished readily, and which goals require extensive engineering or may even prove impossible to achieve. In subsequent chapters I put forth my own conception of the development of the child's mind during early childhood and the way in which this "natural mind" clashes with the agenda of the school. Inasmuch as this conception builds upon and responds to previous portraits of the child's mental processes, it is important to consider these briefly here.

JEAN PIAGET'S PIONEERING STUDIES OF COGNITIVE DEVELOPMENT

In science, as the historian of science Thomas Kuhn has taught us, theories do not die because they are deficient; they fade away when other, more appealing, more compelling, and more comprehensive views come to the fore. For scientists like me, trained after midcentury in the wake of the behaviorist era, the study of child development had received a marvelous breath of fresh air. The air wafted in from the shores of Lake Geneva, where, since the 1920s, a brilliant biologist-turned-psychologist named Jean Piaget had been studying children. For the most part these were normal children, youngsters attending good Genevan schools like the Maison des petits de l'Institut Jean

Jacques Rousseau, as well as Piaget's own three children—Lucienne, Jacqueline, Laurent—whose nursery antics have become familiar lore among students of human development.

True to the spirits of Rousseau and Darwin, Piaget conceptualized the course of human development as lengthy and complex. Children are not born with knowledge, as a Cartesian might have maintained; nor is knowledge simply thrust upon them, as the British empiricist philosophers had argued. Instead, each child must construct his own forms of knowledge painstakingly over time, with each tentative action or hypothesis representing his current attempt to make sense of the world.

Like a watchmaker poring over the many interlocking parts of an intricate mechanism, Piaget embarked upon a lifetime course of observing and explaining the development of the child's mind across a whole host of cognitive domains. The titles of his books communicate his grand research program: a few volumes of synthesis like *The Psychology of Intelligence* and *The Psychology of the Child*, supported by dozens of monographs treating more specific themes like *The Child's Conception of Space, The Child's Conception of Geometry, The Child's Conception of Time, The Child's Conception of Physical Causality,* and *The Moral Judgment of the Child.*

An extremely ingenious observer and experimenter, Piaget bequeathed to the emerging science of developmental psychology many, if not most, of its classic demonstrations. Among the most notable are the conservation problems, in which children must judge, for example, whether two globular mounds once similar in appearance continue to contain the same amount of clay when one has been rolled into sausage (or, alternatively, into pancake) form; the object permanence problem, in which an infant either continues or fails to continue to search for an object that has disappeared from sight; and the intentional moral dilemmas, which ask the child to decide, for example, whether it is worse to break a single dish while one is trying to steal a cookie or to break a whole stack of plates while one is trying to help a friend.

At heart a monist, Piaget discerned a common thread across these domains of experience. According to the Piagetian analysis, every child passes through roughly the same stages in the same order, whether he is negotiating the domain of causality or the domain of morality. Moreover, and crucially, each stage involves a fundamental reorganization of knowledge, a reorganization so profound that the child does not even have access to his earlier forms of understanding.

Once he is out of a stage, it is as though the prior stage had never happened.

During infancy, according to Piaget, the child comes to know the world in a "sensorimotor" way, constructing the first forms of knowledge of time, space, number, and causality in a virtually lock-step fashion. A five-month-old has the capacity to repeat simple actions purposefully, and this capacity obtains across domains; the year-and-one-half-old infant has the capacity to imagine an object when it is no longer present, again across domains.

As the child moves from infancy into early childhood, she now acquires a "preoperational" or "intuitive" sense of concepts like number and causality: She can draw upon them in a practical situation, but she cannot use them in a systematic or logical manner. So, for example, the three-year-old will choose one pile of candies as more numerous because the contents have been spread out over a larger area, and she will change her judgment when the same number of chocolates have been bunched together. Or, to cite another example, the four-year-old will confuse the meaning of the word *because;* she is as likely to say "The sun is shining because I am hot" as to say "I am hot because the sun is shining."

More advanced stages are marked by the two forms of "operational thinking." The young schoolchild of seven or eight is capable of "concrete operational thinking." Here the child has mastered those causal and quantitative understandings that eluded him when he was younger. He can now appreciate that the number of candies in a pile remains constant so long as nothing has been added or taken away; that the same objective scene looks different to individuals who are seated at different vantage points; that an object positioned behind another object will eventually pass it provided that the former object is moving in the same direction at a faster rate. According to Piaget these new understandings are sufficiently powerful that they annihilate earlier conceptions: the "conserving" child can no longer recreate the mental set of the "nonconserver." Note, however, that all of these understandings are embedded in the concrete specifics of the problem; the child must have the opportunity to watch the objects and to try out experiments for himself.

In contrast, for those adolescents at the "formal operational" stage, the presence of concrete stimuli and the need for concrete activities are no longer necessary. A formal operator is able to reason exclusively on the level of propositions; that is, given a set of statements— for example, about the respective speeds and trajectories of objects

A and B—the youth is able to make deductions or inferences and to draw proper conclusions on the basis of those statements alone. Although it may be convenient to have a diagram or an ensemble of objects on hand with which to work, such aids are no longer necessary. The objects can now be construed mentally; the operations that once had to be carried out in the physical realm have now been "internalized" or "interiorized." The mathematician or scientist can progress simply by sitting in her study and thinking, because the requisite operations can now be performed in an abstract, or formal manner.

Such a quick synopsis scarcely does justice to the intellectual power, the breathtaking scope, or the exquisite detail of the Piagetian enterprise, one that he brilliantly launched in the first half of this century and that still provides employment for many enterprising researchers. Not only is Piaget eminently worthy of study; he is beyond question the single dominant thinker in his field, a figure of Freud's stature who happened to focus on the nonemotional, nonmotivational aspects of human development. We now appreciate that Freud's contributions inhere more in the dimensions and scope of his vision than in the accuracy of his specific claims. Similarly, a subsequent generation of researchers, while acknowledging Piaget's genius, has found it necessary to take issue with nearly all of the Genevan psychologist's principal claims.

In light of current understandings of human cognitive development, there are four particularly problematic aspects of the Piagetian world view. First, there is Piaget's core belief that development consists of a series of qualitative shifts in representation and understanding. This claim may well be legitimate with respect to certain domains; for example, the way in which children conceptualize life and death may alter from toddlerhood to adolescence. Yet such qualitative shifts do not seem to obtain across the board. Many basic understandings—for example, the notion that the world consists of objects that have boundaries, move in certain ways, and have predictable effects upon objects with which they impact—are present at birth or shortly thereafter and do not undergo a lengthy developmental process.

A second limitation is Piaget's belief that all major milestones are yoked, with critical events across different domains all locking into place at approximately the same time. There is now copious evidence to suggest that developmental domains are far more independent of one another, with advances in one area often failing to signal comparable advances in other areas. Thus, for example, a child's first meaningful utterances occur well before his first meaningful drawings. Unlike the carefully interlocking parts of a watch, the structures of the mind—and of the brain—seem to be able to evolve in different directions and at different paces.

Third, while Piaget believed that he was studying all of cognition and all of intelligence, there is good reason to think that his field of vision was much more limited. At the center of Piaget's vision were the competences of the scientist, and even within the scientific realm, a great deal of his attention was directed at numerical competence. Like a faithful Pythagorean or Platonist, Piaget seems to have believed that the understanding of numbers lay at the center of the intellect. An appreciation of quantity, an interest in how quantities relate to one another, a mastery of the different kinds of operations that can be imposed upon quantities—these run like leitmotifs through Piaget's analysis. It is an exaggeration, but perhaps a suggestive one, to say that Piaget's major achievement as a scientist was the development of a deep understanding of what it means for a creature to be numerate and that his view of human development centered upon the capacity of our species to achieve sophisticated knowledge about numbers—or Number.

Many if not most developmental psychologists would acknowledge these three limitations in Piaget's work. A fourth consideration is more controversial. I argue that Piaget made a fundamental error in his contention that the older child's more sophisticated ways of knowing eradicate her earlier forms of knowing the world. Such an elimination of earlier conceptions may occur in the case of experts, but research on ordinary students reveals a dramatically different pattern. For the most part, children's earliest conceptions and misconceptions endure throughout the school era. And once the youth has left a scholastic setting, these earlier views of the world may well emerge (or reemerge) in full-blown form. Rather than being eradicated or transformed, they simply travel underground; like repressed memories of early childhood, they reassert themselves in settings where they seem to be appropriate.

THE MIND AFTER PIAGET

Piaget's work continues to provide stimulation even for those who would, for whatever reason, fault his formulations. It would be easy to read this book (and others I have written) as an extended debate with the Genevan master. And it is certainly possible to consider the major competing visions of human development, described below, as commentaries in one way or another on Piaget's central conceptualizations.

The Neo-Piagetians

Those most faithful to Piaget have been dubbed the neo-Piagetians. Prominent within their ranks are my colleagues Robbie Case of Stanford University and Kurt Fischer of Harvard University. According to the neo-Piagetian consensus, Piaget got right the big picture of development—the major set of stages from birth through adolescence, each with its characteristic form or "structure" of cognition. The neo-Piagetian theorists examine a wider gamut of behavior than did Piaget; for example, both Case and Fischer have been interested in emotional development, an area virtually declared off-limits by Piaget, and each has recently been examining artistic capacities as well. Yet, as I read them, they retain a commitment to a fundamental central strand in development, and like Piaget they locate that core in the human sensitivity to number, numbers, and numerical relations. Thus, when considering the social realm, Fischer examines the child's capacity to appreciate a number of social roles and their relationship to one another. Case, when turning to the arts, looks at children's drawings in terms of the number of features they include and the ways in which these features relate to one another.

The neo-Piagetians demonstrate how one can discern continuity across seemingly different domains of development by maintaining a fundamental anchoring in an appreciation of number. This view allows them to impose a powerful lens on a wide set of domains; moreover, it is a useful focus in scholastic matters, where command of numerical relations is often critical. But in my view such a perspective risks distorting domains like the social realm or the visual arts, where number seems an intrusion rather than a central component. To the extent that such researchers come to focus on more central aspects of the social or artistic domains, they risk being unfaithful to the Piagetian vision.

The Information Processors

Piaget is often considered one of the central figures in the cognitive revolution, that series of discoveries and reconceptualizations in the 1950s and 1960s that amounted to a death knell for behaviorism and learning theory, at least when it came to the elucidation of higher mental functions. But because Piaget was born a shade too early to participate fully in the computer age, he must be considered less pivotal than those figures who locate computers and computational mechanisms at the center of their system.

Often dubbed "information-processing" researchers, a phalanx of post-Piagetian students of mind have taken the digital computer as the preeminent model of cognition. In this view the developing child is an individual in possession of a computer—some would prefer to say the child *is* a computer—that changes in various ways over the course of childhood. At all ages, it is legitimate to speak of input mechanisms, storage buffers, short-term and long-term memory stores, internal processing mechanisms, and some kind of an output mechanism. But the size, the efficiency, and possibly the very operations of the computer are believed to change over the course of development.

From personal experience we are all painfully aware of how quickly technology changes. Thirty years ago, all computers were so bulky that they dominated the rooms in which they were housed; a decade ago, desk-size personal computers were just beginning to be introduced; now computers no larger than a book can be seen at meetings, on airplane tray tables, and even on the lunch table. The growing power and versatility of computers is also legendary.

Much the same kind of rapid shift has occurred within the ranks of information-processing students of the human mind. Twenty-five years ago, investigators searched for general problem-solving mechanisms that, à la Piaget, could be called upon to deal with any kind of content. Ten years ago, there was a recognition of "expert systems" in which considerable knowledge about a specific domain of experience (like chess or medical diagnosis) has been "wired in." Now the serial, one-step-at-a-time computers of the past appear to be on their way out as models of mind; as I write, they are being replaced by parallel distributed systems that, brain-like, carry out many small quasi-independent computations at the same time. Reflecting these trends with perhaps a slight temporal delay, the child postulated by information processors in the 1990s is a very different child from the one underlying the research of the 1970s or the 1980s.

The neo-Piagetians are concerned about retaining the overall vision of the master, even as they alter aspects of the portrait and fill in many of the missing details. For the most part, the information processors are more interested in specifying mechanisms of problem solving than they are in ascertaining the accuracy of Piaget's overall conception; for example, they will debate the specific operations involved in conservation of number and how these relate to the appreciation of relations of class inclusion. Whatever their differences with Piaget and with one another, however, both of the post-Piagetian factions have retained his stress on logical and numerical relations. In that sense, they endorse a developmental psychology appropriate to the computer age and adapted to a certain vision of school.

Noam Chomsky and the Biological Perspective

The Piagetian child and the post-Piagetian child both differ notably from the child posited by another major flank of the cognitive revolution, that ensemble of scholars influenced by Noam Chomsky, the eminent linguist long at the Massachusetts Institute of Technology. Chomsky began his scholarly career in the late 1950s by proposing an entirely new approach to the study of language. Instead of comparing exotic languages with one another, or simply describing their rules of operation in the manner of a conventional grammar book, Chomsky embarked on a far more ambitious program. He set out to discover the precise rules that an organism must know in order to master the syntax of any naturally occurring language. In one sense, then, Chomsky can be thought of as part of the computational camp, for he was searching for rules that either a human or a machine would have to "possess" or follow in order to be an adequate speaker-hearer of a language.

Yet, before long, Chomsky revealed that he was as radical in other fields as he had been in the area of linguistics. He asserted that language was a special realm, deeply different from other areas of human cognition. He claimed that much, if not most, of our knowledge is inborn or innate; as such, it needs simply to be activated or stimulated rather than acquired or constructed in a more active fashion. Indeed, Chomsky suggested that language is better thought of in quasi-biological terms, as a "mental organ" along the analogy of other organs, like the heart or the liver. Just as the liver or the heart exhibits its own principles or rules, written into the human genetic program, and expresses these rules in the environment of the body, the "language organ" harbors its own rules as well, which unfold in the environment of other speakers in one's community.

Finally, taking a leaf from the nineteenth-century American philosopher Charles Sanders Peirce, Chomsky argued that human beings are constituted to achieve certain kinds of understandings easily, while others prove difficult or even impossible to attain. Clearly humans can learn arithmetic easily and some can do mathematics in a most advanced way; psychology proves much harder, and Chomsky has often suggested that by virtue of our species membership we may never be able to understand ourselves. The verdict is still out on the study of the rules governing human language, but Chomsky remains cautiously optimistic that the potential for understanding language lies within our understanding.

These extreme views, argued with exemplary eloquence, brought Chomsky into sharp conflict with nearly every research community in the human sciences, among them the Piagetians, the behaviorists, and the computer-influenced information-processing scientists. Chomsky criticized Piaget's neglect of language and his blithe assumption that language simply reflects more general cognitive processes and structures. Chomsky insisted on the special nature of linguistic syntax and questioned whether there are indeed any general cognitive structures. He also contended that it was unnecessary and unreasonable to posit the existence of elaborate knowledge construction or learning devices within the human mind.

Equally alienated from traditional learning theory (his virulent critique of Skinner's learning-theory tract on language is thought to have discredited the entire behaviorist movement) and from Piagetian constructivism, Chomsky questioned the need for any psychology along the lines that we know it. One ought instead to describe knowledge systems per se (language, music, understanding of the physical world), figure out how much knowledge had to be built into an organism's nervous system in order for that organism to acquire these systems of knowledge at all, and then locate the triggering circumstances under which such knowledge can make its appearance.

Chomsky was hardly more moderate with respect to computer scientists and information-processing scientists. Again, he challenged the notion of general problem-solving mechanisms. Expressing his uneasiness with a technology-based model, he encouraged researchers to study the way that systems "unfold" biologically rather than to assume that the operation of a recently invented mechanical device would necessarily elucidate the operation of an organic system. Also, if information or knowledge were already built into the system and simply had to be triggered or stimulated, this situation would call for a view of competences radically difficult from that implied by a mechanism whose operation depends upon the receipt of input from the environment and subsequent elaboration of that initial input.

Chomsky's perspective has posed a challenge to the concepts hallowed by developmental psychologists and to educators. With respect to developmental psychology, Chomsky endorses inborn knowledge at the expense of knowledge constructed over time, domain-specific faculties rather than general problem-solving skills, and the realm of language, rather than number, as the most prototypical paradigm for conceptualizing knowledge. Chomsky's views prove even more troublesome in the educational realm. If knowledge unfolds according to a genetically based timetable, educational interventions are difficult to justify. And if each form of knowledge has its own principles and constraints, it is unrealistic to expect significant transfer from one educational situation to another, let alone from "school learning" to problems encountered in one's everyday environment.

By no means has Chomsky gone unchallenged. Indeed from the philosopher Nelson Goodman, his teacher, from Piaget, with whom he debated in 1975, and from a raft of empirically or computationally oriented researchers, Chomsky has received probing criticisms (to which he has responded with great gusto). Chomsky's own work in linguistics is seen as obscure, tangential, and perhaps wrong headed. His belief in biological models of psychological phenomena has clashed with a scholarly culture in which a black box or a microchip are seen as more promising points of departure. His invocation of different domains, each exhibiting its own principles, is seen as a threat to parsimony. His biologically oriented perspective scarcely recognizes cultural and social factors. And perhaps above all, his conviction that much knowledge is built in collides with an empiricist tradition that has held sway in Anglo-American circles at least from the days of Locke, Berkeley, and Hume as well as with the Piagetian view that higher stages of knowledge are attained only as a consequence of years of active engagement with the physical and social worlds. Still, even those who are troubled by Chomsky's excesses recognize that he has called attention to a whole raft of phenomena and possibilities that deserve further exploration.

In 1967 Eric Lenneberg, a psychologist and a longtime colleague of Chomsky's, published a technical monograph called *Biological Foundations of Language*. In this wide-ranging volume, Lenneberg laid out the case for language seen as a biological system, indeed one housed in certain regions of the left cerebral hemisphere; Lenneberg saw certain left-hemisphere structures as particularly important for syntactic operations. He claimed that many linguistic functions were directly mediated by a timetable under genetic control and that they unfolded in the same manner as other biological systems like walking. He suggested, in addition, that "critical periods" govern language acquisition, such that the task of language learning, or of recovery from language disorders, would become increasingly difficult once an individual had reached adolescence. He indicated that adults who suffer from lesions in left-hemisphere areas of the brain would become aphasic and in most instances would need to evolve compensatory mechanisms of communication. Most speculatively, he explored the relation of language to communication, on the one hand, and to other cognitive operations, like conceptualization of number, on the other.

Lenneberg's book evoked a good deal of controversy. The great linguist Roman Jakobson praised it for its courage but said that there were errors on every page. Biologists challenged the claims about critical periods, even as neuropsychologists accused Lenneberg of insensitivity to the considerable degree of localization that in fact characterizes language *within* the left hemisphere. Psychologists were uncomfortable with the reductionism implied in a "brain" analysis of the human faculty of language. Distress at the lack of appreciation of his seminal ideas is sometimes cited as a contributing factor to Lenneberg's suicide some years later.

From my point of view, Lenneberg's book, even more than Chomsky's writings, marked an important turning point in the contemporary study of cognition and cognitive development. Perhaps for the first time, it became widely recognized that domains of knowledge exhibited their own rules and principles and that these might be attributed, in some concrete detail, to structures and mechanisms in the brain. Even if Lenneberg had the details wrong, he was right about the nature of the enterprise. And if he was right, then psychologists and educators interested in cognition would have to focus increasingly on the finely structured principles of specific domains of knowledge and on the foundation of these principles in the human nervous system.

Ideas about the biological foundations of language and other cognitive domains were much in the air in the 1970s. Norman Geschwind, a leading neurologist in Boston, brought to attention important studies made of brain-damaged patients in Europe nearly a century ago. These neuropsychological case studies documented the extreme specificity with which the brain carries out cognitive operations: Punctate lesions can destroy such fine-grained capacities as tune recognition, spatial orientation, face recognition, reading of written language, or short-term verbal memory while leaving other, even theoretically related capacities essentially intact. A figure of comparable stature in the Soviet Union, Alexander Luria, published cases of traumatic brain wounds to illustrate his claim that remarkably specific kinds of aphasia will occur, depending on the precise location of a missile wound. In the face of such documentation, a characterization of the brain as a general information-processing mechanism seemed primitive, and efforts to examine the mind in ignorance of brain factors seemed anachronistic.

SPANNING BIOLOGY AND CULTURE

In 1976 Paul Rozin, a physiological psychologist at the University of Pennsylvania, published an important paper, "The Evolution of Intelligence and Access to the Cognitive Unconscious," in a regrettably obscure series entitled *Progress in Psychobiology and Physiological Psychology*. In this paper Rozin argued that many species have evolved highly specific kinds of mechanisms that allow their members to carry out computations quickly, accurately, and automatically. From this perspective, the human syntactic and phonological capacities central to language are not theoretically different from the pre-wired capacities of birds to learn species songs, or of squirrels to bury nuts, or of bees to communicate the location of nectar to others in the swarm.

Human beings differ from lower organisms in two crucial respects, and these can be said to characterize our peculiar form of intelligence. First, we humans have the capacity to join together two or more of these originally separate mechanisms or systems in order to perform a new task. For example, the reading of an alphabetic language links the human capacity to recognize distinctive visual forms (*b, a, d*) with the capacity to analyze sound streams into their component parts (which can be transcribed as /buh/aah/duh/). This linking capacity, which (so far as we know) was mobilized only a few thousand years ago, has radically increased the intellectual compass of the species.

Second, it is possible for human beings to become aware of the operation of such mechanisms and to use that knowledge productively; as Rozin puts it, we can come to gain access to our systems of information processing. Thus, in learning to read an alphabetic system, humans gain conscious access to the properties of our phonological system; they "sound out" words and connect particular sounds to particular graphic symbols (in English the squiggle *a* makes the sound /aah/ or /ah/ or /ay/). The development of intelligence in our species consists of ever-greater access to elements of our cognitive repertory. So, for example, humans can not only learn to read an alphabetic system but can learn to appreciate the nature of the grapheme-phoneme mechanism that undergirds reading and can draw on this understanding to learn new languages, to devise their own artificial languages, and even to come to understand the operation of natural and artificial languages in the style of a Chomskian linguist.

With more or less effort, most human beings seem able to master the operations involved in a skill like reading. Those who find it especially difficult to couple their auditory and visual analytic systems, or to attain some kind of access to the principles that underlie sound organization, end up at a distinct disadvantage in a realm of human activity that has attained enormous importance. Recently we have come to call these people "dyslexic." Dyslexics would not be recognized in an illiterate society or in a society where reading occurs with ideographs, but if a person at risk for dyslexia is born into a literate society that happens to use an alphabetic system, he must somehow overcome his limitations if he wishes to participate fully in his culture.

Writing as a physiological psychologist—one who studies the brain for a living—Rozin was able to refer with some specificity to the kinds of neural mechanisms that allow for careful visual and auditory analyses. In that sense he was being a proper member of the guild, building upon the elementary operation of sensory and motor systems. His adventurousness began with an acknowledgment that humans are not simply at the mercy of their senses; we have the potential to become aware of the operations carried out by these analytic mechanisms, to "go meta" in the current jargon. Through the elaboration of higher-order cognitive mechanisms, we can understand and perhaps even control the manner of operations in our brains; we are not merely a reflection (or a reflex) of elementary neural mechanisms.

Rozin's paper stands out in particular because of the way in which his argument straddles the usually disparate realms of biology and culture. Nothing in humans is more quintessentially biological than the kinds of discriminatory powers needed to see the difference between a *b* and a *d* or to hear the differences between the opening sounds in /bin/ and /din/. As we will observe in the next chapter, these capacities are heavily constrained by our biological makeup. Yet at the same time, these capacities are mobilized in the service of a culturally invented activity—reading—which in no meaningful sense can be said to have been the *reason* motivating prior evolution. Of course, we could not read unless we could see, hear, and relate certain kinds of information; indeed, our powers to effect such discriminations are subtle and targeted. But it is difficult to sustain an argument that millions of years of evolution were governed by the possibility that a certain kind of decoding strategy would be invented in the Middle East a few thousand years ago.

Work by researchers like Chomsky, Lenneberg, and Geschwind helped to redress an imbalance in empirical science of the behaviorist era by restoring an appreciation of the importance of the human nervous system in all manner of human activity. Moreover, work in this tradition called attention to the surprising specificity of brain functions and to the particular cortical locations at which they were carried out. To phrase it in the language of this book, these neurologically oriented researchers underscored the constraints under which human development operates.

Humans are creatures of the brain, but not solely so. Unlike all other organisms, we participate in a rich culture, one that has had its own evolution over many thousands—though probably not millions—of years. Indeed we have no choice; we are as much creatures of our culture as we are creatures of our brains. As anthropologist Clifford Geertz has argued most eloquently,

> The accepted view that mental functioning is essentially an intracerebral process, which can only be secondarily assisted or amplified by the various artificial devices which that process has enabled man to invent, appears to be quite wrong. . . . Rather than culture acting only to supplement, develop, and extend organically based capacities logically and genetically prior to it, it would seem to be ingredient to those capacities themselves.

A cultureless human being would probably turn out to be not an intrinsically talented though unfulfilled ape, but a wholly mindless and consequently unworkable monstrosity.

In invoking explicitly the concept of culture, we touch here on the one remaining area of developmental psychology that has emerged with great vigor in the post-Piagetian period. Growing most centrally out of the work of the innovative Soviet psychologist Lev Vygotsky and reinforced by such American supporters as Jerome Bruner and Michael Cole, an increasingly influential group of developmental scientists has made the case for the centrality of cultural factors in any consideration of human development. According to these thinkers, Piaget, Chomsky, and other "mind-" or "individual-centric" investigators have omitted at least two crucial factors in the equation of cognitive development: the contributions of cultural artifacts and inventions, on the one hand, and the contributions of other live human beings, on the other.

In this view, encapsulated in the Geertzian formulation, an individual restricted to his own devices is unthinking, if not unthinkable. From the moment of birth, when parents react to the sex of their newly sighted offspring, the child enters into a world that is rich in interpretations and meanings, all introduced courtesy of the assumptions of the culture in which he happens to be born. The other humans in that world introduce him to physical satisfactions— warmth, food—and to psychological nutrients—love, conversation, humor, surprise. They expose him to language and demonstrate its uses. They present him with the artifacts valued by the culture, be they technology like pens or computers, toys like rattles or dolls, art works like stories or songs, or wisdom in the form of rituals, sayings, or moral precepts. Much of the story of human development must be written in the light of cultural influences in general and of the particular persons, practices, and paraphernalia of one's culture. And chief among these, of course, in any complex culture will be such educational institutions as apprenticeships or formal schools.

The shifts that have occurred most recently in the study of the human mind pull students of cognitive development in two opposite directions. On the one hand, researchers have probed more deeply into the human brain, the apparatus or organ that severely constrains the parameters and shape of any kind of human growth. The behaviorist notion that human beings can learn—or forget—anything seems as naive as the initial computational faith that all problem solving is of a piece. Language is but one of our special realms of knowledge, and even within language, such operations as syntactic analysis of speech and reading of alphabetic text might operate quite differently from one another.

At the same time, however, it has become evident that the ways in which culture interacts with the nervous system cannot be ignored or taken for granted. Over the centuries human beings have constructed complex cultural environments, containing ingenious artifacts and much accumulated knowledge, prejudice, ideology, and even wisdom. A world with powerful "thinking machines" available instantaneously to all persons, with scientific instruments probing the stratosphere, and with the potential for travel to any spot, conversation with anyone anywhere, and virtually total destruction at the press of a button was unthinkable even to the most prescient utopian writers a few centuries ago. In no meaningful sense can this knowledge be said to be built into the genes.

Of course, all cultural invention must take place within the parameters set by the human genes, though there is great disagreement about the range and rigidity of these parameters. The deep problem for the developmentalist attempting a synthesis is to understand the relationships among the constraints imposed by nature, the constraints imposed by culture, and the degree of human inventiveness that nonetheless manages to emerge. Failure to address the factors that permit human cultural inventiveness to occur and take hold over the millennia is Chomsky's Achilles' heel, even as explanation of such creativity remains a challenge to psychologists and educators.

Accepting whichever constraints are immutable, the society must construct procedures and institutions whereby the young can acquire a dizzying array of competences and knowledges: systems of morality, skills like reading and calculating, crafts like musical performance, rituals like religious observations, bodies of knowledge in the sciences and the humanities. And, for their part, the young must somehow draw, bootstrap fashion, on their own neural mechanisms, consciously as well as unconsciously, in order to master the modes of living presented in their culture. According to our new and expanded understanding, mind exists equally within the skull, in the objects strewn about in the culture, and in the behaviors of other individuals with whom one interacts and from whom one learns.

While the field of developmental psychology is difficult to envision apart from the initial vision of Charles Darwin and the pivotal legacy of Piaget, it has in fact moved far beyond them. Careful theoreticians and ingenious empirical researchers have sorted out the more enduring from the less reliable of Piaget's claims. The invention of the computer has provided a powerful if ever-changing model of cognition and an invaluable tool in simulation, data analysis, and conceptualization of the human mind. The exploration of specific domains like language has revealed their intricacies, their neural specificity, and the surprising constraints that influence the unfolding and operation of human cognitive activity. The renewed attention to cultural artifacts has underscored the extent to which human development is incomplete—perhaps even inconceivable—in the absence of consideration of cultural and social influences and contrivances. The work of Paul Rozin nicely encapsulates these divergent themes, which once led the Nobel laureate Peter Medawar to quip that human behavior is 100 percent under the control of the genes and 100 percent under the control of the environment. We end up with an emerging theoretical and empirical perspective far more complex than Piaget or Darwin might have wished for. If we are fortunate, this perspective may provide a more comprehensive view of human development and guide us in fashioning a more appropriate and a more effective educational system.

As children grow, their lives become entirely enmeshed with cultural institutions. While those institutions are not absent at birth, their presence is less salient. Through a closer look at the young infant, therefore, we can best position ourselves to appreciate those constraints and opportunities that are built into the human genes. Such initial predisposing factors set the limits and lay out the possibilities for the society that would—and perhaps must—educate its offspring.

CHAPTER 3

Initial Learnings:
Constraints and Possibilities

THE PHILOSOPHICAL AGENDA

When the pre-Socratics first began to ponder philosophical issues, they focused on the nature of the external world. In particular, they sought to ascertain the fundamental elements out of which our world has been constructed. In the dialogues of Socrates and the writings of Plato, interest in fire, water, earth, and air gave way to more abstract concerns: the definition of virtue, the nature of knowledge, the purpose of education, the attainment of the good life. For over a thousand years, these topics remained at the center of philosophical discourse and, in a sense, they have been neither resolved nor supplanted. Yet it can be said that at least two new epistemological issues arose in the Renaissance and Enlightenment eras.

First, René Descartes focused directly on the nature and functioning of the human mind. In his view, the mind had an existence apart from the body, came equipped with considerable innate knowledge, and exhibited powers of mathematical reasoning. These rationalist views proved anathema to Descartes's successors in the British empirical tradition; looking instead to the world of external sensory experiences, philosophers like John Locke and David Hume questioned the inborn nature of knowledge, the alleged disjunction between mental and physical substance, and the primacy of reason. Immanuel Kant, seeking a synthesis of these perspectives, put forth a more comprehensive scheme. He laid out the framework within which all experience and all phenomena had to be apprehended—the categories and "schemas" that were intrinsic to any knowing of which human beings were capable.

The ways in which these issues came to be framed by major philosophers have had extraordinarily powerful effects on subsequent considerations of human nature. For example, Piaget's focus on logical thought had a distinct Cartesian flavor; moreover, his long-term research agenda entailed tracing the developmental history of the Kantian categories—space, time, causality, and the like—as they unfolded in the experience of the young child. Even among individuals who are unaware of the venerable philosophical tradition, the tension between the rationalist and the empirical traditions is manifest. Within the area of psychology, for example, it matters enormously whether one assumes that all infants come to the earth equipped with specific knowledge about the world in which they will live, whether they possess general frames or schemas that make knowing possible, or whether they are relatively "blank slates" upon which a variety of disparate messages could comfortably be etched.

By the same token, the tacks adopted by those charged with educating young minds will differ, depending on the educators' epistemological predilections. For example, if (rationalist-style) they assume significant constraints on how one comes to know the world, they may avoid certain topics or feel that these topics must be approached in a prescribed way; if (empiricist-style) they acknowledge wide latitude in how information is apprehended or interpreted, they may be more willing to experiment in curricular and pedagogical matters.

Over a century ago William James speculated about the "blooming buzzing confusion" that constitutes the world experience of the young infant. Even if the usually modest James were pleased by this turn of phrase, he would assuredly be surprised by how often it has been quoted (even as it has often been misquoted as a "booming buzzing confusion"). James would be even more surprised to learn that it is quoted nowadays chiefly as a strawman, for one of the firmest demonstrations in recent times has been the degree of solid preparation for knowing with which every normal infant comes equipped. Far from being a blank slate or a vortex of confusion, the infant emerges as a remarkably well-programmed organism. Subsequent learning must build upon the constraints and biases that every normal infant brings into the world.

THE FINELY TUNED INFANT

That the reflexes of the infant are in good order is perhaps least surprising. After all, one could reasonably expect that evolution has succeeded in preparing an infant to turn away from noxious stimuli, to search for a nipple on which to suck, to suck comfortably as long as she feels hunger, to respond sharply when her grasp begins to loosen or when she is subjected to pain.

The degree and nature of preparedness of the child's sensory systems is less readily anticipated, perhaps because discriminations among visual or auditory stimuli are less evident than responses to a pinprick or a source of milk or because they seem less linked to survival and more psychological or cognitive in nature. Nonetheless, the techniques developed by experimental researchers have made it possible to gain quite specific information about just which distinctions are noticed by the young child.

As a start, a researcher can display two or more stimuli and simply monitor how long the child attends to each one; so long as a difference in attention span occurs, one can assume that at least some distinguishing feature has been noted. A somewhat less direct but more revealing measure comes from observations of the course of the child's attention span. Exposure to the same or similar stimuli eventually results in a loss of interest, so one can tell, by noting when boredom sets in or, alternatively, when interest is rekindled, which stimuli are deemed by the child to be similar (and hence boring) and which are registered as distinct (and hence worthy of renewed interest). It is also possible to monitor surprise, not only by observing facial or bodily reactions but also by using electrophysiological measures, including heart-rate deceleration and variation in skin responses, two measures invoked for the detection of lies in the testimony of older people.

Equipped with an armamentarium of such indices, researchers

have demonstrated a set of strategies and understandings that would have been difficult to anticipate from Darwinian cribside observations or Jamesian alliterative asides. At birth or soon after, infants can distinguish an astonishing ensemble of forms, shapes, and line configurations from one another. They can also learn to recognize visual or auditory patterns, or schemas, and will then register heightened interest when these schemas have been altered by an experimental manipulation. Infants prove especially sensitive to facial configurations and will respond differentially to normal and distorted faces. Within a few months, and perhaps even within a few weeks, an infant can recognize his own mother from among other female adults.

For our purposes the most revealing demonstrations illuminate the kinds of processing biases or constraints built into the infant's perceptual systems. That the infant should be predisposed to focus on facelike configurations is not surprising, given the evolutionary stake in an early and secure bond to the mother. Of great psychological and epistemological importance is the fact that infants also divide or "parse" higher-level sensory continua in much the same way as do adults. In the case of color, for example, infants do not process colors as a continuum, in the way that empiricists would have to predict. Rather, infants see the color spectrum as divided at the same points in the continuum as do adults, recognizing the existence of focal colors (a "good" red, a "representative" blue, a "marginal" blue/green). They are more likely to group together two different blues (450 and 480 nm) than a blue and a green (480 and 510 nm), even though the differences in wave lengths (30 nm) between the two members of each set are exactly equivalent in a mathematical sense. They discriminate colors in the same way as a color-seeing person and in a manner different from a color-blind person.

It is highly implausible to think that the three-month-old has learned from experience how to differentiate a "good" from a "poor" red, or to consider the two different blues as members of the same overarching category; much more plausible is the conclusion that visual receptors have been designed to recognize, and respond most powerfully to, certain representative hues. The fact that chimpanzees select the same prototypical colors as human beings clinches the argument that such perceptual biases are built into the neurophysiology of the visual system.

Equally striking biases are observed in the operation of the auditory system. Here it is useful to distinguish between responses to linguistic stimuli, such as consonant-vowel clusters, and responses to nonlinguistic stimuli, such as musical tonal sequences. In the area of linguistic signals, one encounters a revealing analogy to the color continuum. On a purely acoustic basis, there is a smooth shift of voice onset time from an "unvoiced" /p/ to a "voiced" /b/. Yet, despite the fact that the timing onsets of the frequency components of sounds vary continuously, linguistic signals are dichotomized by the auditory perceptual system so that they are heard as either /p/ or /b/, rather than as intermediate signals. Two sounds that have the same psychophysical difference between them (for example, twenty milliseconds' voice onset time) are both heard as /p/ if they fall within a certain voice onset continuum, but if they straddle the permissible range, then one will be heard as /p/ and the other as /b/.

Now, as with color, it could be the case that infants at first hear these sounds continuously and only gradually learn to group them into discrete categories. But research has refuted this possibility. From the very first, infants, like adults, treat all /b/s as /b/s, and all /p/s as /p/s, with categorical perception overwhelming the detection of purely physical differences in voice onset time. Such a built-in bias in the nervous system is helpful, if not essential, if human beings are to learn to understand and speak natural language. Again it is extremely difficult to imagine how the young organism could learn to divide the speech continuum in this useful manner or to master an artificial language that failed to honor categorical perception. The fact the infants from widely different speech communities parse the continuum similarly in the early months of life provides yet more decisive evidence that nature has constrained the perception of auditory-linguistic stimuli.

Even in areas that may seem less crucial for human survival, one finds strong predispositions built into the infant's perceptual repertoire. At birth, a newborn will turn his head in the direction of a sound. By the age of three months, he hears a series of taps as organized into distinct rhythmic configurations. By five months he can recognize a pattern of pitches, sorting out instances where the melody is the same and only the key has been changed from instances in which the actual intervals that constitute the melody have been altered, and by six months he can sing back tones at approximately the same pitch.

Nor, contrary to standard empiricist dogma, must infants pass through a lengthy process before they can relate information gleaned through one sensory system to information received through another. One-month-old children can associate an object they have seen to an object they have felt; three-week-olds associate loud sounds to bright lights; and four-month-olds know which sounds go most appropriately with characters in a movie, including a male voice with a male frame and a female voice with a female frame. These sensory discriminations and associations, rather than being learned in any meaningful sense, seem to be the inborn basis on which subsequent learning must be constructed.

PIAGET'S PORTRAIT OF INFANT COGNITION

Conducting research during an era when methods for studying sensory discrimination and integration were not highly developed, Piaget simply assumed that the young child could see, hear, and associate percepts sufficiently well for her purposes. Though Piaget did not address the issue, he would presumably have been comfortable with an acknowledgment that at least sensory information about how to parse the world was part of the human biological heritage. For Piaget, the important issue was not how the senses work but rather how the organism apprehends more formidable concepts and problems. Working with his own infants, he conducted an extended clinical investigation of how children come to understand the existence and operation of objects in the world, their behavior within a spatial-temporal framework, and the ways in which one can attain goals by joining one's knowledge of the behavior of human agents to one's understanding of the nature and trajectory of inanimate objects.

Piaget's portrait of the "infant's construction of the world" has proved amazingly robust, more so, perhaps, than any other portrait that he rendered. This fact is especially remarkable when one considers that Piaget's research population consisted of only three children—and, for that matter, his own!—at a time when the technology for experimentation was essentially limited to such objects as rattles, rubber ducks, and a beret for hiding them. Piaget felt that he had disproved the rationalists' claims for inborn knowledge. He had challenged this Cartesian vision by showing that the child's understanding of time, space, causality, and the like, rather than being present a priori, had to be constructed in a painstaking six-stage process that unfolded over an eighteen-month period.

It is indeed true that, posed problems of a Piagetian flavor, infants of a given age will reliably fail. Shown an interesting demonstration (say, a duck that quacks), six-month-olds will flail their bodies about in an effort to get the effect repeated, rather than honing in on the sources of the demonstration directly (grabbing and squeezing the duck's tail or directing someone more dexterous to do the same). By the same token, when a desired object is hidden in one place but then moved overtly to a second location, the ten-month-old will with amazing persistence continue to search in the original locus of the object. In light of demonstrations like these, Piagetians concluded that the infant has large areas of ignorance (or, to adopt the terminology of this book, persistent misconceptions or misunderstandings).

The limitation of the early infancy researchers (including Piaget) lay in an underestimation of what the infant knows—information that can be elicited when the infant is "questioned" more directly and more appropriately about specific bodies of information or knowledge. It turns out that even a four- or five-month-old will register surprise when an object with one appearance passes behind a screen and emerges in different form or disappears altogether. Under some conditions, even three-and-one-half-month-old infants realize that objects continue to exist after they have been hidden and that they cannot traverse a space already occupied by another object. A six-month-old has a clear sense of what an object is, ignoring surface characteristics like color or texture in favor of the deeper and more reliable clues of a single uninterrupted contour and a stable rigidity. Infants as young as six to nine months of age show an incipient sense of number, being able to distinguish a set of two objects from a set of three, even when the spatial configurations of the sets have been deliberately rearranged so that a response based simply on a familiar visual-spatial pattern will not suffice. And youngsters in the first year of life can also demonstrate a mastery of some facets of causality, appreciating, for instance, what makes an object fall down or under what conditions of contact one object can cause another to move. It is worth underscoring that all of these abilities emerge well before children have developed language, complex series of motor activities, or a system of interpretation specific to their culture.

Too much ink has already been spilled on the question of whether these early strands of knowledge can be said to be inborn in a Cartesian (or Chomskian) sense or whether they simply have been acquired very early in life, as a traditional empiricist would insist. From my perspective, it really does not matter whether one calls them inborn or very early learning; to put it more positively, only an organism of a certain genotype, reared in an environment of the sort found—and expected—all over our world, would be able to exhibit these forms of knowledge while it still remained helpless in so many respects.

What is important to stress, for the purposes of our inquiry, is the extent to which these early elicited behaviors illustrate—indeed epitomize—strong constraints upon early cognition. The experimentation of the past decades reveals how the human organism has been designed so that it can readily make sense of the world. It is essentially *unthinkable*—in fact, this may be the most appropriate gloss of that word—for infants to evolve unless they parse the world of colors, linguistic sounds, and musical patterns pretty much in a way that they have been shown to do, and that they have as well a readiness to make certain assumptions about the structure and behavior of physical objects, the operations of causal relations, the salience of numerical quantity, and the like. These very early and deeply entrenched understandings form the basis of robust theories of matter that emerge during the following years; and these theories in turn are the views with which formal education must contend if disciplinary understandings are ever to supplant intuitive ones.

That these early proclivities and forms of understanding were less recognized in the past was due, in part, to the strong empiricist tradition that undergirds experimental science. It is also likely, however, that few researchers bothered to think about how one could ever construe the world in a sensible manner *save* in the light of such strong and effective initial assumptions about matters of matter. Piaget claimed that he had shown that what Kant had claimed to be present a priori was simply present a posteriori. The philosopher Gottfried Wilhelm Leibniz, responding to Locke's claim that "nothing is in the intellect which was not first in the senses" agreed but then added "except the intellect itself."

KNOWING THE SOCIAL WORLD

So far, we have stressed the cognition of the world of physical objects, a Western cultural bias going back at least to Cartesian times and possibly traceable to the era of the pre-Socratic philosophers. An equally remarkable story can be told about the extent to which the human organism is pretuned to come to know the world of other persons. Beginning with the inclination of the newborn to focus on facelike configurations and the tendency of the two-month-old to smile when encountering another human being, infants emerge as incipient social psychologists, fascinated by other members of their species, no less than as fledgling physical scientists interested in the world of nonliving objects.

In addition to a nearly compulsive attraction to other beings, infants are capable in the first months of life of engaging in quite elaborate social interchanges with competent adults. In one such familiar early script, the adult will initiate an interchange by smiling or sticking out a tongue, and the young child will respond by reproducing or responding to this opening move. Such an interchange can continue for up to several minutes, with a complex ballet of action and reaction taking place on the part of both participants.

At first these interchanges have a predominantly ritualistic flavor, but before long they can become the occasion for more specific modes of communication about feelings, intentions, and/or fears. That these exchanges soon extend beyond the ritualistic is illustrated by the fact that two- to three-month-old infants become upset if exposed to a taped rather than a live interacting adult. By the middle of the first year of life, the child can communicate desire or upset to the adult, the adult can communicate pleasure or concern to the child, and each participant can reasonably expect that her meaning has been conveyed.

Anyone who has observed such interchanges—and we all have participated in them, at least as infants—will recognize that these moments are potent. The attachment of the young organism to another human being, and especially to a parent, is of special importance for many reasons. The most convincing demonstration of the importance comes from the strong emotions exhibited by the infant when the loved person suddenly leaves the field, or when a stranger attempts to initiate such contacts as a substitute for the parent. Although the exact nature and extent of shyness, wariness, separation anxiety, and stranger anxiety vary considerably within and across cultures, the existence of these phenomena and their reliable appearance toward the end of the first year of life confirm the potent constraints operating upon human development, this time in the social and emotional domains. By the same token, the absence of these phenomena, in infants who have been neglected or abused or who exhibit disorders like infantile autism, suggests a child whose future development is likely to be severely impaired.

A strongly charged set of emotions accompanies interactions in the personal realm, an ensemble of feelings that may be qualitatively different from those evoked in mundane interactions with rubber ducks or paternal berets. Anxiety at the disappearance of a parent and delight at his return often seem more marked than comparable emotions at the loss or reappearance of a toy. A central reason for taking into account the child's relation with other human beings is to underscore the extent to which the child is an organism of feeling and of feelings centered around the social world, as well as an organism of discrimination, conceptualization, and disciplined understandings focused on the physical world.

Whether these early intensive social exchanges between adult and infant constitute a rehearsal for later verbal communication remains controversial. Emphasizing the "autonomy" of the linguistic system, those of a Chomskian stripe have voiced skepticism that the mastery of language presupposes such early ritualistic interactions. But even if the Chomskians are, in a strict sense, correct—even if one can master syntax without ever having smiled, babbled, and cooed in reaction to a loving adult—it seems clear that subsequent interpersonal intercourse, viewed more broadly, builds upon these early social interactions. The child wants to talk and to understand language because this is nature's and culture's way of continuing the conversations of infancy. (Quite possibly, autistic youngsters are incapable of carrying out this form of person-to-person communication, even if they can eventually master the grammar of their language.) It is likely that subsequent face-to-face exchanges between human beings are being rehearsed in the peek-a-boos of the crib. It also seems highly likely that the young child's gradual conceptualization of self—her emerging understanding that she is a human being in her own right— is eased into place by coming to know other selves in this way. To put it succinctly, the theories of life, mind, and self that have coalesced by school age originate in the constrained but playful interchanges of early infancy.

FIVE FOOTNOTES TO SENSORIMOTOR KNOWLEDGE

As we have noted, Piaget termed infancy the "sensorimotor stage" and stressed the extent to which early forms of knowing depend upon the activation and deployment of the range of sense organs and the variety of motoric activities. If one is going to label eighteen months of life with a single term, "sensorimotor" seems as apt as any other characterization, but it needs to be footnoted in several ways.

First, there are forms of knowledge that go beyond the world of objects and that extend particularly to the child's communications with others, emotional life, and incipient sense of self. These forms of knowledge build upon sensory and motor capacities but direct them to a quite distinct realm of experience: the human world, as contrasted with the inanimate world. Piaget was of course aware of these other realms but, perhaps reflecting the biases of the Western philosophical tradition, deliberately chose to underplay them.

Second, while the systems of sensing and acting are clearly a privileged means of acquiring knowledge, they are not uniquely important. Children can come to know earthly realms even when particular sensory systems have been blocked; thus blind children not only acquire language in a relatively normal way but even prove capable of appreciating the spatial nature of the world. Moreover, to an extent that might have surprised Piaget, knowledge can be acquired even in the absence of functioning motor systems. Children born without limbs because of the damage wrought by the drug thalidomide still construct the forms of understanding needed to deal with a world of physical and human objects.

Third, within the cognitive realm there are forms of understanding that have a distinctly abstract flavor and that the child seems pretuned to appreciate. Understandings of causal relations, of the nature and constituents of objects, and of the world of numbers can all be elicited in the first year of life. While sensory or motor information may have been necessary to trigger these understandings, there is nothing particularly sensory about concepts like "having one more unit" or "impossible to be in two locations at the same time" or "grasping what I have been trying to communicate." Rather, these understandings seem part of what it means to be a human being living on the planet Earth. While it is premature to speak of the infant as having an elaborated theory of anything, it seems entirely legitimate to point to these early understandings as forming the basis of soon-to-emerge theories about the physical, social, and personal worlds.

Fourth, Piaget focused in his work on those "universal" stages and understandings that can be expected to characterize all normal children around the world. As a research strategy, this universalist tack is an entirely appropriate one; developmental researchers are the wiser because Piaget adhered to it. At the same time, however, it must be pointed out that during the first year or two of life, significant and even striking differences can be observed among youngsters: differences in temperament, in personality, in speed of information processing, in sensory acuity and motor capacity, and perhaps even in cognitive strengths and styles.

There is a final, highly important footnote. Whatever inborn individual differences may exist soon come to interact with quite powerful cultural configurations. Both within and across cultures, there are quite varied expectations about what babies are, how infants do (and ought to) behave, how adults should interact with them, how such predictable phenomena as feeding, crying, playfulness, or anxiety should be treated. For example, the Kaluli who live in the rain forests of Papua New Guinea see babies as helpless creatures bereft of understanding. Rather than speaking to their infants, Kaluli mothers speak "for them." This attitude stands in dramatic contrast, of course, with the stance of American middle-class parents, aware of the newly discovered competences of infants, who engage in extended interchanges with their youngsters from earliest childhood and who in some cases start to teach at birth, or even before. In another example, Gusii mothers in southwestern Kenya hold their infants three times as much as do American mothers, while American middle-class mothers spend far more time talking to and looking at their infants. Ultimately, Gusii children will be expected to remain enmeshed in familial relationships and to act restrained in the presence of their elders, whereas American children will be encouraged to express themselves freely and to go out and explore the wider world.

Beyond question, such strongly contrasting cultural practices and expectations accumulate over time to yield children and adults who are characteristic of their own culture and who may appear dysfunctional in a culture that embraces a divergent or opposing set of assumptions. While the human genetic program expects certain features in the environment of the infant, it also depends on others that may or may not emerge, depending on the values and priorities of the community. By the same token, even though infancy remains the period in which the biological heritage can be examined most directly, one must remember that part of the emerging mind already exists beyond the skin of the child, in the games, customs, and symbols that adults are directing at a growing future member of their community.

The study of infancy is exciting in part because it is one of the rare domains where new forms of technology provide at least provisional answers to questions about experience that have vexed philosophers for millennia. Certainly, we now appreciate that infant development is constrained in ways that would have surprised nearly all scientific researchers merely a few decades ago. Yet, ultimately, the most entrenched questions—such as the relationship between nature and nurture—may not permit of a definitive answer. Instead, we must be content with a deeper understanding of the ways in which the genetic constraints and the cultural pressures unfold and interact over the course of a human life.

In the years that follow infancy, the child will come to exhibit many new forms of knowledge, some arising in the course of ordinary interactions in the culture, others as a result of the explicit program provided by educational institutions. These packets of information, concepts, and practices, increasingly susceptible to conscious examination, will constitute the overt knowledge and memory of the growing individual. By virtue of the fact that the infant cannot capture his knowledge in symbolic forms or reflect upon his categorizations, the experiences of infancy become unavailable to him; we all suffer from "infantile amnesia." It would be a serious miscalculation, however, to assume that because these experiences cannot be remembered, they cease to be important. In all probability, these primordial experiences and understandings make all subsequent knowing possible. And, as we shall see, they continue to underlie our apprehension of the world, often remaining more powerfully entrenched than the "revisionist" notions that educators seek to impart during the years of school.

CHAPTER

4

Knowing the World Through Symbols

Monsieur Jourdain, a character in Molière's play *Le bourgeois gentilhomme,* expresses surprise when he learns that he has been speaking prose all his life. It is perhaps equally jarring for most of us to apprehend the extent to which we have been trafficking in a swarm of symbols for nearly all our lives. Sitting at my word processor, I am first of all peering at linguistic and numerical symbols; various graphic and iconic symbols could be readily activated were I to switch to another program or to another computer system. I look at my watch to see how much time I have before I have to hop into my car and confront a series of traffic signals on the way to the supermarket, whose shelves and products are punctuated by an ever-expanding set of symbolic codes.

Leaving the relatively scholastic setting of my office to interact with my five-year-old son Benjamin in his room, I encounter a different ensemble of symbols. We talk, we tease, we wink; we draw, make constructions out of blocks, play cards and board games, enact short or lengthy sequences of dramatic play. In the course of a day, Benjamin in his world and I in my superficially quite different one are each awash in a sea of symbols, some common to us both, others peculiar to our respective daily routines.

SCHOLARS OF SYMBOLS

Despite (or perhaps because of) the ubiquity of symbols, most traditional philosophers paid little attention to these meaning-suffused forms of exchange. Indeed, Charles Sanders Peirce was probably the first major thinker in the modern era to ponder the nature, range, and operation of the manifold symbols, and systems of symbols, that permeate our lives. Working in the philosophical tradition founded by Peirce, Ernst Cassirer and Susanne Langer helped to map out the terrain of symbolic forms and functions, with special reference to the "softer" realms of myth, ritual, and art. More recently, Nelson Goodman, my longtime teacher and colleague, helped to place the realm of symbolic understanding on more rigorous ground through his articulation of a theory of symbols.

If the label "sensorimotor" reasonably spans the first eighteen months of life, the label "symbolic" is at least as adequate to cover the remainder of the preschool years—the period, say, from two to six or seven years of age. During this period all normal children the world over come readily and naturally to master a whole gamut of symbols and systems of symbols. They learn to speak and to understand natural language, using it not only to make requests and to execute commands but to tell stories and jokes, to taunt and tattle, and to amplify their understanding of the social and physical world. By the time of their entry to school, five-, six-, or seven-year-olds are full-blown symbolic creatures.

Few would question the choice of language as the symbol system par excellence, but it is important to underscore the potency of other symbol systems. Much knowledge is apprehended and communicated through gesture and other paralinguistic means. Depiction of aspects of the world through drawings, constructions in blocks or clay, or other iconic vehicles is a symbolic avenue of great significance in early childhood. Variations of pretense play and rule-governed play are favorite pursuits everywhere. An introduction to the concept of quantity and to the names and operations associated with numbers is part and parcel of the first years of childhood. And various customs, rituals, games, and other social interactions are rife with symbols of various sorts, whose meanings are at least partially accessible to—and in all probability highly potent for—the preschool child.

Scholars of The Symbol—who often style themselves, after Peirce, as semioticians or semiologists—call attention to three central aspects of symbolic systems, which every aspiring user of symbols must come to master. There are the rules that govern the ordering and organization of the symbol system itself—what is termed the grammar or *syntax* of the system. There are the explicit meanings or denotations of the symbols, the relation between the symbols and the objects, ideas, or "referents" to which the symbols refer—what is termed the *semantics* of the symbolic system. Finally, there are the uses or functions of the symbols, the reasons that they have been invoked in a given context—what is termed the *pragmatics* of the system. Though challenging to explain, the task of the child in the early years is straightforward to describe: He must come to master the syntax, semantics, and pragmatics of those symbol systems that are valued in the surrounding culture.

The word *culture* deserves underscoring here. Whereas, as we have seen, the culture is certainly present in the object-hidings and social interactions around the crib, variations across cultures may not be crucial for the acquisitions that occur during the first year of life. Not so for symbolic acquisitions, however. The particular symbol systems favored—or spurned—within a culture form the agenda that the child must master in the "semiotic," "symbolic," or "representational" stage. And just as important a part of the child's learning at this time are the particular ways in which the symbol systems are used. Indeed, in observing the child's acquisition of symbolic competence, we witness that continual interplay between inborn proclivities and cultural options that characterizes human development forever after.

Where the semiotic period may differ from subsequent periods, however, is in the extent to which biology and culture conspire to make full-blown symbolization readily available for all human beings. In this sense, the learnings of the semiotic period are differentiated from the universal learnings that characterize infancy and equally different from the distinctly cultural learnings that come to dominate subsequent periods. Particular symbolic competences will reflect the peculiar practices of one's culture or subculture, but symbolic competence is a universal achievement of early childhood.

Once the importance of symbols had been recognized within the academy, researchers concerned with human development reached a consensus that this period of development is best termed a time of "symbolic mastery." Such otherwise disparate scholars as Jean Piaget, Heinz Werner, Alexander Luria, and Jerome Bruner would all concur with this characterization. Indeed, so great is the consensus that one wonders whether possibly everyone may inexplicably have overlooked some competing issue—one as manifest as the prose that was missed by Monsieur Jourdain. In what follows, I will take advantage of this consensus and simply assume that this characterization is uncontroversial.

Two other matters *are* controversial: the extent to which symbolic development is sharply constrained and the extent to which symbolic development occurs in similar fashion across diverse symbolic domains. All later education, whether formal or informal, builds upon a presumption of symbolic competence, so it is crucial to uncover the facts surrounding this developmental milestone. Because this has been the area of my most intense research over the past two decades, I draw heavily on findings from our research laboratory in the discussion that follows.

LANGUAGE AS A SYMBOL SYSTEM

For nearly all investigators, language is the prototypical system of symbolization; indeed for some it is the only system worth study. For these reasons, a great deal of knowledge has been accumulated about the syntax, semantics, and pragmatics of language, both in its mature adult state and in the contours of development as observed in children emerging from the sensorimotor stage. Research about other symbol systems is typically modeled upon the procedures and analyses used in studies of language. Yet despite the considerable knowledge base, the controversies about language acquisition remain sharp and anticipate much of the discussion about symbolization across a variety of media and domains.

Syntax and Learnability

As we have already seen, Noam Chomsky has elected to mount his campaign about the nature of cognition and the mind on the basis of his studies of language. And a powerful campaign it has been! With respect to the study of linguistic development, the troops have mustered under the banner of "learnability."

Learnability is a technical, mathematically oriented area of analysis that attempts to lay out the knowledge that a mechanism (human or inorganic) must have if it is to be able to acquire a natural language on the basis of the samples (strings of words) that it encounters. According to proponents of learnability theory, it would be impossible for any organism ever to be able to master the kinds of languages that all human beings master if that organism had to consider every conceivable set of rules that might govern that language. Indeed, the facts of the matter (say the theorists) are precisely the opposite. Human beings learn languages with ease precisely because, on the one hand, they come to the task equipped with powerful assumptions about what any natural language must be like, and on the other, they do not even consider the countless rival hypotheses about what might in fact obtain with all conceivable (but non–naturally occurring) languages.

What kinds of assumptions are made by all normal language learners? To name just a few, language learners assume that strings of sounds can be broken down into specific pockets of sounds called words or morphemes (the smallest meaningful units, which include *s*, *ed*, and *ing*); that these word strings refer to aspects of the environment or of personal experience; that a given string of words, when reordered, can carry a sharply different meaning (*man bites dog* versus *dog bites man*); that groups of words function together as phrases that have specific meanings; and that modifications and other linguistic operations may be—and typically are—applied to phrases as a whole.

Learnability theorists have put forth a range of claims. Perhaps the most intriguing formal claim holds that there exists a whole class of languages, called "natural languages," that cannot be learned from scratch without negative evidence—that is, evidence of impermissible utterances. Yet it turns out that children are not exposed to reliable information about impermissible utterances. Either this means that children cannot learn language (a fact we know to be empirically incorrect!) or it means that children must come equipped with various built-in assumptions about how to master the language that is spoken in their midst. On a learnability account, children learn to speak their native language even in the absence of negative evidence because particular assumptions about the nature of natural languages are part of their innate knowledge.

As an example of a more specific claim, let me cite in some detail a particular phenomenon studied empirically by Peter Gordon. The claim (and its supporting evidence) may seem unduly technical, but in fact it is representative of learnability work.

Analyses of adult language show that there is a surprisingly orderly three-level procedure for building more complex words out of simpler words. Level 1 rules allow changes in pronunciation and unusual semantic outcomes. For example, a level 1 rule permits one to convert *red* to *reddish*, *Spain* to *Spanish*, and *book* to *bookish*. Note that the vowel cluster sounds different in *Spain* and *Spanish* and that *bookish* does not mean "like a book." In contrast, level 2 rules do not allow changes in pronunciation, and they have predictably consistent semantic effects. One level 2 rule, for example, permits one to add a suffix like *-ness;* others govern compounding. By definition, level 2 rules are applied after level 1 rules; thus one can have *bookishness* but not *booknessish.* Level 3 rules are those that are applied after level 1 and level 2 rules; they include the rules for regular pluralization, as in the form *rednesses.*

Consider the application of this theory of word structuring within a small meaning set. Conversion of *mouse* to *mice* reflects level 1, because the pronunciation has changed; conversion of *rat* to *rats*, a regular pluralization, reflects level 3; the words *rat-eater* and *mouse-eater*, formed through compounding, are examples of level 2. Because the levels must be applied in order, *rat-eater*, *mouse-eater*, and *mice-eater* are all possible words, but *rats-eater*, though it seems to be constructed in the same way as the other terms, is actually impermissible because its formation would violate the usual order by invoking level 3 pluralization before level 2.

How do all these possibly plausible technical distinctions relate to child language performance? Gordon designed a parlor game for preschool children. The subjects were given a puppet and told "Here is a puppet who likes to eat———. What would you call him?" Gordon provided some model responses so that the child would become aware (or be reminded) of the "x-eater" compound form.

The research revealed that children responded in the same way as adults. That is, they called a puppet who was fond of eating a mouse a *mouse-eater* and a puppet who liked to eat a rat a *rat-eater;* a puppet who liked to eat rats was also called a *rat-eater.* Crucially, the children almost never termed the latter puppet a *rats-eater.* Moreover, even when children used improper plurals in their own spontaneous speech (*mouses* instead of *mice*), they treated these in the same way as legitimate regular plurals (like *rats*) so they never called the puppet a *mouses-eater.*

Unfortunately, the route from this interesting demonstration to a claim that such knowledge is inborn is hardly direct. Gordon's evidence comes from a study of the kinds of forms that children regularly hear and the kinds of forms that they would have had to hear to be able to play this game correctly on the basis of instances to which they had already been exposed. He claims that children would have been unlikely to hear the necessary instances in their environment—for example, *mice-eater* but not *rats-eater.* His findings embolden him to claim that the youngsters perform correctly because some version of the level-ordering constraint seems to be innate.

I am probably not alone in believing that this claim requires a stretch of faith. And I believe I am being fair to the data in reporting that other individual studies along this line are no more convincing in themselves. Nonetheless, I find the general claim of constraints on learnability to be persuasive. The learnability literature contains dozens of examples of utterances that children might plausibly make but simply never do. For example, they do not convert the statement *The man who is tall is in the room* to a question form *Is the man who tall is in the room?* nor do they say *John put* rather than *John put it away.* And learnability researchers chronicle all kinds of errors that children routinely make— "he goed" or "he wented" rather than "he went," *childs* rather than *children, I'm unthirsty*—even though these incorrect forms have not been modeled in their presence. The long list of possible errors that children never make and of unmodeled mistakes that they predictably make point to powerful constraining forces at work in children's language learning routines.

Moreover, there are all sorts of conceivable linguistic moves that human beings would never consider making, unless they were involved in some kind of formal game. For instance, human beings would never pay attention to the meanings of words—or strings of words—spoken in reverse, nor to meanings based on attention to every other word, or every third word, nor to meanings based on a concatenation of all members of a class (such as all prepositions in a sentence). Children seem to know instinctively that rules of modification operate upon whole clauses or phrases rather than on the second or on the fourth through sixth words in a sentence. These hypothetical strategies strike us as bizarre, but that is in fact the point. Just as scientists (according to Peirce and Chomsky) seriously entertain only a fraction of the innumerable hypotheses that could possibly account for a physical phenomenon, so too language learners consider only that relatively tiny set of hypotheses that presumably have become part of the "language organ," thanks to the long-term processes of evolution.

As this discussion has conveyed, most of the work undertaken by learnability theory occurs squarely in the area of syntax, the heartland of Chomsky's demarcation of language. It is hard to dispute Chomsky and his associates on this, their home base, and only a few experts in developmental psycholinguistics have been knowledgeable enough or brave enough to publish their reservations. Syntactic analysis in some ways resembles a reflex; it emerges readily and it proves impossible to stifle, so individuals in search of inborn constraints move readily to this arena of examples. Nonetheless, it is probably the case that most psychologically oriented investigators would prefer to avoid the strong assumptions of learnability theory if they could help it. As Nelson Goodman once pointed out to Chomsky, the fact that it is difficult to figure out how something is learned is not sufficient grounds to conclude that it must be innate.

Semantics

The controversy about learnability has in fact echoed in the other two regions of language acquisition. In the case of semantics, for example, Ellen Markman and other researchers have suggested a strong bias built into early language acquisition. According to the "mutual exclusivity" principle, language learners assume that each object has one name and one name only. Thus, once aspiring learners of language have given a single object a name (say, *chair*), they doggedly resist the temptation to apply another name to it. Accordingly, they assume that a second name spoken in the vicinity of the object applies to something else, rather than being, say, the name of part of the object (*leg*), the name of a superordinate category (*furniture*), or a synonym for the object (*stool* or *rocker*). In support of the mutual exclusivity principle, Markman and her colleagues have conducted a number of ingenious studies in which children are asked to apply artificially contrived names to familiar or novel objects and the researcher observes how those arbitrary names are actually mapped onto those objects.

On the surface of it, the claim of mutual exclusivity seems plausible enough, at least as plausible as the assumption that humans have evolved to invoke in prescribed order the three levels of word-structuring rules. Yet this claim has evoked considerable controversy as well as a growing number of attempts to disprove it empirically (by showing that the youngest children do not observe it) or to constrain its generality (by showing that children observe it only if there is no reason not to observe it). As I write, the dispute has not been settled to anyone's satisfaction.

I discern three reasons for these strong reactions. First, the claim of mutual exclusivity does not require esoteric knowledge about learnability in order to be understood, addressed, and rejected. Second, semantics is seen by most psychologists as closer to the heartland of language-and-mind; it is thus of greater interest and importance than the seemingly marginal (and clearly esoteric) territory of syntax. Third, any acknowledgment of an inborn constraint in the area of language acquisition is considered a slippery slope by antinativist empirical investigators; once they acknowledge that so mundane an activity as the naming of objects might be subject to some kind of inborn strategy or constraint, then perhaps no area of human cognition will remain sacrosanct. Object naming today, political voting patterns tomorrow.

Pragmatics

An analogous battle has been waged with respect to the pragmatics of language acquisition, although this time the forces are differently aligned. Any number of investigators, dating back at least to Jerome Bruner, have insisted that language would never be mastered if the child were simply exposed to samples provided by, say, a perpetually operating tape recorder. In addition to a Language Acquisition Device, there must as well be a Language Acquisition Support System. Such researchers point to the early intensive social interactions between parent and infant as a prototype of such support. They go on to invoke numerous examples of ways in which parents, and especially mothers, engage in lengthy, carefully nuanced exchanges with their youngsters, modeling phrases for them, asking children to repeat things that were not well understood, and offering corrections for errors of various sorts, from grammatical mishaps to factual blunders. Such "motherese," it is claimed, is requisite to successful language acquisition.

No one, not even dyed-in-the-wool Chomskians, questions that a supporting parent may make the task of language learning more enjoyable and perhaps easier. The controversy instead swarms around the issue of whether such motherese-style support is necessary or just nice. According to the more rabid nativists, such support is simply not essential; any organism exposed to a sufficient sample of language will readily learn to speak in an appropriate manner. The fact that all children do seem to learn language, despite the varying conditions of households and cultures, suggests that it is difficult at best to thwart the language learning process. Even the Kaluli youngsters, whose parents reportedly do not speak directly to them at all, end up speaking their native language in a perfectly appropriate way. Yet the fact that (happily) experimenters cannot manipulate environments to prevent *any* kind of social support means that it will be difficult ever to satisfy the more militant disputants in this case.

That children learn language readily, given at least a modest degree of environmental support, is the most dramatic instance of early learning in our species. As I noted in the introduction to this book, the learning of a first language continues to be the behavior that is most impressive for our species, and the one that both adult language learners and teachers in all settings look upon with the greatest envy. Even if we can never demonstrate that specific constraints of learnability are built into the human genes, it seems clear that we as a species are predisposed to learn language in an orderly fashion with remarkable ease. In the wake of work by Chomsky and his students, few would maintain that the learning of language is an unconstrained activity.

Even if language should turn out in some respects to be a special case among human faculties, it is one that must be understood. Language not only is the prototype for the gamut of human symbol-using capacities more generally; it is clearly the symbol system that dominates early schooling, particularly during the period when the acquisition of literacy and formal concepts is at a premium. Whatever constraints obtain with respect to language, therefore, will affect large segments of formal education, ranging from the kinds of meanings students attribute to new terms to the ways in which they master a formal-mathematical or a second "natural" language.

CATEGORIZING OBJECTS AND EVENTS

Language proves crucial in categorizing the many objects, elements, and entities in the world. As the philosopher Willard Van Orman Quine pointed out many years ago, the fact that we can consensually

name and categorize objects is a remarkable feat. To use his capti-
vating (and by now well-worn) example, the word *gavagai* uttered in
the neighborhood of a passing rabbit is endlessly ambiguous: In addition to referring to the passing rabbit, it could equally well denote
a rabbit part (say, 'tail' or 'tail and half of the hind quarters') or some
odd space-time combination (say, 'animal that passes by me while I
am walking in a certain direction or at a certain moment'). As Quine
commented, "Point to a rabbit and you have pointed to a stage of a
rabbit, to an integral part of a rabbit, to the rabbit fusion, and to
where rabbithood is manifested." That no one seems seriously to
entertain such glosses suggests that our naming and categorizing
practices must reflect biases and constraints.

Careful studies of human classificatory procedures have completely
dismantled the so-called "classical" view, which held sway until a
generation or so ago. There is little or no evidence in ordinary behavior for the textbook version, according to which objects are class-
ified according to a defining set of necessary and sufficient
characteristics (a rabbit is a big furry animal with a tail and long
ears; a chair is a piece of wood furniture with four legs). An obvious
refutation of this approach is the fact that a rabbit would remain a
rabbit even if its tail were cut off, and a chair with three or five legs
is still a chair.

In contrast to this classical picture, categorization actually seems
to occur in a quite different way. Two principles are at work. First,
categories are customarily organized around representative examples—what psychologist Eleanor Rosch terms "prototypes" or "good
versions" of an entity. We all carry around in our heads schematic
images (in some medium of thought) of what makes a rabbit, a tree,
a chair, a bird, and the like, and of what makes a "splendid instance"
of these entities. To the extent that a particular instance seems relatively close to the prototype on a reasonable number of dimensions
or in overall appearance, we are likely to recognize it as a member
of that category and to do so with rapidity and confidence, but should
the deviation prove too extreme on too many dimensions, should the
instance appear too "peripheral," we become loath to make that
classification.

Complementing the prototype strategy is the level of specificity at
which we are inclined to produce names. Human beings seem predisposed to name objects at the so-called "basic level"—that level of
categorization that is commonplace, recognizable by depictable instances, relatively comfortable to see, feel, and to operate upon,

generic without being too general. Thus a rabbit is far more likely to be named as a "rabbit" than as an "animal" (superordinate category) or "this particular middle-sized short-eared rabbit" (subordinate category). Similarly, a chair is more likely to be called a "chair" than a "piece of furniture" (superordinate) or a "Chippendale" or a "Morris" (subordinate).

Just what determines the recognition of categories in general, and instances of category membership in particular, has for some time been an area rife with controversy. Some authorities stress the importance of perceptual features (A looks like B) or functional features (A1, A2, and A3 are all used in the same way—perhaps to hug). Other authorities believe that even young children can overlook these "surface" aspects and pay attention to underlying structural or relational features. (A is called a *bik*, and therefore it must be grouped with other *biks*; A, B, C are all used to contain; or A, B, C are all very important to me.) In all probability, each of these approaches can be applied by children, and each continues to play a role at times as children tackle the classificatory tasks of school.

Naming and classifying are central aspects of language. Commentators as diverse as the blind and deaf writer Helen Keller and the German psychologist Wilhelm Stern have reminded us that the capacity to name objects opens up an entire universe of meaning to the young child. For some children, this opening occurs in the first year of life; for Helen Keller, it came into its own only at the end of her first decade. Once it has come into place, however, it becomes an indispensable cognitive tool.

Names help to introduce new areas of experience, directing children to notice common features or differentiating features they might otherwise have missed; the word *wing* may call the child's attention to a previously ignored feature on a fly or an airplane and may also stress their common function. But names can sometimes serve to limit the user as well; when there is prejudice or stereotyping in the air, the labeling of a person or an object in a certain way may prevent one from approaching that entity in a fair and open manner. And the capacity to issue a name or list a set of features is sometimes mistakenly taken as a measure of deeper knowledge of an entity or a concept. In the United States there are too many students whose knowledge of a term is sufficient for picking the correct answer on a standardized test but who could not otherwise use that term appropriately or generatively.

Another use of language, equally important and highly generative, involves the description of recurrent events. Borrowing a practice from mainstream cognitive science, the developmental psychologist Katherine Nelson has named this area "the use of scripts." Just as single-word naming reveals the child's categorization of common objects in the world, so too the enunciation of scripts reveals the child's determination of important familiar sequences of events in her environment.

Generically, a script entails the identification and ordering of those features that are reliably associated with a recurrent event. For example, the script for an American-style child's birthday party includes, at a minimum, the arrival of guests, some common activity (such as playing Pin the Tail on the Donkey), consumption of food (such as pizza and a birthday cake), the opening of presents, and the singing of "Happy Birthday to You." Frequent options include handing out favors and, in more affluent circles, the surprise arrival of a professional magician.

Appreciation and mastery of scripts is not necessarily a linguistic activity in itself. As early as fourteen months of age, children can already point to those objects that belong to a recurring activity, for example, dressing in the morning or grooming oneself before going out of doors. Soon, however, script knowledge becomes enmeshed with linguistic competence. By the age of two or three, children prove able to describe scriptlike events—those that happen in their own lives and those about which they hear (a trip that they are going to take with their family; the treatments administered by an evil stepmother in a fairy tale). These scripts serve as an entry point to storytelling and story understanding, even as they allow children to conceptualize and to report what has happened to them in their own lives.

Perhaps most important for our purposes, scripts serve as a generic set of sequences of events against which newly encountered events are judged. Thus when the child encounters a storybook in school or observes a sequence of events in a science lab, he seeks to measure this novel series against the scripts with which he is already familiar. Linguistic versions of scripts are called upon regularly in scholastic contexts, but those observed in nonlinguistic contexts (for example, in a televised cartoon, at the automobile repair shop, or as part of daily farming chores) may be activated as well. Scripts can be extremely powerful cognitive screens; they are a convenient aid to memory, but they can often cause students (as well as nonstudents) to misperceive events or to misremember them later. That is, one may revert to features of the generic script rather than faithfully preserving its variations, elaborations, or deviations.

The anthropologist Shirley Brice Heath portrays in compelling fashion how youngsters living in three different communities put scripts and practices of language to strikingly different uses. In Trackton, a predominantly poor black community, storytelling is favored, and the ability to tell a "tall tale" is especially cherished. In Roadville, a community of impoverished whites, stories are intended to recount actual events as they actually happened; deviation from strict literalness is spurned and even punished. In Gateway, a middle-class white community, imaginary tales are acknowledged and praised *so long as they have been explicitly marked as fantasy;* a confusion of fantasy and reality is disdained, and young students soon learn which of the two forms is appropriate for school and which is preferred on the playground or around the campfire. Encountering what is objectively the same narrative or script, children from these different communities may assimilate it quite differently, even as they subsequently invoke it in characteristically distinctive ways.

Throughout one's life, scripts continue to play an important role, helping one to assimilate new experiences and allowing one then to make them one's own. The mind of the five-year-old is already chock-full of serviceable scripts, many of which will be drawn on for decades to come. If other aspects of knowing and understanding may decline somewhat with age, the capacity to utilize scripts proves amazingly robust, even surviving considerable damage to the brain. Indeed, older individuals are a virtual repository of scripts, which can be called upon appropriately to help deal with situations that may be unfamiliar to younger citizens. At least part of wisdom may involve a rich stock of scripts that the individual is able to invoke and deploy appropriately; in senility, the scripts are simply rehearsed without reference to context.

Yet, just as is the case with naming and categorization, certain entrenched scripts may prevent people from making fresh and un-contaminated judgments about individuals or events they encounter. Or prior practices may cause a script to be utilized in ways that make sense to one social group but not to others. For example, the public praising of a child who has performed well at a recital may be seen as an appropriate sign of love in one social group and as bragging by another. By the same token, what is important about an event may be its deviation from a common script; thus, a so-called "political revolution" in a third-world country may be misclassified as similar to the American or French revolutions, when it is actually closer to a replacement of one elite by another, the resolution of a family dispute, or the installation of an even more reactionary regime.

PLAY, IMAGINATION, AND THE BIRTH OF THEORY

During the early years of life, much of script knowledge is manifest in the kinds of symbolic or "pretend" or "pretense play" sequences in which children engage alone, with child-sized props, or with peers or parents. Just as children can behave appropriately at birthday parties, and just as they can answer experimenters' questions about these scriptlike events, they are also capable of staging "make-believe" parties with dolls or with friends and of re-creating portions of these events in their drawings and even in daydreams and night dreams. In many societies symbolic play constitutes a primary form of symbol use for young children, one in which they have an opportunity to experiment with roles and behaviors that they will ultimately assume in the adult world or in tandem with "big kids."

Like Monsieur Jourdain's prose, the symbolic play of young children has often been taken for granted, at least in contemporary Western society. Just as young dogs and cats predictably cavort with one another on the street, young children dress up as Mommy or take their favorite stuffed animal on a mythical car ride or trip to the store. Thanks to the Scottish psychologist Allan Leslie and his colleagues, we now have a better understanding of the considerable achievement involved in pretense play and the extent to which this activity may represent another species-specific, highly constrained sample of behavior.

Adopting a line of analysis first put forth by the philosopher Jerry Fodor, Leslie assumes that infants already possess a "language of thought"—some kind of "mentalese" in which they represent to themselves facts about the world (that is a chair, this dog is nearby, I want that food, I feel lousy). Of course infants do not use such symbolization overtly (otherwise they would be symbolizers in our sense), but their cognition of the world presupposes some kind of medium in which to represent the input from their senses as well as some kind of "internal language" that acts upon such representations.

Whether or not one accepts the Fodor-Leslie version in just this way, the following point seems clear. When a child engages in pretense, she becomes involved in a kind of mental activity different from straight "first-order" representation. Where once she was observing a banana and labeling it to herself—"This is a banana"—she now makes a different mental move. Holding the banana to her mouth and "speaking" into it, she is activating a second-order or higher-order representation, in which she asserts *I pretend* that this banana is a telephone, and I am treating it as such for now." Such pretense play thus involves a recognition that a banana is usually one way and a telephone is usually another way, but that for certain clearly marked purposes, one can treat the banana as if it were a telephone. On other days, for other reasons, one might as likely treat a telephone as if it were a banana.

Treating one object as if it were another is a cardinal form of "metarepresentation." In pretense play other metarepresentational orders may be encountered as well. One can treat nothing as if it were something: "I will drink the tea out of this cup" even though the cup is in fact empty. One can treat something as if it were nothing: "I will talk about Susie as if she were not here." Or one can distort a property so it is treated like another property: "I will treat this short hair as if it were long hair and wear it in a pony tail." Operating in each of these cases of metarepresentation is a recognition that what is apparently the state of affairs can be intentionally bracketed, so as to bring about another state of affairs that the player wants to evoke. Even as the child must be aware that she is doing this (one cannot pretend unless one is aware of this pretense), she must also acquire the awareness that others can pretend (otherwise she would constantly be fooled) and that pretense can be appreciated by others as well as by oneself (or the behavior of the pretender would strike an audience member as bizarre).

As Leslie points out, this state of affairs is peculiar on the face of it. One might well think that it could be extremely disconcerting, at the very time when the child is learning what a banana is and what roles it usually fulfills, to challenge this new knowledge and treat the newly familiar yellow fruit as if it were suddenly and magically a black piece of plastic. By the same token one can readily envisage a situation in which children could become extremely distraught when—to reverse our example—another person took a telephone and pretended to peel it and serve it to an eager monkey. The very fact that children are rarely confused by such behavior—that they more typically revel in it—provides persuasive evidence that this behavior is clear and important to the human being, both in terms of the knowledge it makes possible and the pleasure that it invokes.

There is no need to argue here that pretense play is itself a universal phenomenon, though it may well be, or that it is constrained to operate in certain ways, though that seems to be true as well. What I am claiming is that within the first few years of life, all children pass a crucial milestone. Moving beyond the ability to think directly about the world of experience, they now become capable of imagining. They are able to envision a state of affairs contrary to the one that is apprehended by their senses, to capture that imaginative activity in public symbolic form, and to continue to elaborate upon that imaginative capacity. Such metarepresentational capacity is certainly remarkable; it need not have evolved, and certainly it does not appear to exist in any interesting form of other species. The capacity to take a stance toward everyday reality—to confirm, deny, or alter it—confers enormous new power on the child. As I shall argue in the next chapter, it soon allows the creation of works of imagination—be they artistic products or theories about the world. These free and flavorful inventions populate the world of the preschooler, and they continue to exert strong influence throughout the child's schooling, which, after all, presupposes that the child can learn about events and processes that are remote from the context. When the formulations contrived by the child happen to coincide with those put forth by teachers or by experts in a discipline, substantial understanding emerges; often, however, the symbolic products and explanations arrived at by the child veer off in quite another direction. And so, for example, if the child's own personally elaborated view of the solar system happens to resemble that arrived at by astronomers, he is likely to assimilate information about the sun, the moon, and the planets quite readily; to the extent that the personal and the disciplinary pictures diverge, however, the child may become confused or hold onto two quite incompatible world views.

A STUDY OF EARLY SYMBOLIZATION

Until this point, while I have made forays into the realm of preverbal scripts and pretense play, I have remained comfortably within the sphere of language. Naming, classifying, enacting scripts, and pretending make heavy use of language and are difficult to conceive of in the complete absence of language, although they are certainly found in deaf people as well as in people with pronounced impairments of language. It is perhaps not surprising that the quasilinguistic activities examined here turn out to be quite closely tied to linguistic milestones; sophistication of pretense play progresses in tandem with language sophistication, just as classification activities mobilize and reflect extant language abilities.

Yet, as we noted earlier, the symbolic repertoire of the preschool child extends well beyond language and its close relatives in the communication sphere. The young child engages as well in symbolization in the realms of drawing, modeling with clay, building with blocks, gesturing, dancing, singing, pretending to fly or drive, trafficking with number, and a host of other symbol-studded domains. While these other realms have not been studied to same degree as have language and language-related fields, one can discern surprising regularities in their development. Someday—or perhaps even sooner!—investigators may feel emboldened to speak of the same kinds of inborn constraints in music or gesture as have been discerned with respect to linguistic or pretense activities.

Were one to adopt a strict Piagetian perspective, one would have to assume that all these semiotic activities are yoked; that is, a milestone in one area co-occurs with (or directly presages) milestones in other arenas. It is possible, however, to adopt a contrasting developmental stance. Following the line of reasoning favored by Chomsky and Fodor, one would expect a much more domain-specific picture of symbolization. In this account, events in one realm—say, language—might turn out to have only a distant or accidental relationship to milestones in other domains—say, music or drawing or number.

When my colleague Dennie Wolf and I conceptualized this issue about fifteen years ago, little relevant empirical evidence was available. Accordingly, we and a number of colleagues at Harvard Project Zero* decided to carry out a naturalistic study of early symbolization. Inspired by the approach that Piaget had taken with his own children, we elected to follow a cohort of nine first-born children on a regular basis for seven years, roughly from their first to their eighth birthdays. (To make sure that our conclusions in this longitudinal investigation were not too parochial, we included an additional seventy youngsters as controls in a cross-sectional study.) Our focus was deliberately broad: We looked across the range of symbol systems, including lan-

---

*Our colleagues are listed in the endnote keyed to this page.

guage, pretense play, two-dimensional depiction (drawing), three-dimensional depiction (modeling with clay and building with blocks), bodily expression, and music.

We also included a seventh important symbolic system, number. Number served three related purposes. First, among the symbol systems we were examining, number was least likely to be used in an esthetic way. It thus served as a kind of control or comparison with the other symbol systems, each of which is highly susceptible to use in an artful way by young children. Second, among our symbol systems, number could also serve as a kind of Piagetian (or neo-Piagetian) marker: It is, as I have argued, the one symbol system most crucial to the standard "unitary" account of cognitive development. If Piaget and the neo-Piagetians are correct, then numerical sophistication should drive the rest of the system; if, however, the domain-specific hypothesis has legitimacy, then number should prove no more dominant than any other symbol system. Third, number (along with language) is the symbol system most prized in school. Interest in the precursors of scholastic facility dictates the monitoring of numerical skills.

Life is less predictable than one might like; science observes no principle as faithfully as Murphy's Law (What can go wrong, will go wrong). The story of symbolic development turned out to have far more complexity than we had initially expected—a complexity that, we may infer, characterizes other areas of cognition as well. It turned out that our findings touched on four separate aspects of symbolic development.

Streams of Development

Of comfort to a Chomskian position was our discovery of the existence of definite *streams* of symbolic development. We define a stream as an aspect that seems inherently tied to a specific symbol system and that exhibits no apparent link to any other symbol system. Thus, for example, a stream in the area of music involves the child's discovery of the organization of tonal pitch structure—the appreciation that there exists a basic, organizing key and that certain tones (tonic, dominant, and so on) occupy privileged positions within that tonal structure. Children work through their understanding of this musical stream in the first years of life, and all make considerable progress; but progress in this aspect of music seems unrelated in any straightforward way to progress in other symbolic domains.

Nor is this phenomenon restricted to the area of music. Each domain seems to have its own stream-like properties, notably in regions that, like tonal structure in music, it seems legitimate to term *syntactic*. In language, there is not only the literal mastery of syntax but also the capacity to construct narratives of different degrees of complexity. In three-dimensional constructions, the capacity to master and vary spatial layout turns out to have streamlike properties. Even in the neighboring domain of two-dimensional depiction, learning the properties of line, contour, and color arrangement has no evident relationship to milestones in other domains. It is my conclusion that the syntactic aspect of symbolic development is severely constrained within each domain—perhaps for genetic reasons—and that one syntactic trajectory has no close relation to other syntactic trajectories. Subsequent mastery of disciplines or domains valued by the society may well draw upon appropriate streams of competence, with the musician drawing on musical streams, the scientist on numerical ones, and the like.

Four Waves of Development

We maintained our aquatic metaphor when we encountered an entirely different set of properties, properties that are more reminiscent of a Piagetian position. At yearlong intervals, beginning at about the age of two, children pass through a series of developmental crests that we have termed *waves*. While streams adhere within the boundaries of a symbol system, waves are less readily regulated; by their nature they are inclined to spill over the banks that purportedly define their domain. Thus our waves of symbolization, which are basically *semantic* in nature, characteristically begin within a single symbol system but then extend to other symbol systems, even ones in which they are not considered to be appropriate.

The first wave of symbolization, which we called "event-" or "role-structuring," has already been noted in passing. Somewhere between the age of eighteen months and two years, the child becomes capable of capturing in symbols his knowledge that there are events, that these involve agents, actions, and objects, and that these events have consequences. The point of origin of this symbolic capacity is in language, more specifically in those aspects of language that are mobilized in symbolic play. Rather than remaining within these limits, however, the understanding of roles and events spills over to other domains. Given a marker and asked to draw a truck, for example, an "event-structurer" will clutch the marker, hunch over the paper, and murmur, "Vroom, vroom" as he passes the marker back and forth across the paper. Rather than creating a graphic equivalent of the truck, he instead converts the depicting moment into an enactment of the process of driving a truck along the road. And so the event-structuring wave has invaded a domain (that of representational drawing) where it is not conventionally utilized.

An analogous kind of appropriation occurs in each of the subsequent waves. Around the age of three, a second wave, called "topological mapping," can be widely observed. In topological mapping, the symbol captures certain dominant relations of size or shape drawn from the field of reference. At first this form of mapping is noted in the domains of two- and three-dimensional depiction, where the child becomes able to capture in a plastic medium the dominant spatial relations of a corresponding real-world referent. For example, the child can draw two abutting circles, one above the other, and label the top one the head and the bottom one the body, or he can build a model house out of a row of blocks and superimpose a crowning block that is designated as a roof.

Once again, this ability to appreciate spatial or topological relations comes to be mirrored in other forms of symbol use. Asked to create an ending for a story that has a number of characters, the child will collapse the characters into two contrasting roles (such as a good mother and a naughty daughter), thus preserving an overall topological relationship but not the explicit details and nuances. Or, seeking to master a song with an elaborate pitch contour, the child will simply observe when the contour undergoes a large shift in pitch direction and convert the song into a series of sharply rising and falling melodic contours.

The third wave of symbolization typically occurs around the age of four. Where topological mapping captures the general temporal or spatial relations of a configuration, "digital mapping" captures precise numerical quantities and relations. For the first time, the child can actually enumerate a small group of objects explicitly and appreciate the commonality between, say, four instances of one kind of object and four instances of the same or of another kind of object. This ability of course builds upon the numerical sensitivity of infancy but goes well beyond it in terms of the size of quantities appreciated and the deliberateness of the quantification.

Often with surprising speed and ferocity, the world now comes to be seen as an arena for counting. Here is where the wave properties become manifest. Children want to count everything—facial features in a drawing, tones in a melody, characters in a story. In many ways this digital tack represents progress, yet sometimes counting is not particularly relevant to the symbol system in question or the symbolic task at hand. For instance, it is more important to give the overall impression of a full head of hair than to enumerate each strand; it is better to capture the mood of a song than to focus exclusively on the number of note or beats. Indeed, the four-year-old in the grip of digital mapping reminds me a bit of an overenthusiastic Piagetian looking everywhere for evidence of numbers.

The final wave of early symbolization is in many ways the most important in any consideration of education. Around the age of five, six, or seven, children show an attraction toward "notational" or "second-order" symbolization. Given a game to play or a sequence to enact in pretense, they often have recourse on their own to some kind of scheme that can help them remember or codify information of relevance. For example, they will invent a tally system to keep track of their progress in a game, or, asked to go on a pretend vacation, they will draw pictures to remind them of which objects to take along.

Of course, the extent to which such notational behavior is engaged in will reflect in part the prevalence of notational systems in a culture. Presumably children would invent marking systems much less frequently if they had not seen adults around them indulging in such activities. Thus does culture color symbolization as clearly as it taints every other realm of early child development. Yet I would claim that the *impulse* to create a second-order symbol system—a set of marks that itself refers to a set of marks—is a deep human inclination that will emerge with relatively little provocation. Surely the universal decision to begin formal schooling around the age of five to seven is no accident: it presumes comfort with first-order symbolization and readiness to use symbols or notations that themselves refer to other symbols.

Moreover, this wave of symbolization opens up a Pandora's box of a most powerful sort. Once one has devised a symbol system that itself refers to other symbol systems, the possibility of embeddedness emerges; completed systems can be systematically absorbed as component parts into ever more powerful systems, as, for example, when multiplication presumes addition or when algebra presumes arithmetic. Such second- and higher-order systems of notation lie at the center of many scholastic activities. The capacity to engage readily in such metasymbolic activities is certainly an aid to scholastic success; indeed, it is too often equated with it.

A number of points should be made with respect to this sequence of four waves of symbolization. First, while it is uncertain whether these represent the *only* universal forms in which meaning is made, these four do represent a very promising synopsis of the major kinds of meanings that people make. Telling stories about the world, capturing spatial or temporal relations of importance, appreciating number and numerical relations, and creating notations that can themselves refer to other first-order symbols add up to a very rich set of capacities for dealing with a complex world of meaning, whether within or outside the context of school.

Second, so far as we can tell, every normal human being is capable of these forms of symbolization. Moreover, they seem to be acquired with relatively little formal tutelage, in the period before schooling and in the order that I have described. Nearly every five- or six-year-old has a "first-draft" knowledge of stories, songs, dramatic sequences, counting games, drawings, dances, and other emblems of the regnant cultural system. Children of this age are well equipped for later adventures in the symbolic realm even if they have never spent a day inside a school. (Notational symbolization might be better thought of as a transitional form here; we do not know about the extent to which children try to create tally systems or other second-order types of reference in a society that has been untouched by schools.)

Third, the discovery of the waves of symbolization, while made independently at Project Zero, shows encouraging correspondence with other reported pictures of early symbolization put forth by major theorists. For instance, it is reminiscent of Jerome Bruner's suggestive sequence of enactive (read "sensorimotor"), iconic (read "topological"), and symbolic (read "arbitrary" or "conventional") forms of representation. Moreover, the specific crests described in our studies are consistent with those reported in recent years by other researchers. Many investigators, like Elizabeth Bates and Malcolm Watson, have noted the coalescence of knowledge about events and roles around the age of two and the ability to capture them in simple scripts during the years that follow. Judy de Loache has carried out revealing studies in which children around the age of three rapidly become able to relate objects in a miniature version of a room to the "same" objects placed in a larger adjoining model room—a telling instance of topological mapping. And several investigators of cognitive development have recently confirmed the coalescence around the age of four of a basic understanding of counting procedures and simple numerical competence.

A final point with reference to waves of symbolization. If these waves do indeed represent the major ways in which human beings construe meanings, they may have powerful implications for education in and out of school. We may expect that students will be predisposed to learn materials that are presented in forms that highlight event-structures (stories), topological maps (relations of size, space, or time), digital maps (quantitative aspects), and/or second-order symbolic forms (notations that refer to other forms of knowledge). We can anticipate as well that, irrespective of how materials are initially presented, students may themselves represent the information—and later recall it—in terms of these principal modes of human symbolic reference. And we may presume that major projects in which students become engaged, from writing essays to shooting films, will use these symbolic forms as prototypes. Teachers, curriculum developers, and students would be well advised to become aware of these forms of symbolization, lest they invoke them inadvertently in inappropriate ways—for example, confusing a concept that functions in quantitative manner (like density) with one that exhibits narrative properties (like the life cycle).

Channels of Development

The study of early symbolization opened our eyes to some issues that go beyond "waves" and "streams." Reverting again to our aquatic metaphor, the Project Zero research team noted that around the age of five or six, children have an incipient sensitivity to "channels"—distinctions within each symbolic system. The three-year-old draws in essentially only one way, but the six-year-old can not only distinguish drawing from writing but also differentiate among kinds of drawings such as maps, cartoons, photographically faithful depictions, and designs. The three-year-old tells only one kind of story, but the six-year-old can distinguish between a newspaper report, a straightforward story, a fairy tale, a joke, and even a shaggy dog story. We see, then, that the child on the doorstep of school is already aware of genre practices within a particular symbol system; she can recognize instances of the genre and also create incipient instances of those genres. Obviously the specific culture will determine the kinds of genres that are detected, the educational system will determine which genres are mastered, and the vocational and avocational systems will determine which genres are pursued in later life; but sensitivity to "genre channels" seems a natural emergence at about the time that school begins. Again, educators can either exploit these newly emerging sensitivities or risk being entrapped by them, as happens when drawings and written texts are inappropriately lumped together.

Pragmatics of Symbol Use

A final aspect of symbolization pertains to the pragmatics of symbol use—the ends to which symbol systems are marshaled. Usage is not a major issue in syntactics, of course; that aspect of symbolization simply involves a sensitivity to the regularities and patterns that obtain among a string of symbols. The mastery of different kinds of meanings—the semantics of the system—can also be achieved without appreciable reference to purpose or function. Once one thinks about the roles of symbols in a world of human beings, however, it becomes apparent that symbol systems—and their ensemble of genres—are created and mobilized for definite purposes: to instruct, to entertain, to insult, to acquire or display knowledge. Alas, in our original studies, we were not sufficiently alert to the pragmatics of symbolic knowledge. Thus we still know too little about the uses that youngsters have in hand or mind when they tell stories, sing songs, or create notations. Yet because such uses of knowledge play so important a role in any educational environment (indeed, in any human environment), I want to comment briefly on them.

More than a few parents have been struck by the fact that youngsters in middle childhood or adolescence often express boredom and lament the absence of projects that engage them, whereas preschool children only rarely voice such sentiments. It has been my own experience, as parent, teacher, and psychologist, that three- or four-year-olds need little stimulation to want to interact with symbolic media; to employ our aquatic model for the last time, they take to words and pictures, to block-building and music-making, as a duck takes to water. Of course, children are not blind to instrumental usages, and when they find that a particular pattern of reward or punishment has come to surround a specific symbolic activity, they will certainly factor this knowledge into their subsequent behaviors. (Enthusiastic young "performers" tend to have "stage mothers" or "stage fathers"!) Yet for the most part, young children seem to obtain intrinsic enjoyment from symbolic activities, and further explorations of rich symbolic systems, often in the context of child-initiated projects, provide their own rewards.

This characterization should be kept in mind when we consider the many problems attendant upon motivating somewhat older youngsters to display even a modest degree of enthusiasm about school. For some reason, perhaps for many reasons, a large number of schoolchildren do not appreciate the rationale for the kinds of symbolic and notational practices featured in school. Nor, regrettably, do most of them find that kind of symbol use to be intrinsically interesting, in the way that so many preschoolers enjoy drawing or singing for the sheer pleasure of those activities.

PLURALIZING AND INDIVIDUALIZING THE WAYS OF KNOWING

In addition to the insights regarding symbolic development that emerged from our early symbolization study at Harvard Project Zero, this research also had a profound effect upon my own thinking about cognition. Specifically, when considering this research in conjunction with related work with brain-damaged adult patients, I became convinced that the general notions of intelligence and cognition held by most investigators were unduly restrictive. Owing both to the tradition of intelligence (and other kinds of) testing and to Piaget's pervasive and persuasive arguments about "general structures" of mind, most investigators have adhered to two fundamental assumptions: (1) that human cognition is basically unitary, and (2) that individuals can be adequately described and evaluated along a single dimension called "intelligence." Our research findings persuaded me that there exists a much wider family of human intelligences. As I explain in *Frames of Mind*, I was eventually stimulated to create a theory of "multiple intelligences."

To qualify as an intelligence in my scheme, a capacity has to satisfy a number of requirements: Among other things, it must feature a clear-cut developmental trajectory, be observable in isolated forms in populations like prodigies or autistic youngsters, and exhibit at least some evidence of localization in the brain. In the end, after considerable reflection and collaborative research, I posited the existence of seven human intelligences. In my view, all normal human beings develop at least these seven forms of intelligence to a greater or lesser extent. As noted in chapter 1, we are a species that has evolved to think in language, to conceptualize in spatial terms, to analyze in musical ways, to compute with logical and mathematical tools, to solve problems using our whole body and parts of our body, to understand other individuals, and to understand ourselves. An interesting and especially relevant facet of these intelligences is that each is susceptible to capture in a symbolic or notational system.

Even as all humans possess and exhibit these seven intelligences, the intelligences also serve to distinguish us from one another. Individuals possess varying amounts of these intelligences and combine and use them in personal and idiosyncratic ways. Just as we all look different and exhibit different personalities, we all possess different kinds of minds. This fact has decisive implications, particularly, as I have come to believe, for the ways in which we carry out educational endeavors.

Until now, most schools in most cultures have stressed a certain combination of linguistic and logical intelligences. Beyond question that combination is important for mastering the agenda of school, but we have gone too far in ignoring the other intelligences. By minimizing the importance of other intelligences within and outside of schools, we consign many students who fail to exhibit the "proper" blend to the belief that they are stupid, and we do not take advantage of ways in which multiple intelligences can be exploited to further the goals of school and the broader culture.

As I have argued in many writings and as I elaborate in the final chapters of this book, an education built on multiple intelligences can be more effective than one built on just two intelligences. It can develop a broader range of talents, and it can make the standard curriculum accessible to a wider range of students.

During the sensorimotor years, hints of these other intelligences can already be discerned. Infants distinguish melodies from one another, interact with other persons, gesture toward things they desire, and so on. But like other aspects of cognition, the multiple intelligences really come into their own and become enwrapped with cultural artifacts during the years immediately before school. Not surprisingly, the culture also determines the importance placed on the various intellectual competences: In general, Ugandans value slow-paced, careful involvement in activities, Mexicans stress interpersonal sensitivity, and the Chinese value mastery of large bodies of factual information. By the age of six or seven, each of the human intelligences has already developed to a high degree in any normal child, and the child has absorbed the culture's prototypes of the intelligent individual.

In addition to identifying the flowering of several intelligences in the opening years of life, our research has also revealed how these different intelligences develop into increasingly distinctive configurations over the course of childhood. Indeed, in Project Spectrum, a research project described in detail in chapter 11, we have determined that even four-year-olds exhibit quite distinctive cognitive profiles or, one might say, distinctive configurations of intelligences. Thus some four-year-olds approach the world regularly through the symbol system of language; others are more likely to take a spatial or visual orientation; and still others are already absorbed in the world of relations with other people. These differences, too, eventually exert profound effects upon the child as student, determining, for example, which "entry point" (a story, an image, a hands-on activity) is most likely to be effective for a given student in encounters with new material and, less happily, which concepts are likely to be confused with one another.

As should be evident, I consider the period from age two to age six or seven a fascinating period of human development. In my view, in fact, it harbors more of the secrets and power of human growth than any other comparable phase of growth. The first instances of symbolic competence are mastered. Habits of body and mind are set. Artistry and creativity in general are unleashed—or blocked—at this time. Perhaps most significantly in light of the argument put forth this book, powerful biases and constraints are mobilized and oriented in one or another direction. I have shown in some detail the lines of these constraints in the symbolic spheres of language and pretense play, suggesting as well that analogous kinds of constraints may obtain across the board in human symbolic activities.

Yet the description I have given thus far is necessarily fragmented. Syntactic capacities, the building blocks of cognition, abound. The child tells stories, counts objects, makes drawings, and begins to devise notations. At the same time, however, the child is attempting to make overall sense of the world; she is seeking to integrate the waves, streams, and channels of her own complex of intelligences into a comprehensive version of human life that encompasses the behavior of objects, interactions with other human beings, and an incipient view of herself. She is strongly constrained to carry out this integration, for survival could not take place in the absence of some coherent version of the world.

In the next chapter, which concludes part 1, we revisit the pre-school child, not as a collection of syntactic capacities or symbolic skills or distinct intelligences (though she is all of these things), but rather as the successor to the sensorimotor infant, a growing child trying to comprehend the world in terms of first-order or "natural" symbols. Mastering and synthesizing this knowledge is crucial, for it is the knowledge that the child will bring with her to school. As I have already suggested, this knowledge is also robust; its durability will help the child assimilate formal knowledge that is consistent with it but will hinder the child in mastering knowledge that conflicts with these basic, deeply entrenched ways of making sense of the world.

CHAPTER
5

The Worlds of the Preschooler: The Emergence of Intuitive Understandings

C ultures differ markedly in the attention they pay to the formal education of the young child. In Sweden, many children attend preschools, but, at least until now, the training of literacy skills has been put off until the age of seven. In the People's Republic of China, on the other hand, instruction in reading musical notation can often be observed in classes for three-year-olds, and the characters used in writing are frequently introduced to four- or five-year-olds. Diverse as ever in its educational means and goals, the United States features a full gamut of options, all the way from Glenn Doman's Institute of Human Potential, where children are drilled on written flashcards when they can barely walk, to developmentally oriented schools where children do not learn to read until they themselves take the initiative.

Even in those cases where formal or informal schooling is not an option, however, children acquire a great deal of knowledge. Through regular, active exploration of the world, they acquire what we have called *intuitive understandings* about the world. By combining their sensorimotor ways of knowing with first-order symbol-using capacities and emerging intelligences, young children come to think of the objects, events, and persons around them in a coherent way.

By the age of five or six, children have developed robust senses of three overlapping realms. In the world of physical objects, they have developed a theory of matter; in the world of living organisms, they have developed a theory of life; and in the world of human beings, they have developed a theory of the mind that incorporates a theory of the self. These theories are supplemented by skill in different kinds of performances, mastery of a wide set of scripts, and an ensemble of more individualized interests, values, and intelligences. Children bring this formidable "homespun" set of theories, competences, understandings, and penchants with them to school, and, of course, these in turn strongly influence the way in which the young students apprehend newly encountered materials.

In this chapter, I describe the theories, understandings, and constraints that characterize young children in the West. We have every reason to believe that similar world views characterize young children elsewhere, but children in other cultures have not been studied sufficiently to allow us to invoke the term *universal* with confidence. For the sake of economy, I will speak throughout of the "constraints" that lead to "theories of mind, matter, and life." But it should be stressed here that these shorthand references to theories cover a wide range of more specific biases, prejudices, and options, rather than a single type of constraint.

A word about the use of the term *theory* is appropriate here. In the sciences, the word is generally reserved for a set of propositions that relate systematically to one another and that can be captured in formal notations and operationalized in the laboratory. Clearly, in speaking of children's theories, I do not intend to suggest so integrated or self-conscious a framework. Yet, like a number of my colleagues, I find it suggestive to denote children's organized beliefs about the world as incipient theories, for children utilize these ideas regularly and generatively and draw inferences consistently from them. So long as the term *theory* is not taken too literally and is glossed as 'organized beliefs' or 'consistent world view,' it functions as a helpful shorthand for denoting the child's emerging understandings of the world.

These theories or world views are serviceable and powerful. They allow children to make at least provisional sense of most of what they encounter in the world. Part of their power is insidious. Because neither children nor their elders have been aware of these theories, the theories tend to be ignored once formal schooling begins. Yet rather than dissolving, as Piaget and some educators might wish, the intuitive theories remain as prepotent ways of knowing and are likely to reemerge with full force once the person leaves a scholastic milieu. Only if these intuitive theories are recognized and engaged is it possible for the child (and her teachers) to determine under which circumstances they ought still to obtain, when they are not relevant, and when they are actually at odds with more formal knowledge or beliefs that have been developed in the culture and that should be at a premium in school.

Whether the nativists are right and such knowledge is a priori, or Piaget was correct and such knowledge must be constructed during the first two years of life, there is no question that the two-year-old has already achieved a working sense of the physical world. She appreciates that objects exist in time and space and continue to exist even when they have been removed from sight. She is aware that an object in a given location can be approached by a variety of routes. She has clear expectations about the behaviors of specific objects; a ball thrown up into the air will fall down, but a ball tossed out of the room will not come back to her unless it is retrieved or tossed back by someone else. It is upon these sensorimotor understandings that the child's initial theories of matter, life, and mind are constructed.

THE CHILD'S INTUITIVE THEORIES

Ontological Theories

In the years succeeding age two, the child's initial knowledge of the physical world undergoes a series of changes and finer differentiations. One area that has been carefully studied is the child's emerging *ontology*, the types of entities that he recognizes and the kinds of distinctions that he comes to draw among them. At first the distinctions are quite gross—for example, between objects that are tangible (balls, candy) and entities that are not (time, weather, love). Next, distinctions come to be drawn within categories; some objects move and some do not, some move under their own impetus and others must be propelled by some kind of external agent. Children appreciate that one can speak of or think about any kind of object or entity, tangible or not; that one (or at least *someone*) can lift any tangible object; that objects that move under their own impetus are "alive," whereas those that must be impelled by others are generally not; that among living objects, some feel and a smaller proportion can think or read or tell a lie.

That children draw such distinctions is perhaps not surprising. But as Frank Keil has shown, the child's ontology does not inhere in simply drawing ever-finer distinctions. Children also make determinations of which inferences are permitted about, within, and across categorical boundaries. Thus, once having decided that something is inanimate, they deem it as incapable of having feelings, thoughts, or wishes. Distinctions cannot violate broad classes of objects: Thus, just as machines can't feel sad, human beings can't be fixed at the shop. The capacity to make such distinctions not only provides a rough-and-ready guide to which sorts of expectations can legitimately be entertained about an entity (a child may be disappointed, but time cannot be); it also lays the groundwork for an appreciation of metaphor, in which the attributes usually reserved for one category of objects (say, machines) can, for certain communicative purposes, be mapped onto a contrasting set of objects (a rigid teacher, a well-oiled speaker, thoughts that have become jammed up).

The child's emerging ontology is important for two reasons. First, the ways in which children come to think of classes of entities affect the kinds of theories they develop about these classes and the kinds of inferences they are prepared to draw. Children's theories of mechanics, for example, apply to entities they consider to be machine-like, whereas their theories of mental phenomena gradually become restricted to those they group under "feeling entities" or "living entities." As the boundaries of these groupings shift, so do the entities to which the respective theories are applied. But—and this is my second point—these groupings and inferences are by no means arbitrary. In making such groupings, children honor very powerful constraints; once they have classed a certain set of entities as being, say, nonliving, they will steadfastly refuse to think of those entities as exhibiting the features associated with entities they have classed among the living. Only the most powerful authorities—such as an ensemble of teachers, parents, and textbooks—have any hope of challenging these entrenched distinctions. And even these authorities often fail to convince students that a tomato is actually a fruit, a whale is actually a mammal, or a virus straddles the usual line between living and nonliving.

Theories of Number

Developing alongside the proclivity for parsing entities into "kinds of beings" is a capacity to deal with them in a numerical way, to conceptualize them as belonging to sets of different sizes. Infants, as we have seen, already exhibit a primitive sense of number, and our digital-mapping four-year-olds are prone to enumerate everything. But an important additional ensemble of understandings also emerges in the normal preschooler.

Rochel Gelman, perhaps the major contemporary student of numerical understanding, has spoken of widely available "principles" of number. Four-year-olds appreciate that each item in an array must be labeled by one and only one number word; that the order of number words (or tags) must remain stable; that the last spoken number in a set is also the number of items in that array; that one can count any set of entities; and that the order in which a given member of the array is tagged is irrelevant, so long as each object is tagged but once. In general, young children are drawn to assessing number, finding it more salient than the seemingly more accessible perceptual properties of color, shape, or size. They readily notice changes in the number of elements in a set.

Neo-Piagetian researcher Robbie Case has postulated the existence of knowledge of "number lines"—mental models that allow any entity to be assessed in terms of its numerosity. It is perhaps an exaggeration to speak of such understandings as being inborn, but it is perhaps equally misleading to suggest that they are learned or taught in any traditional sense. Rather, assuming that youngsters live in an environment where some account of number is taken by other people, the understandings seem to emerge as a matter of course in the preschool years.

As in the case of language, it is difficult to imagine how a young child could cope with the environment in the absence of incipient numerical capacities. How would the child ever keep track of the games, books, food, or even friends in her environment? The child would be able only to react to whatever object or objects happen to be within her surrounding at the moment. Nor is it readily imaginable what life would be like if numerical competences were radically different in scope. Say, for example, that every kind of entity had to be counted in a different way, or that counting depended upon whom you were speaking to or for what purpose you were enumerating. More radically still, what would life be like if the whole concept of counting did not exist? Under such circumstances, it would seem as if we were dealing with a different kind of human, or even a different species.

Given the child's early and strong tendency to recognize a domain of number and her preparedness to enumerate in a proper way, the question arises why more formal areas of mathematics often pose such problems for students. (This question echoes the disjunction between virtually universal facility in oral language and not infrequent difficulties with reading, writing, and/or spelling.) We will consider the problems in mathematics in chapter 8. At this point, it may be helpful to point out that dealing directly with quantities in one's environment is not the same thing as performing operations on notations that denote quantities not present in the milieu. Moreover, some of the strongly encouraged practices in the realm of number can interfere with formal numerical tasks. For example, the practice of adding sets to one another can create problems in learning to add fractions; students are tempted to add the numerators, add the denominators, and treat the resulting fraction as the correct sum.

Theories of Mechanics

Life in a world composed of enumerable objects is accompanied by certain basic conceptions about the behavior of matter. As outlined by the physicist-educator Andrea DiSessa, these ideas are quite powerful. Borrowing a nice figure of speech from Goethe, he terms these ideas "phenomenological primitives." Among these basic ideas that arise readily in young children are a division of objects into those that are rigid and those that are "springy"; a belief that an increase in impetus will always lead to an increase in noticeable results (even as an increase in resistance will lead to less potent results); and a conviction that objects will proceed in the direction in which they have been aimed, independently of the speed and direction in which they were previously headed. For most everyday purposes, these assumptions about the behaviors of objects are just fine; indeed, they may well have been acquired and become consolidated over the millennia precisely because they prove so serviceable in the everyday world. As DiSessa notes, however, each of these ideas and a host of others eventually conflict with principles that, according to physicists, actually govern the behavior of objects in a Newtonian world.

Certain of these primitive ideas prove especially powerful in coloring the ways in which preschool children think about the objects around them. One has to do with the principles that govern the activity of an object. From the age of three or so, children distinguish between those objects that appear to move on their own volition and those that do not. According to Rochel Gelman and her colleagues, the former objects are thought to have "innards," internal mechanisms that cause them to be able to move intentionally and on their own. The other set of objects can only move when propelled by external forces; they are susceptible to the impetus of an external agent. The power and effectiveness of these distinctions are underscored by the fact that young children appreciate that a doll, which looks like a person, is in fact subject to the external-agent principle, and so, for that matter, is a mechanical monkey. In contrast, a weird new animal, never seen before, is assumed to be able to move by virtue of its possession of the requisite "innards."

It might be thought that these ideas are latent in children, only to emerge when an experimenter poses a problem. It is my experience, however, that children readily and spontaneously invoke these mechanical principles when faced with a problem. On the very day that I was preparing this chapter, I complained to my wife that my car was stalling again and that I did not know what was the matter. Our son Benjamin, then aged four and one-half, piped up unasked with the following suggestion: "I know what. Maybe when you were driving on the highway, a stick bounced up and ran into the motor and that makes the car stop sometimes." When I probed further, Benjamin was not able to tell me the source of his hypothesis. The fact that he was nonetheless able to volunteer such an explanation with conviction underscores the extent to which he assumed that there was a mechanical source of the difficulty and that it could in principle be identified and rectified. More generally, as this example illustrates, children's mechanical understandings are not restricted to known exemplars; rather, as Ann Brown has shown, they are readily applied to novel machines, tools, or situations, even in the absence of perceptual cues that they might be relevant.

Theories about the World of the Living

Perhaps the most powerful discrimination made by children posits two classes of entities: those objects that move on their own, considered to be "alive," and those objects unable to move without external impetus and considered to be "dead" or "nonliving" (these are initially equated). The prototypical living organism is the human being; the more closely an organism resembles a human (particularly in physical appearance), the more it is assumed to possess the attributes and behaviors of human beings. This presumption obtains even when the child has not heard of the attribute in question. Thus, told that humans have spleens, children infer that monkeys must have spleens and dogs probably do as well; they are uncertain whether mice or fish have spleens, and they conclude that flies and butterflies probably do not. Even four-year-olds will chuckle at the thought that a pencil or a stone might have a spleen.

As Susan Carey has shown, these distinctions lead to an intuitive or folk biology, with characteristics discrepant from the discipline-based biology to which one is introduced in school. According to the intuitive theory of life, animals are alive, but plants are not, because they do not move. Organisms that look alike (fish and whales) are assumed to have the same organs and to carry out the same functions, while those that look different (penguins and robins) are presumed to have different organs and capacities. Carey reinterprets Piaget's early claims about childhood "animism" as evidence that properties like motion (clouds move because they intend to go somewhere) are more potent than evidence about internal structure (clouds do not have a nervous system and, in the absence of "innards," cannot initiate motion).

Generally sympathetic to a domain-specific view of development, Carey puts forth the interesting proposal that young children develop incipient theories about perhaps a dozen kinds of phenomena in the world. These include the nature of physical causality, the distinction between appearance and reality, and the operation of naive psychology, reflecting the intentions of a thinking agent. Such understandings have quite wide scope. Carey speculates further that these basic structures may ultimately give rise to scholarly disciplines (like physics, philosophy, or psychology) that seek to synthesize formal knowledge on these same topics. Should this be the case, it should be possible—and it would be educationally effective—to have students directly confront the discrepancies between their intuitive theories and those that have been developed by experts in the disciplines. Indeed, unless such confrontation takes place, it is likely that the intuitive theories will continue to exist, potentially to reemerge and dominate once the expert theories are no longer supported by the trappings of school.

Thus, by virtue of living in a world composed of many kinds of matter that they can classify, count, and conceptualize, children construct reasonably viable theories of matter and theories of life. These theories honor at least rough distinctions between living (or animate) matter and nonliving (mechanical) matter, and they contain more specific claims about what living and nonliving entities are like. Preschool children can also appreciate the difference between objects that have a natural existence in the world (so-called natural kinds, like plants, animals, or minerals) and those that have been made by human beings (artifacts like machines, toys, or buildings). Moreover, they can make inferences based on these distinctions; for example, if something is alive but not moving, it might be sleeping or pretending or injured.

For most intents and purposes, such distinctions will suffice. As Bertrand Russell remarked with respect to the nonintuitive nature of the theory of relativity, "Since everyday life does not confront us with such swiftly moving bodies, Nature, always economical, had educated common sense only to the level of everyday life." In preliterate traditional cultures, the understanding of the five-year-old may be quite close to that of elders in the community. In the modern Western world, however, the rough distinctions made by young children are now quite remote from distinctions based more solidly in a disciplinary understanding of how machines and organisms (and, for that matter, astronomical bodies) are actually constructed and how they actually operate.

Theories of Mind

Just as children develop intuitive theories of living and nonliving entities, they develop serviceable frames for thinking about the human mind. Appreciation of the complexity of a full-blown theory of mind was brought home to me when, primed to think about these issues, I attended a performance of Shakespeare's *Richard II*. As a first approximation, *Richard II* can be thought of as an early, historically grounded version of *Hamlet*. King Richard is a weak and egocentric ruler with some of the spirit of the poet and the intellectual. When he imposes an apparently unfair punishment on his relative Bolingbroke, the latter sets in motion a series of events that culminates in Richard's downfall and in the ascendancy of Bolingbroke—now Henry IV—to the uneasy throne.

An unusual feature of this Shakespearean history is that, until the end, when Richard II is murdered, virtually no blood is shed among the principals. The decision by Richard to abdicate the throne is made simply and at one point is almost reversed. Richard is trying to read Henry's mind—to envision what Henry might do if Richard does or does not renounce the throne—and, reciprocally, Henry is trying to read Richard's mind. Richard realizes that being king goes beyond a dubbing ceremony; it is also important who is *considered* by others to be the king. The power that inheres in attribution, in the "intentional states" (or beliefs) held by important persons, is patent.

We encounter here striking illustrations of theory-of-mind thinking. Human beings have the capacity to appreciate the existence in other human beings of those entities that we call minds. When Richard is trying to figure out what Henry is thinking, he is illustrating what is often called a "first-order" belief— a belief about someone else's thought processes. When he also tries to figure out what Henry is thinking that he (Richard) is thinking, he is illustrating a "second-order" belief—a belief about someone's thoughts about one's own (or a third party's) thought processes. Even higher-order beliefs are possible; for example, Henry could be thinking about what Richard is thinking that Henry is thinking about what Richard is thinking! And of course Richard is also attempting, Hamlet-like, to know his own mind.

The play of minds extends beyond the stage. Shakespeare wrote the play during the reign of Elizabeth I. Like Richard II, the Virgin Queen had no offspring, and there was great debate about who was to ascend the English throne after her death. It is difficult to believe that Shakespeare did not have Elizabeth on his mind when he wrote a play about Richard II; in fact, as though to settle any lingering doubts on that score, Elizabeth once remarked to William Lambarde, the keeper of records in the Tower of London, "I am Richard II, know ye not that?"

The play of minds also extends to other eras. Take a mid-1990 production in Britain occurring during the "reigns" of Margaret Thatcher and of Elizabeth II. Questions about the time and identity of succession swarmed about both formidable women, and it is entirely possible that current actors and directors may have had these comparisons in mind as they mounted a production on a British stage.

Clearly, the kinds of embedded understandings described here are not within the ken of the young child. Indeed, even the adult writing these lines has to step back and think intensively once he attempts to extend the mentalistic chain beyond second-order beliefs. Yet in recent years, evidence has accumulated that the young child develops a quite robust theory of mind, even in the years before entering school. The theory encompasses other persons, with their minds, and oneself as an agent, with a body and a mind. While one could therefore speak of theories of minds, bodies, others, and self, I will for the most part use the overarching phrase "theory of mind."

According to the picture that is emerging from research, the two-year-old child is already aware of himself as a separate entity and of others as discrete persons. Charming evidence of this self-awareness comes from the fact that the two-year-old, when he spies himself in the mirror, will try to rub off rouge that has surreptitiously been placed on his face. Neither the one-year-old nor most animals will show any such inclination, perhaps instead treating the reflection as a fellow member of the species. By the third year of life, children are already speaking about wishes, desires, and fears, which are at least "soft signs" that they are aware that they have minds and that they can impute some kinds of mental states to others.

Preschoolers develop as well a strong sense of themselves. To a considerable extent, this sense is rooted in the physical; the child has attained a certain size and stature, has hair and eyes of specific colors, wears certain clothes, and cherishes certain possessions. But self-knowledge transcends the superficial. The five- or six-year-old already knows that he is better in some pursuits than in others, that he has certain wishes and fears, that he is capable of obedience and disobedience, selfishness and altruism (although he may not use those words).

Especially pertinent to our inquiry, the young child is already developing incipient theories of himself as an agent in the realms of learning and thinking. He forgets certain things, to his annoyance; he remembers other things easily; if he practices an activity, he expects to get better at it, although he considers other activities "just too hard" for him. Often included in his theory is a perception of how learning occurs: You go to school, a smart person tells you something, and you are expected to learn it and remember it, and if you don't, you are stupid. Rarely is there any conception of learning as a long process of experimentation, reflection, and self-improvement; rather, learning depends upon having certain abilities or, more broadly, having a good mind. Especially in the scholastic milieu, one's merit as a self is closely allied with assessment of how good your mind is. (Consistent with my belief in the durability and potency of the five-year-old's mind, I note that this model of schooling and learning is held by many parents and teachers as well.)

In developmental psychology, scientific advances are often achieved following the surprising demonstration that children fail to exhibit a certain skill or understanding or that they construe the world in a way quite different from most adults. (A large number of such demonstrations constituted the empirical facet of Piaget's genius.) In recent years, a most striking demonstration has come from studies of "false belief" conducted by Josef Perner and Heinz Wimmer.

In a typical study, a young subject observes a sequence of actions carried out in front of him by the experimenter and an accomplice. For example, the child and the accomplice both see a box of chocolates on a table. The accomplice then leaves the room. In his absence, the experimenter removes the chocolates and places pencils inside the box instead. When the accomplice has returned to the room, the observing child is asked what the accomplice expects to find in the box. Until the age of four, the child will insist on the accomplice's expectation that there are pencils inside the box. Because the child has been privy to the exchange of pencils for chocolate, he seems unable to conceive that the accomplice is not also privy to that information. In other words, the child assumes that all minds have access to the same information.

By the age of four, however, a crucial change takes place. The child becomes capable of appreciating that the accomplice was not privy to the exchange. Thus the accomplice will continue to believe, falsely, that the box still contains chocolates. By his correct response, the observing child shows that he is able to represent to himself the content of another's mind—in this case, the lingering false belief that the box contains the chocolates that were originally there.

One might ask why it is necessary to pose such a complex task, simply to demonstrate the existence in young children of an awareness of other minds. (Indeed, many experimenters have asked this question, and some have provided evidence that children have at least an incipient understanding at an earlier age.) But there are good reasons for using the false belief task. So long as the child and the apparently ignorant "other" both have access to the same information, it is impossible to tell whether a child really understands the mind of the other or is simply answering based on his own knowledge. Once the knowledge base of the child and the other are apparently different, however, it becomes possible to determine whether the child actually appreciates that he and others may see the world differently.

The ability to appreciate that another person has a set of beliefs different from one's own represents a considerable advance, just as the ability to appreciate that one previously held a contrasting set of beliefs oneself constitutes a milestone. Once the principle of different belief structures has been established, the potential exists for more finely differentiated "maps" of the beliefs of others, of the sort ultimately achieved in an appreciation of a drama like *Richard II*. Such a sensitivity also underlines the capacity to go beyond stereotypes and to appreciate that others may legitimately see the world in ways very different from one's own perspective.

It must be stressed, however, that these further advances in theory of mind take place only gradually. Even the older child, for example, has difficulty appreciating that a person might say one thing even though he believed another, in order to make an ironic point. And even the mature adult often falls into the habit of assuming that another person has the same beliefs as he himself, probably because an assumption of similar beliefs represents a comfortable "default position." In the realm of mental phenomena, no less than in the domain of physical objects, the theories of early childhood may persist indefinitely.

Stages in the Development of a Theory of Mind

A number of investigators, David Olson prominent among them, have attempted to place the emerging theory of mind within a more general picture of the child's symbolic competence. It is useful to think of the child as becoming capable, over the course of early childhood, of several ordered levels of symbolic sophistication:

1. The child at the end of the infancy period has a "mundane" symbolic capacity. She can appreciate that words or pictures refer to entities in the world, and she can begin to use words and graphically wrought lines to refer to such entities.
2. The child becomes able to employ sets of symbols within a single system. For instance, during the initial wave of symbolization, the child can understand and produce simple sentences that refer to event sequences or to an agent's actions in the world.
3. The child becomes able to appreciate that symbols represent a

point of view, the mental state of the particular person who has issued the symbolic statement. Thus the statement "This dog is Fido" represents an individual's belief that a certain state of affairs is extant—specifically, that the individual believes a particular dog in question is named Fido. The realm of symbol use has now extended beyond a simple description of a state of affairs to the acknowledgment that a description—indeed any description—reflects the perspective of an agent and has a certain true or false value.

4. The child now recognizes that the point of view of an individual, while sincerely held, can nonetheless be contrary to the actual state of affairs. This is what happens when the child masters a false-belief task. The observing child now is able to hold in mind the actual state of affairs (the box contains pencils) while simultaneously appreciating that another person may legitimately—and even tenaciously—subscribe to an erroneous belief (the box continues to hold chocolates).

5. The child comes to appreciate that one may deliberately state something that is contrary to a state of affairs, for example, to fool someone or to enlist his solidarity. In the case of a lie, the statement "This is a lovely day" represents an attempt to hide from someone the fact that it is actually raining. In the case of sarcasm, the statement "This is a lovely day," made when the rain is pouring down, represents an attempt to comment on an undesirable state of affairs and thus to adopt a common critical stance with reference toward an area of mutual disappointment. Appreciation of irony or sarcasm seems to require second-order beliefs: The speaker must know that the listener knows that the actual state of affairs is different from that which has been explicitly coded in the utterance. The child is approaching (even though she has not yet quite reached) the complexity of the mental struggle between Richard II and Bolingbroke.

This account of stages in the development of a theory of mind may seem a bit abstract, drawing as it does on the results of laboratory research. I can assure the reader that it reflects as well genuinely changing stances in the daily world. As an inveterate developmental psychologist (and a doting, if sometimes intrusive, parent), I have always asked my children questions to which I already knew the answer. Recently, Benjamin, aged five and one-half, has begun to call me on this. He now says, "Dad, you know the answer to that question. You know that I know the answer to that question. So why do you ask me it anyway?"

Human beings have evolved to survive in a world that itself obeys particular physical principles (such as gravity), contains man-made objects that follow certain principles (machines that can be impelled in given ways), and features other human beings with whom they must interact productively but who sometimes engage in behavior or discourse that seems deviant in light of the current state of affairs. It is therefore not surprising—and it may even be necessary—that young human beings evolve robust theories of matter, number, life, mind, other, self, and the like that allow them to deal with the workaday world. We have seen that such theories seem to arise spontaneously in the course of early childhood; as we shall have occasion to observe shortly, these theories play an important role—sometimes facilitative, but sometimes counterproductive—as students attempt to master more formal disciplinary and scholastic forms of knowing.

While the term "theory" perhaps promises more coherence than is actually the case, it is important to stress that children are able to use these emerging frameworks in order to make sense of new phenomena. Indeed, the typical experimental paradigm in this domain involves introducing the child to a machine, an animal, a statement, or a state of affairs that he has never encountered before and then, by means of an interview or some other procedure, eliciting the child's theoretical stance toward the entity in question: Is it living or dead? Does it have a mind? Is the mind privy to the same evidence as my own mind? It seems quite legitimate, too, to invoke the term "understanding." The child is appreciating newly encountered phenomena and relationships on the basis of understandings that have already evolved. The new understandings may of course be deficient (as is the ultimate fate of all understandings) but they are typically not the result of either rote memory, sheer imitation, or simple guessing. In fact, they often involve chains of inferences, which devolve from the basic tenets of the theory or theories on which the child is drawing.

OTHER EARLY PREDISPOSITIONS

Early understandings of mind and matter are a crucial part of the mental equipment that children bring to school, and by and large, they represent the ways in which children think about scholastic topics unless deliberately instructed to conceptualize them in a different manner. But such theoretical conceptions are by no means the only kinds of skills, competences, tendencies, and attitudes that color children's future learnings. We will consider here a few others.

Canonical Events and Stereotypes

Children's understandings of mind and matter strongly affect their scripts about the most universally encountered objects and events in the world—the falling stone, the sad friend. But youngsters also have script knowledge of many other frequently encountered, if somewhat more idiosyncratic sets of events. Their scripts include not only the birthday party but the wedding, the confirmation ceremony, and the funeral; not only the trip to the restaurant but also the family vacation, the visit to the museum, the jaunt to the toy store, the ride in the car, train, or airplane, and countless other familiar sequences of events; not only events they have witnessed with their own eyes but also plots and characters they have seen on television or at the movies or learned about in books.

Children expect to read and hear about instances of these scripts—or variations of them—in their school curricula. To the extent that what they are taught is consistent with canonical sets of events, that material will be readily assimilated, but to the extent that newly encountered sequences of events clash with well-entrenched scripts, children may distort them or have difficulty in assimilating them. Thus, if children are accustomed to scripts that feature "good guys," "bad guys," a chase and a happy ending, they will tend to interpret historical events like a civil war or literary texts like *Oliver Twist* along these lines, and they may well reduce more complex scripts to these sound-bite capsules of reality.

As a result of daily experiences and of media presentations, children also develop robust images of kinds of characters and personalities. Such stereotypes may be quite positive or neutral (the mother as a warm and loving person, the policeman as someone who offers protection), but they may also contain misleading assumptions (all doctors are male, all nurses are female) or generalizations that are false and even dangerous (all Jewish men are smart or crooked, all black men are strong or prone to violence). From an early age, children develop stereotypes that seem to be especially flagrant in the area of sex roles and that prove quite resistant to change. Not surprisingly, information that conforms to these stereotypes is readily assimilated, but where the stereotypes are countermanded, students may either miss the contrary clues or even deny their own perceptions.

Performances

As we saw in our earlier discussion of symbolization, children about to enter school have also mastered a set of performances that embody their command of several symbolic media. They can tell (and appreciate) stories, sing songs, and enact dramatic or bodily sequences. Some, indeed, already qualify as miniature performers, able to seize the interest of an audience and to carry out quite elaborate series of actions. Such competences are revealing, not only because many schools value skilled performances but also because they illuminate children's conceptions of what it means to "know" or "understand" something—that is, to carry out a performance of one or another sort.

For the most part, performances of young children fall under the rubric of rote, ritualized, or conventional patterns of behavior, but children sometimes go beyond the models that they have seen, and their performances may embody genuine understandings. In such cases children are able to utilize symbol systems to create performances that reveal sensitivity to a variety of perspectives or express their own feelings or beliefs about a state of affairs. As psychiatrist Robert Coles has shown, children caught in political or social crises are especially prone to exhibit their understandings through works of literary or graphic art, and these works may reflect both a rounded sense of a controversial issue and the creator's personal response to it.

Esthetics and Values

Both as audience members (who attend puppet shows or watch television) and as fledgling performers (who tell stories or jokes, sing songs, and dance to music), children evolve a sense of what makes for an effective or artful presentation. In many cases, these esthetic standards are quite specific: A painting should look like its subject; a poem should rhyme; a joke requires a loud noise and a grimace; a story must have a clear beginning, middle, and ending. These standards also highlight certain features (bright colors and funny names), even as they perforce reflect insensitivity to others (subtlety in portraiture and use of figurative language). At times, these esthetic rules of thumb may come to interfere with the appreciation of works that violate the canons in one or another particular.

More broadly speaking, the milieus in which children spend their early years exert a very strong impact on the standards by which they subsequently judge the world around them. Whether in relation to fashion, food, geographical environment, or manner of speaking, models initially encountered by children continue to affect their tastes and preferences indefinitely, and these preferences prove very difficult to change.

Closely related to standards of taste are an emerging set of beliefs about which behaviors are good and which values are to be cherished. In most cases, these standards initially reflect quite faithfully the value system encountered at home, at church, and at preschool or elementary school. Values with respect to behavior (you should not steal, you should salute the flag) and sets of beliefs (my country, right or wrong, all mommies are perfect, God is monitoring all of your actions) often exert a very powerful effect on children's actions and reactions. In some cultures, a line is drawn early between the moral sphere, where violations merit severe sanctions, and the conventional sphere, where practices are simply a matter of taste or custom; in other cultures, all practices are evaluated along a single dimension of morality. Even—and perhaps especially—when children are not conscious of the source and of the controversy surrounding these beliefs and values, unfortunate clashes may occur when they meet others raised with a contrasting set of values. It is assuredly no accident that Lenin and the Jesuits agreed on one precept: Let me have a child until the age of seven, and I will have that child for life.

Children carry around in their consciousness a large number of scripts, stereotypes, models, and beliefs. Examined analytically, these conceptual schemas may harbor many internal contradictions: Boys are better than girls versus I love my mother and hate my father; teachers are mean and bossy versus I want to be a teacher when I grow up. Rarely, however, are these contradictions noted, and even when they are, they rarely trouble the child. I would suggest, further, that adults carry about with them a similar set of conflicting statements and sentiments (for example, in the political sphere) whose contradictory nature rarely proves troublesome in everyday life. It should be apparent, however, that contradictory perspectives can interfere with formal learning. Not only may they be logically contradictory to one another but one or both may clash with findings that have been established within a discipline. A person who believes that all art ought to be representational and who also believes that abstract designs ought to be symmetrical is not going to have an easy time relating to contemporary abstract expressionist art.

Temperament and Personality

One additional aspect of the child's world view will have consolidated to a significant extent by the end of the preschool years. Extending beyond the usual definition of the cognitive, extending even beyond beliefs, standards, and values and yet of crucial importance for all subsequent learning are the child's temperament and personality characteristics: the ways in which the child tackles problems and puzzles; the kinds of interests he has already developed (as well as areas that he fails to appreciate or actively fears); the models of learning he has witnessed at home or on the playground; the amount of energy he has available and the ways in which he customarily harnesses and directs it; and the particular history of interactions he has had with others as he attempts to learn a new skill (like riding a bicycle) or to unravel an enigmatic physical phenomenon (what makes something float). In this arena, of course, each child differs from every other child, and the differences that children bring with them color the ways in which they handle (or fail to handle) the milieu and the lessons of school.

FIVE CONSTRAINTS ON LATER LEARNING

In this chapter, I have introduced a wide range of factors and phenomena that, taken together, constitute the world view of the young child. There are her incipient (but already powerful) theories of mind, matter, life, and self; the various scripts and stereotypes (sometimes contradictory to one another) that she has absorbed; and the aspects of esthetic standards, values, personality, and temperament that also contribute to her apprehension of the world. For the purposes of summary, I find it useful to consider all these factors as constraints or biases, which influence, guide, or restrict the child in any kind of subsequent educational experience. These constraints may be thought of as representing five different degrees, with the power of the constraint ordered here from most to least intractable:

1. *Kantian-Einsteinian constraints*. Of greatest potency are what might be called Kantian-Einsteinian constraints. I refer here to the *necessity* of conceptualizing the world in terms of objects, space, time, causality and to the impossibility of even conceiving of the world in other than these terms. Kant posited the centrality of these categories of knowledge; Einstein serves to remind us that our understanding of these concepts does change, thanks to scientific investigation, although such revised (and often enhanced) understandings are not easy to promulgate, particularly when they deviate from intuitive theories of the world.

2. *Ontological constraints*. Second only to the built-in limits on knowing are the particular categories of objects and entities of which the world exists. Objects are defined and recognized in certain ways, and they belong to certain broad categories, such as tangible or intangible, living or nonliving, feeling or nonfeeling. Once one has parsed the world in terms of such ontologies, certain kinds of groupings and comparisons become possible, whereas others are precluded, and the transfer across domain that is inherent in metaphor can be mobilized.

3. *Constrained theories*. As a consequence of the history of her interactions in the world and the particular objects that she has constructed, the young child comes to formulate basic theories about the physical and social world. In the terms adopted in this book, she develops theories of mind, matter, life, self, and other ontological realms. Not derived from formal study or from any preexisting disciplines, these naive, folk, or intuitive theories nonetheless achieve considerable potency; they come to color subsequent interpretations of persons, events, and concepts, within and outside of a formal schooling context.

4. *Strengths, tendencies, and styles*. Whereas the first three constraints affect all human beings in quite similar ways, the last two serve to differentiate human beings within and across cultures. One type of constraint includes those biases in information-processing strength and style that can be observed in early life. Children exhibit different kinds, arrays, and degrees of intelligence, even as they evolve characteristic ways of approaching problems and challenges. These cognitive tendencies will be invoked when youngsters enter school; they

presumably will cause problems or furnish opportunities, depending upon the compatibility between the child's own cognitive and stylistic profile, the demands of the subject matter, and the manner in which the material is presented.

5. *Contextual constraints*. A final significant form of constraint reflects particular contextual elements in the child's personal background. Considerations of ethnicity, social class, parental styles, and values will affect the kinds of materials with which the child becomes involved, the ways in which the materials are engaged, and the preferences and standards applied to them. As we saw earlier, students living in adjacent communities can acquire astonishingly different perspectives on storytelling, depending upon the models they have encountered at home and on the street. By the same token, assumptions made about what practices are moral, how children should relate to one another and to their parents, and what counts as proper dress or good food are also absorbed in early childhood. It is probably the case that, of our five clusters of constraints, these preordaining factors are most open to change in the school setting. They are especially readily changed when people are aware of them and want, for whatever reason, to change them, as, for example, when immigrants wish to be assimilated into the host culture. In the absence of a firm recognition and confrontation of such predisposing factors, however, youngsters may find themselves uncomfortably remote from the agenda of school. Such a disjunction is especially likely to happen when the family and the school reflect the standards of quite different communities and when neither is aware of the extent of the gulf.

Constrained by species membership, the physical constitution of the world, the structure of the nervous system, and more specific facets of individual personality, cognitive tendency, and sociocultural background, the preschooler prepares to enter the more formal educational institutions prescribed by his culture. What will happen in school cannot be predicted exactly in any given case. Recent insights into the process, however, reveal how difficult it is for most children to master the agenda of school, particularly to the extent that its mode of operation clashes with, or is irrelevant to, the biases and constraints that have emerged during the first half decade of life. The story of that clash will concern us throughout the remainder of this book.

A DEVELOPMENTAL FORECAST

Ideally, any scientist bent on understanding the operation of an institution like school seeks to factor out its effects. In principle, such factoring could best be achieved by defining a population, assigning a randomly-chosen half of the children to attend school, and assigning the remaining half to remain completely apart from any formal educational setting. Of course, in such a "blue-sky" exercise, it would be desirable as well to examine the effects of apprenticeships, different kinds of schools, home schooling and other comparable pedagogical variants, and relevant control groups. Only under such ideal laboratory conditions could one with confidence factor out the effects of school from those of natural development.

As I have already conceded, the category of "natural development" is a fiction; social and cultural factors intervene from the first and become increasingly powerful well before any formal matriculation at school. The fiction seems a useful one to maintain in the preschool years, however. For one thing, most children do not receive any kind of formal instruction at that time; for another, the regularities across children continue to be quite impressive. Once the child reaches the age of six or seven, however, the influence of the culture—whether or not it is manifested in a school setting—has become so pervasive that one has difficulty envisioning what development could be like in the absence of such cultural supports and constraints.

For these reasons it is simply not feasible to present a picture of development after the age of seven, were one to be able to follow it in its pristine form. Piaget seems to have thought otherwise. He apparently believed that he was tracing natural development when he described the "formal operator" of adolescence. But nearly all informed observers now concur that Piaget was actually describing the development of habits of thought and mind gained in school, such as the discovery of certain ways of testing hypotheses and manipulating variables that are conventionally taught in the general science laboratory. As many investigators have shown, Piaget-style formal operational questions simply make little sense when posed in a completely nonscholastic setting.

Two other options are available to the researcher. One is to compare the task performances of youngsters raised in schooled societies with the performance of youngsters raised in societies that feature little or no schooling. The results of dozens of studies over the last few decades are quite consistent here. When Western-style school tasks—the kinds that appear on standardized tests—are administered to both populations, schooled children typically perform much better. (In fact, it would be difficult to envision any other outcome.)

But when unschooled children are given materials from their own environment with which to work, when they have become familiar with the circumstances of the testing, or when their own behaviors are examined for evidence of the sought-after capacities (like memory or inductive capacities with respect to practices of importance for survival in their culture), the apparent differences across schooled and unschooled populations either disappear altogether or are radically reduced. It seems that the basic human cognitive capacities in which psychologists have traditionally been interested—attention, memory, learning, classification—can be assumed to develop, so long as the individual does not live in a grossly impoverished environment. Not surprisingly, so long as the comparisons are restricted to the particular information taught in school, schooled children continue to display their superiority in all measures.

The other option is to examine some of the trends that clearly develop in Western schoolchildren but that seem to have less to do with the specific agenda of school and more to do with the experience of simply living in a world and having to cope with its problems, contingencies, and opportunities. Presumably such trends should characterize children in every culture.

All children everywhere will become more skilled in those pursuits that engage their interests and their efforts and that are valued by adults and peers in their environment. Skill develops not only in areas of vocation and avocation but also in the simple activities of living— telling stories, estimating large numbers, handling disputes, instructing a younger person. Which areas show the most improvement, and how rapidly the improvement occurs, will reflect the accidents of culture and individual, but a steady improvement, at least for a while, can be counted upon.

Children not only think better as they mature; they also become capable of thinking about their own mental processes. Memory capacity may not expand in any real sense, but children (and adults) learn how to boost their recall by various strategies, ranging from the ways in which they group or store things to the kinds of tally systems they utilize on paper or in their heads. Children also learn to think about their own problem-solving activities: How can I best handle a new challenge? Which system or which tool would be useful?

Who can I turn to for help? What is relevant and what is irrelevant to a problem I am trying to solve or a principle I am seeking to discover or master? Often these lessons are learned by watching others reflect on their memories or their thinking processes, by mastering practices common in the culture, or by following oft-repeated adages; even left pretty much to their own devices, however, it seems reasonable to assume that nearly all youngsters will improve somewhat in these "metacognitive" areas between the age of seven and adulthood (which itself begins at markedly different ages across cultures).

Whereas improvement can be expected in most areas, it is not an automatic occurrence. Among the intriguing sets of phenomena described by developmental psychologists in recent years are the so-called "U-shaped curves" of development. The basic idea is straightforward: Children sometimes get worse in a performance as they get older, and then at least some children, and in certain cases nearly all, recover from the dip in the U and ultimately perform at a higher level.

U's have been discovered in many domains of development, and there is no reason to believe that they all reflect the same causal mechanism. In the arts, for example, young children often prove to be better metaphor makers and to produce drawings with more originality and flavor than older children mired in the so-called "literal stage" of esthetic production. Some children remain at the trough in the U, some cease drawing or metaphorizing altogether, and selected others eventually produce fine drawings or innovative metaphoric figures.

In language, U's have been discovered in early life. Young children typically produce irregular terms correctly; they say "he went," "she sang," "three blind mice," and the like. Then, seemingly as a result of the effort to find and apply general rules, a torrent of errors follows; the child begins to utter such never-modeled phrases as "he goed," "she singed," or "three mouses." In this case the dip in the U is transient, with nearly all children eventually mastering both the laws of the past tense and of pluralization, as well as the exceptions to these rules.

Still other kinds of U's have been observed in scientific learning. The young child will show an intuitively correct response to a problem, whereas a somewhat older child will allow this common sense to be overridden by a compulsive application of a rule that happens to be inappropriate. For example, in probing children's conceptions of intensive quantities like temperature, Sidney Strauss has shown children two beakers of water, each 10 degrees in temperature, and then combined the contents of the two beakers. When the young child is asked the heat of the now-commingled bodies of water, each 10 degrees, he unhesitatingly answers that the water remains the same temperature, and he may be able to quantify the answer as "10 degrees." He succeeds because he knows—indeed, understands—that water added to water of the same temperature does not change temperature. A somewhat older schoolchild, however, posed the same problem, is likely to respond "20 degrees." Upon reflection, the reason for this response seems patent. As I noted in reviewing early numerical skills, children evince a strong urge, almost a compulsion, to add any two numbers presented together in a school context. Thus, notational fluency ends up overriding common sense.

Strauss has reported another finding that is highly relevant to our concern here. When these and similar phenomena are tested with unschooled children, one does not encounter the same strong U dip. Instead, the dip occurs at a somewhat later age and proves neither as deep nor as ubiquitous as that encountered in schooled children. The reverse side of the story is that there is also less of a complete recovery. While one hesitates to make too much of a single finding, Strauss's research may signal that U-shaped phenomena are a part of normal development but that they are exacerbated by some of the procedures highlighted in a school setting. A natural proclivity to look for rules and to strive for quantification is reinforced by the practices and expectations of school.

Annette Karmiloff-Smith has observed a similar kind of progression across disparate developmental domains. In the course of learning a procedure, youngsters go through a phase where it seems important for them to "mark" some aspect of the emerging knowledge, so that it is totally clear to them. For example, when a single word or phrase can have two meanings, the child sometimes adds a completely unnecessary morpheme or word, just to make it absolutely clear to all concerned—and particularly to herself!—that she has not confused the two meanings. So, for example, the young child learning to speak French says unnecessarily "une de pomme" to mean "an apple" just to show that she does not confuse it with "une pomme" meaning "one apple." Ultimately, the child gains sufficient handle on the distinction that she no longer has to add this extra marking.

According to Karmiloff-Smith's analysis, the mature understanding then becomes automatized, so that the child is able to use the correct expression in each context without having to think about it or mark it in any way. In this manner, the child actually proceeds from an initial unconscious performance to a period of conscious awareness of possible confusions, which results in this overmarking activity, to a final, less reflective but more confident kind of knowledge. This procedure can be observed in language learning, drawing, the operation of machines, and presumably other domains as well. As bicycle riders or skiers have long observed, it is most comforting when activities that once required attention and conscious problem-solving faculties can be assigned confidently to the realm of well-routinized neural sequences.

This brief survey of certain competences and capacities that emerge following the sensorimotor and symbolic periods suggests that cognitive development does not cease merely because a growing child fails to attend school. (Indeed, the more rabid Rousseauians might contend that more or better development ensues in such a context and that school is actually an impediment to further development. I will not defend that romantic position here.) We can confidently expect children around the age of eleven or twelve to be more skilled, more reflective about thinking and memory, and more effective in their problem solving.

We can also speculate that certain transient declines in competence can be expected, as youngsters attempt to master the rules of the society as scrupulously as possible, as well as some "errors of growth," as children attempt to avoid certain formerly appealing responses or behaviors that seem to them inappropriate or potentially confusing in the current context. At least in some domains, the dip in the U should prove short-lived, but it is possible that in the arts a seemingly temporary dip in performance may become permanent for most children.

For the most part, these developmental trends cannot be observed in untrammeled form. By the time the child has reached the age of seven or so, his development has become completely intertwined with the values and goals of the culture. Nearly all learning will take place in one or another cultural context; aids to his thinking will reside in many other human beings as well as in a multitude of cultural artifacts. Far from being restricted to the individual's skull, cognition and intelligence become distributed across the landscape.

THE POWERS AND LIMITS OF THE FIVE-YEAR-OLD MIND

Just as Freud stressed the degree to which the adult personality harbors within it the complexes and strivings of the Oedipal child, I maintain that students (and nonstudents) continue to be strongly affected by the practices, beliefs, and understandings of the five-year-old mind. Because this is a potent—and in some respects novel—assertion, it merits a few additional concluding remarks.

To begin with, the child of five, six, or seven is in many ways an extremely competent individual. Not only can she use skillfully a raft of symbolic forms, but she has evolved a galaxy of robust theories that prove quite serviceable for most purposes and can even be extended in generative fashion to provide cogent accounts of unfamiliar materials or processes. The child is also capable of intensive and extensive involvement in cognitive activities, ranging from experimenting with fluids in the bathtub to building complex block structures and mastering board games, card games, and sports. While some of these creations are derivative, at least a few of them may exhibit genuine creativity and originality. And quite frequently in at least one area, the young child has achieved the competence expected from much older children. Such precocity is particularly likely when youngsters have pursued a special passion, like dinosaurs, dolls, or guns, or when there is a strain of special talent in areas like mathematics, music, or chess or simply a flexibility, a willingness to try new things.

As this chapter amply documents, the child's performances and understandings also exhibit limitations. In many ways, the theories are simple, if not simplistic; the stereotypes, esthetic preferences, and moral codes rarely exhibit subtlety or complexity. Cultures have achieved much knowledge and sophistication over the millennia; these are not available to the young child, and there are quite legitimate reasons for instituting formal or informal education, even if that education proves more difficult to achieve than teachers in earlier eras may have thought.

Indeed, it is perhaps best to think of the mind of the five-year-old as a curious blend of strengths and weaknesses, powers and limitations. In its theoretical resourcefulness and intuitions, it is powerful; in its artistic endeavors, it can be creative and imaginative; in its adventurousness, it is exemplary; in its tendency to stereotype and simplify, it is distinctly limited. Because the mind is not yet well organized into discrete chambers—still (in Freud's terms) polymorphous perverse—it can extend in many, often contradictory ways, waxing wise at one moment, foolish at a second, and bizarre, nonsensical, or wholly mysterious at a third. It contains a swirl of symbols, scripts, theories, and incipient notions and concepts, which can be invoked in appropriate ways but which also remain to be sorted out in a more secure manner. Much of the effort of the next few years is to calm or civilize or harness this raw mind; in some ways, such regularization can have a positive effect, but it may also limit the child's imagination or reinforce biases and stereotypes that at this point have not yet become thoroughly entrenched.

I intend a deliberate ambiguity in the phrase "the mind of the five-year-old." Counter to the usual stereotypes—the five-year-old as a spontaneous genius or the five-year-old as a repository of misleading theories—I wish to emphasize both of these apparently contradictory properties. In some sense, the purpose of education should be to revise the misconceptions and stereotypes that reliably arise all around the world in the first half decade of life. But at the same time, education should try to preserve the most remarkable features of the young mind—its adventurousness, its generativity, its resourcefulness, and its flashes of flexibility and creativity.

In the remainder of the book, I will use the expression "the mind of the five-year-old child" to refer to the kinds of understandings and beliefs that have been described to this point. It should be stressed that this is to some extent a shorthand characterization; it would be more precise to say "the mind of the five- to seven-year-old," and at least some of the properties to which I refer do not fully emerge until the age of ten or so. Nonetheless, I stand by my major claim that the mind of the five-year-old persists in most of us, in most of our daily activities, with only the disciplinary expert escaping fully from its powerful clutches in certain areas of expertise.

In many ways, of course, assertions about the importance of the early years and the power of the young mind have been common coin in Western philosophical circles. The Jesuits and Lenin were not alone in concurring on the desirability of corralling the child while he is young; such sentiments have been underscored by Nietzsche, who said, "In true man, there is a child hidden, who wants to play" and by Freud, who maintained, "It has long since become common knowledge that the experiences of the first five years of childhood exert a

decisive influence on our life, one which later events oppose in vain."
I am especially fond of a stanza by Lepicié, which inspired Chardin's
painting *House of Cards*, on display in the National Gallery in London:

> *Charming child occupied with pleasure,*
> *We jest at your fragile endeavors,*
> *But between ourselves, what is more solid,*
> *Our projects or your castles?*

The present account goes beyond these earlier characterizations in
at least two respects: (1) the specific description of the mind of the
five- to ten-year-old, and (2) the stress on the disjunctions between
the intuitive and the scholastic minds, disjunctions that threaten to
overwhelm the effects of school unless they are directly confronted
in the course of the educational process.

Nearly all cultures have evolved specific ideas about education,
although only in modern times does education prove to be virtually
coterminous with formal schooling. Ultimately, the natural paths and
forms of development place many children in a difficult bind, as
students begin to address the quite different agenda of the schoolroom
and the particular structure of the scholastic domains. Before we can
appreciate the tension that often surrounds the child in school, however, it is necessary to consider on its own terms the nature of education and the peculiar place within it of those institutions called
schools. Such constitutes our task in Part II.

Understanding Educational Institutions

CHAPTER

6

The Values and Traditions of
Education

Suppose that you live in a society rich in information, knowledge, traditions, skills, and understandings—Athens in the time of Socrates, for example, or Florence during the Renaissance, or Vienna at the beginning of the present century. Suppose that, cataclysmically, all the normal avenues of education are suddenly terminated, perhaps because all the elders have been killed by a plague or because all institutions have been shut down by a vengeful conquerer, who has since been destroyed. You are privy to the glory that was Athens (or Florence or Vienna), but once your generation is gone, all will vanish. Your assignment: Design a system of education that can ensure that those newly born will be able to participate fully in the traditions and the understandings achieved by your culture and perhaps even build upon them in the future.

EDUCATIONAL OPTIONS I: WHAT IS TO BE TAUGHT?

Consider your options. First, you must determine the realm of society that seems most crucial to preserve. You can decide to focus on the fulfillment of certain societal roles (How does one learn to be a parent, a priest, a poet?); on the transmission of cultural values (What does it mean to be a virtuous person? What is the good life? Which behaviors are approved of or at least permitted? Which sanctions must be invoked if laws are violated?); or on passing on different varieties or forms of knowledge that have been achieved over the millennia (the printed word, the craft of magic, the findings of science).

Each of these options can be explored further. There are many social, vocational, and avocational roles, each of which could be worthy of transmission or emulation. A society features all manner of conventions, rituals, tastes, legal schemes, moral precepts, preferred behaviors, and cherished values, and each of these could be the subject of a targeted education. Finally, there are diverse directions you could pursue in defining the dimensions of knowledge. Because this book focusses especially on the cognitive realm, it is appropriate to direct our attention to the options there.

In any society, knowledge will be encoded in a variety of forms. There will be many skilled performances, much factual information, and numerous, sometimes competing concepts and theories about the world. Thus one option would be to focus on the performances* that are desired in a mature adult. In a Confucian society, for example, you would make sure that youngsters were instructed in how to render calligraphic characters, how to play a musical instrument, how to pour tea, how to draw a bow, and how to dress like a member of the gentry or a warrior. The well-educated person in such a society can carry out exquisitely a whole set of performances—possibly only performances that have been executed many times before, but perhaps ones that evolve in new directions as well.

You might decide, on further reflection, that a host of highly proficient performances is less desirable than the possession of considerable bodies of information. After all, there is so much to be learned, and life evaporates so rapidly. You would then make sure that starting

---

*In the present discussion, the term *performances* is used as a shorthand for ritualized, rote, or conventionalized performances in which the exact dimensions of a desired behavior, response, or answer have been prescribed (see pages 9–14).

116

very young, youngsters committed to memory as much information as possible. They would learn the words and rules of many languages, both living and dead; gain familiarity with numerous stories, works of music, and works of art; master the various arithmetical tables, geometric proofs, and scientific laws that have been established; commit to memory lists of facts and figures about past and contemporary societies, practices, and achievements. By adulthood, a graduate of such a program would resemble a well-stocked vessel, capable of exhibiting the knowledge that we associate with a successful quiz show contestant or a winner in a game of Trivial Pursuit.

A third tack would be to minimize skilled performances of valued cultural practices and/or the mastery of prized facts, striving instead for the attainment of a rich understanding of the concepts and principles underlying bodies of knowledge. According to my formulation in this book, the person who understands deeply has the capacity to explore the world in a number of ways, using complementary methods. She arrives at concepts and principles in part on the basis of her own explorations and reflections, but she must ultimately reconcile these with the concepts and principles that have evolved in various disciplines. The test of understanding involves neither repetition of information learned nor performance of practices mastered. Rather it involves the appropriate application of concepts and principles to questions or problems that are newly posed. In terms of our earlier discussion, the "compleat understander" can think appropriately about phenomena of consequence in her society, particularly ones that she has not previously encountered.

ASPECTS OF UNDERSTANDING

At any given time, the experts in a society determine the nature of current understanding. One who understood physics in Aristotle's time applied a different body of principles in a different way from one who understood physics in a Newtonian age, and the breakthroughs associated with relativity theory and quantum mechanics have brought about further alterations in the contemporary understanding of the physical world. Understanding about the world of people does not evolve in so dramatic a fashion; Sophocles is far closer to Shakespeare than Aristotle is to Galileo. Yet just as the wise elder possesses deeper insights into human nature than does the bright youngster, knowledge obtained from social and cultural studies has altered our notions of the human individual and of human society. For example, in light of psychoanalytic discoveries, a developed understanding of human behavior involves recognition of unconscious motivation.

Finally, while the notion of understanding has usually been applied to conceptual or theoretical realms, it also has its niche in areas like the arts, athletics, or entrepreneurship. Experts in those domains possess skills, intuitions, and conceptual frameworks that distinguish them sharply from novice or journeyman practitioners.

Each domain or discipline features its own forms of understanding. To phrase it in our earlier terms, theories that purport to explain the mind and theories that seek to illuminate matter are quite different from one another, and both differ from understandings about other living organisms or understandings of oneself as an agent. To express the same point in terms of formal disciplines, an understanding of physics is quite a different matter from an understanding of poetry, painting, politics, or psychology. Accordingly, generalizations about understanding are elusive, and those that can be made are necessarily expressed at a high level of abstraction.

In surveying a range of domains in later chapters, I will sketch out in greater detail something of the nature of relevant understandings. At this point, it may suffice to point out that one who understands can exhibit at least some facets of the knowledge and performances associated with an adult master-practitioner in that domain. As such models of competence change, so too do our notions of understanding. Therefore, understandings in a preliterate society are generally restricted to a fusion of sensorimotor knowledge, first-order symbolic knowledge, and folk definitions and concepts. In contrast, understandings in a modern scholastic society typically run beyond, and sometimes counter to, these intuitive forms of understanding. In particular, they will entail the mastery of formal notions, concepts, and modes of argumentation that have evolved within the discipline over the centuries. Ultimately, scholastic and disciplinary forms of knowing need to be reconciled with earlier, partial (and partially misleading) forms of understanding; otherwise a deleterious mismatch between schools and minds will persist.

Of course, in your position as educational architect, you are likely to say that you wish to achieve all three forms of knowledge representation. Is there any need to choose? In all probability any complex society must feature an amalgam of skilled performance, rich information, and deep understanding. And yet, if one observes societies of the past, it is clear that they have varied enormously in the forms they have featured and the capacities they have valued. China and other societies in the Confucian tradition have veered sharply in the direction of performances; many contemporary societies, including ours, have placed a high premium on the achievement of vast storehouses of information, on which one can be readily examined; and certain remote societies (such as ancient Athens) and certain subcultures in today's world (such as graduate programs in the liberal arts or the natural sciences) have accentuated the achievement and deployment of understanding. Achieving an appropriate balance proves a challenging matter, and most societies veer from one type to another, either across ages or across eras, rather than maintaining a comfortable blend.

EDUCATIONAL OPTIONS II: HOW IS KNOWLEDGE TO BE TAUGHT?

Yet another point of decision concerns the issue of how knowledge, of whatever form, is to be transmitted to the young person. Here different societies have accentuated one of two alternative routes. In what has been called "mimetic" education, the teacher demonstrates the desired performance or behavior and the student duplicates it as faithfully as possible. A premium is placed on precise mastery of information or slavish duplication of models, and any deviation from the model is immediately challenged and rejected. In our terms, such cultures value performances that are rote, ritualized, or conventional.

A contrasting tack in education has been termed the "transformative" approach. In this approach, rather than modeling the desired behavior, the teacher serves as a coach or facilitator, trying to evoke certain qualities or understandings in the students. By posing certain problems, creating certain challenges, placing the student in certain situations, the teacher hopes to encourage the student to work out his own ideas, test them in various ways, and further his own understanding.

The contrast between mimetic and transformative modes is clearly related to another, perhaps more familiar contrast—between an emphasis on basic skills and an emphasis on creativity. Adherents of a basic-skills approach stress the need to master certain literacies and skills, such as the venerable three Rs, and a body of factual knowledge of, say, history, geography, and science. Any additional learnings must be erected upon this solid basis; basic-skills proponents have often insisted, "One must crawl before one can walk."

Those more sympathetic to a creativity stance view education as an opportunity for individuals to invent knowledge on their own to a significant extent, to transform what has been encountered in the past, and perhaps eventually to contribute new ideas and concepts to the collective wisdom. Supporters of a creativity stance tend to downplay basic skills, in the belief that they are unnecessary, that they will be acquired anyway, or that they should be a subject of focus only after an ambience of creative exploration has been established.

At first glance, the basic-skills approach aligns more closely with a mimetic educational tack, whereas the creativity approach is akin to the transformative approach to learning, but other pairings are conceivable. One could value basic skills and yet seek to inculcate them through transformative methods—for example, by having children learn to write by keeping their own journals or learn to compute by supervising their own little shopping centers. Alternatively, one could espouse a highly creative education and yet favor the initial learning of basic skills or the use of mimetic methods in which the teacher embodied various creative approaches, techniques, or goals.

The relationship among skilled performances, mastery of information, and attainment of understanding also warrants consideration. Ultimately, any form of learning requires performance, be it a copy of the master's rendition of a song or a transformation of that rendition in an original form; production of a rote or a reconfigured network of data; recitation of a fixed body of scientific principles or a use of such principles to solve—or even define—a new problem. But only in the latter of each of these pairs is it legitimate to speak of a certain kind of performance—namely, a *performance of understanding.*

By now you, as the mythical designer of educational environments, have your hands—or your mind—full. There are too many decisions, too many options. Of course, no one ever faces this array of decisions in such bald form, because there is always an educational procedure already in place. Whether it is functioning well or functioning poorly, any changes in it must be configured in the light (or the shadow) of what already exists. Even in Communist China, which sought to erase all signs of the scorned feudal past, "revolutionary education" had to build upon methods that had evolved over thousands of years, and in many respects those methods proved far more robust than recent importations by the Communist party.

AN INSTITUTION THAT EDUCATES:
THE APPRENTICESHIP

A separate set of issues concerns institutions through which educational regimens have been effectively conveyed over the millennia. In this case the history of education provides a reasonably constant guide, with a certain sequence apparently honored throughout the world.

In the simplest, most traditional societies, education takes place largely within the family environment of young children. Often these families are extended, including assorted kin at each of several generations. In such traditional environments, it is assumed that children will follow in their parents' steps, sons typically carrying out the same vocational practices as their fathers, and daughters emulating the child-rearing, household, and vocational practices of their mothers.

From an early age, children witness their elders carrying out these roles, often in models drawn from several generations, spanning the gamut from great-grandparents to siblings. Most learning occurs through direct observation, although such learning-by-watching will certainly be punctuated on occasion by overt instructions, the invoking of specific rules, or explicit demonstrations of procedures that may not be readily observable or have even been considered secret. The society may well mark important transitions with explicit ceremonies, such as rites of passage into adulthood, but these serve as a symbolic affirmation of learnings and understandings that have already been assimilated or at least thoroughly prepared for. A society that had to begin totally from scratch would be likely to rely heavily on these most firmly established—and possibly most natural—means of rearing the young.

As societies grow more complex, with valued skills attaining a high degree of intricacy, it is no longer possible for youngsters to master the requisite roles simply by "hanging around." Under such circumstances, all over the world, the institution called the *apprenticeship* has come into being. The core idea of an apprenticeship is that a young person goes to work for, and often to live with, an adult expert

121

in a trade or vocation. Typically the young person has no biological relation to the master, although there may well be informal familial links, and typically the arrangement has a legal or quasi-legal status. The overt purpose of the apprenticeship is to learn the skills of a vocation, but apprenticeships have long been seen as an introduction to the world of work and as a transitional niche en route to becoming an adult member of the society.

During a period of time that often stretches over several years, the novice gains mastery in the designated trade or skill. Much of the learning is observational, either of the master himself or of other, already trained workers who still remain under the tutelage of the master. The master will occasionally point out errors or make special demonstrations, and the apprentice is also expected to use his own emerging critical capacities to correct and improve his performance. There may be a fair number of tasks and assignments unrelated to the explicit subject of the apprenticeship, as the master uses the apprentice for his own purposes; in return, the master may acquire ancillary obligations, such as teaching the apprentice certain literacy skills or religious practices.

Most crucial for our purposes is the fact that the learning in the apprenticeship is heavily *contextualized*—that is, the reasons for the various procedures being taught are generally evident, because the master is in the process of producing goods or services for which there exist an explicit demand and an evident use. Moreover, because the trade is the source of livelihood for the master and those in his charge, there is a premium on achieving the goals in an efficient way and in conveying the desired skills in an effective manner. As Michael Polanyi has pointed out,

> The apprentice unconsciously picks up the rules of the art, including those which are not explicitly known to the master himself. These hidden rules can be assimilated only by a person who surrenders himself to that extent uncritically to the imitation of another.

Apprenticeships of any length and complexity typically feature landmarks of growth. Explicit problems or assignments will be posed at various levels of competence, to make sure that the apprentice has learned the requisite skills and that he is ready to move on to the next, more advanced rung on the ladder. Often the apprentice will produce a simple object whose worth can be tested on the marketplace. Apprentices certainly differ in their aptitudes and their degree of application; thus the master must monitor the progress of each one. Ordinarily there will be a premium on advancement and turnover of the apprentices, although there are certainly cases where an apprentice is held back because the master wishes to exploit him further. Ultimately, of course, the apprentice is expected to produce a "masterpiece"—a product that demonstrates to the world that he has mastered the skills and achieved the understandings that will allow him henceforth to proceed on his own.

Most traditional apprenticeships—and especially those with legal standing—involved male apprentices and masters, but similar procedures have often been used with girls. For instance, among the Zinacanteco Indians in Chiapas, Mexico, young girls first gain familiarity with weaving by watching their mothers at work. Later they help boil the threads and dye the wool. At about the age of eight, they make their first serious efforts to learn to weave. The mother initially provides considerable guidance, a mix of talking and demonstrating. But as the child gains facility, the overt instruction diminishes until, by the age of eleven or twelve, the preadolescent girl is able to proceed pretty much on her own.

Apprenticeships continue until this day all over the world. Even in the most advanced industrialized countries, certain trades and professions are best learned by working alongside a master, observing what he does, and passing through a graded set of challenges and opportunities. Indeed, in some technologically advanced countries like Germany, there has been a tendency to revert to apprenticeships as part of a student's secondary school training; over half of all German adolescents participate in some kind of an apprenticeship, in which scholastic competences are tied as closely as possible to the needs and demands of a workplace. Many vocations and avocations, ranging from the making of musical instruments to household electrical or plumbing repairs, and many roles, ranging from newspaper copyboy to magician or police officer on the beat, are profitably approached through apprenticeship techniques. While not necessarily recognized as such, involvement in intensive large-scale projects, such as staging a play or finishing a contracted job on deadline, often amounts to an apprenticeship; sometimes unwitting novices have the opportunity to observe the spectrum of roles and to pitch in wherever and whenever they are most needed. And revealingly, some of the most demanding pursuits in the society, from graduate study at the university to medical internships to the role of a senior aide in a political or business environment, amount to apprenticeship arrangements.

Why do apprenticeships work effectively? The advantages are several. They provide rich information, nearly all of which pertains in some readily recognizable way to final performances and products of demonstrable importance within a society. They permit aspiring youngsters to work directly alongside accomplished professionals, hence establishing personal bonds as well as a sense of progress toward an end. Frequently they also feature interim steps of accomplishment, with workers situated at different levels of the hierarchy, so that a learner can see where he has been and anticipate where he is headed. Peers and others of slightly differing competences can often help and instruct one another. Apprenticeships often are highly motivating; youngsters enter directly into the excitement that surrounds an important, complex, and sometimes mysterious undertaking, where the stakes for success (and the costs of failure) may be high. Finally, apprenticeships embody centuries of lore about how best to accomplish the task at hand, and this lore can be invoked or exemplified at the precise moment when it is needed, rather than at some arbitrary location in a lecture, text, or syllabus.

Indeed, apprenticeships may well be the means of instruction that builds most effectively on the ways in which most young people learn. Such forms of instruction are heavily punctuated with sensorimotor experiences and with the contextualized use of first-order forms of symbolization, such as natural language and simple drawings and gestures. To the extent that they feature more formal notations or concepts, these are introduced to the learner directly in the context in which they are wanted, and the learner sees for himself the ways in which they may be applied. Here the differences from formal schooling are most salient. Of course, the learner's misconceptions and stereotypes may interfere with mastery, but they are perhaps less likely to emerge, and more likely to be counterindicated when they do emerge, because the learner is working closely with a master who may be experienced in meeting and muting such erroneous beliefs and practices.

Why, then, are apprenticeships far less common, and far less visible, than they were even a few generations ago, and why do apprenticeships have a decidedly mixed reputation? The clouded reputation of apprenticeships probably arises in significant measure from the fact that they were often seen as exploitative of the young charges, who were assigned tasks in addition to their stated responsibilities and were sometimes beaten, punished, or deprived of compensation, virtually at the whim of the master. Abuse of a trusted educational relationship is a certain way to call that relationship into question. Some apprenticeships also stress the most narrow form of imitation of a model, though of course more flexible forms of coaching can also be implemented within an apprenticeship.

My own guess is that apprenticeships have also suffered from the simple fact that they have been around for generations and thus appear to be old-fashioned. They are closely associated with the acquisition of skills in the crafts, and of course crafts have declined in our highly industrialized society. Even in professions or vocations where they would still seem highly appropriate, they have often been replaced by lengthy scholastic regimens that culminate in some kind of official certification procedure that is thought to constitute a positive end in itself and that may appear to furnish the quality control that is difficult to document in an apprenticeship. Apprenticeships may result in adults who are competent but not necessarily articulate or reflective about what they can do, and thus the apprentice-turned-master may seem uneducated or naive. In a related vein, an apprentice may appear to be deprived of that wide range of knowledge and those general problem-solving skills that formal educational institutions are *thought* to provide. In short, apprenticeships may simply be a casualty of another, extremely powerful educational intervention—the institution that we call school.

Apprenticeships do, however, offer the designer of our educational utopia a new and exciting option. Even though they have traditionally been reduced or even phased out, in the context of a scholastic culture, there is no necessity to dismiss them completely. Apprenticeships may harbor within them any number of valuable educational attributes, no one of which should necessarily be scuttled. Indeed, in the concluding portions of the book, I argue that the best chance for an education leading to understanding lies in the melding of certain features of apprenticeships with certain aspects of schools and other institutions, such as children's museums. Such melding may link together disparate forms of knowing, whose separation often cripples efforts to bring about genuine understanding.

CHAPTER

7

The Institution Called School

Although the startlingly realistic and hauntingly beautiful drawings of animals that decorate the caves of southern France and northern Spain are familiar to most people, we understand neither the approaches used by Paleolithic artists nor the purposes for which these likenesses were created. Much controversy surrounds the significance of another marking system of the era, the tiny collections of scratch marks that punctuate foot-long wooden slabs. It is at least plausible that these slabs record calendrical systems; the sets of twenty-seven, twenty-eight, or twenty-nine slashes bunched together may well represent complete cycles of the moon.

Between the period twenty thousand years ago when the cave art and ordered groups of marks were created and the rise of civilization over the past ten thousand years, there are no equally striking records of human cognitive activity. The best evidence suggests that economic imperatives—the need to keep track of the exchange of goods—led to the invention in the Middle East of the first written numerical systems, perhaps six to eight thousand years ago. Such records allowed the recording of financial transactions; tokens of wealth were depicted, and a system of marks indicated the relationships among the tokens (owed, paid, and so on). From roughly the same era emerged hieroglyphic and ideographic symbol systems, which recorded historical sequences about important events and personages, as well as laws, codes, and religious practices that were to be promulgated. It now appears that cultures beyond the Middle East invented systems for recording astronomical events, although the period during which these notational systems were invented remains uncertain.

The most eventful breakthrough in human notational systems occurred sometime in the last five thousand years. The Phoenicians created a marking system in which discrete symbols stood, not for single words, ideas, or objects, but rather for isolated sounds or sound clusters. Instead of needing hundreds or thousands of characters (as remains true in Chinese writing to this day), one could now record any message that could be spoken simply by reordering the same small set of graphemes, each of which denoted a given sound. The Phoenician alphabetic system was taken over by other societies, most notably by the Greeks, who used this writing system not only for the usual economic and political purposes but also to create a literary, historical, and philosophical corpus whose quality has not been surpassed.

THE EARLY SCHOOL

By the time a phonetically based writing system was invented, several cultures had already achieved a high degree of complexity, featuring, for example, considerable division of labor. In all probability various educational regimens, on the order of apprenticeships, had been created by this time. Yet it was the need to instruct young persons, presumably boys, in the skills of literacy that gave rise to the first schools.

I shall define a school here as an institution in which a group of young persons, rarely related by blood but usually belonging to the same social group, assemble on a regular basis in the company of a competent older individual, for the explicit purpose of acquiring one or more skills valued by the wider community. The precise nature and extent of early schools remains hidden in prehistory, yet on the basis of the many schools that have been observed in traditional cultures around the world, the following scenario seems plausible.

Schooling generally began during the second five years of life. The entry to school was often marked by ceremony, for it was an event of signal importance for the community. But while the occasion might be joyous, the actual school regimen was strict, if not fear-instilling. Students were expected to be obedient. They copied letters, numbers, or kindred notational forms over and over again until they achieved facility with them. At the same time they were expected to drill on the sounds of the marks, either on a letter-by-letter basis or by memorizing important letter sequences within words.

More often than not, school was designed to facilitate the memorization of important texts, principally religious ones and not infrequently texts written in a language other than that spoken by the community. Such sacred texts formed the basis of the curriculum, because they were thought to contain ideas and practices important for the survival of the community. Yet this significance was scarcely transparent to the beginning pupil. Certainly the classical Arabic learned by young Muslim scholars, or the Greek, Latin, and Hebrew that were featured in the West after the Renaissance, had little if any meaning to the countless scholars who toiled to master these tongues. While nowadays young students in the West may object to the mastery of languages they can never speak or use, it would have been highly inappropriate, if not unthinkable, to raise such challenges in a traditional school. These practices were central to the community's spiritual welfare; moreover, students simply did not challenge the prescriptions of their elders.

While mastery of sacred texts was one purpose of early schools, other, more practical missions surfaced as well. Students trained in such institutions were expected to master the vernacular, so that they could read about events, rules, and laws in their own culture and so that they could record the information considered important by the leaders of their society. Often they were expected to memorize long lists of objects, persons, or events, a knowledge of which was thought crucial to their eventual facility as leaders, informed citizens, or civil servants. Indeed, some of these young students would eventually become scribes, whose job it was to read and write for illiterate, lazy, or overburdened members of the elite.

Along with the written language, students were also taught rudiments of whatever arithmetical system and notations were employed in their culture. Knowledge of these systems was necessary so that trade and other economic interests could be pursued within the society and with other communities.

This picture does no more than hint at the variety of schools that existed—and still exist—around the world. My definition can extend to encompass "bush schools," collections of youths in West Africa who meet on a regular basis to learn the practices to be used in initiation rites as well as the crafts valued by the society; the off-site instruction given to sailors-in-training in the South Seas, where students commit to memory vast amounts of factual information, such as the identities and locations of neighboring islands and the yearly courses of all the stars; and the instruction in literacy given in off-hours to apprentices learning a particular trade.

It should also be noted that not all schools have evolved for the purposes of inculcating literacy. In Sweden a century ago, for example, many youngsters learned to read at home, and if they attended school, they did so for other social and disciplinary purposes.

Yet, as if guided by an invisible hand, schools all over the world have come to exhibit certain predictable features. They focus on the introduction of complex symbolic or notational systems that require sustained concentration over long hours for mastery and that therefore are unlikely to be picked up simply by observing competent parents or other elders or masters at work in the society. Regular drill, rote memorization, and recitation are featured. The ultimate utility of these skills is not an important concern of day-to-day schooling, and indeed, in contrast to apprenticeships, the school experience is marked by an extreme dissociation from important events or palpable products in the life of the community.

From time to time, the links to the community are confirmed. There are clear milestones of progress, typically marked by some kind of ceremony or recognition; privileges or special positions are given to those who excel at the mastery of the system, even as sanctions, ridicule, or expulsion await those who, for whatever reason, are not able to master the system in its cognitive or social manifestations. Those who succeed often become members of an elite group that itself guards the skills and practices surrounding the notational system; they may deliberately decide to withhold the practices from those whom they desire to exclude from the corridors of power. Moreover, insofar as the community provides support for the school, it reveals its priorities at times when a critical problem arises—for example, when a teacher behaves in an inappropriate way, or when a person from a different background assumes leadership over the community.

THE BURDENS OF SCHOOL

Schools have assumed burdens far broader than the mastery of written or numerical literacy systems prized in their society. Especially in the premodern era, schools were considered a principal venue for the transmission of moral and political values. Teachers were expected both to model proper behaviors and to ensure that students had mastered the relevant rules and regulations. Schools were seen as places for the training of an elite, not merely in requisite cognitive skills but also in prescribed behaviors and attitudes expected of those who would assume leadership positions. Training in religious practices and specific preparation for the assumption of a position in the dominant church were other common purposes of schooling. In a parallel vein, an appreciation of the economic order and preparation for assuming a position within it also fell within the purview of the schools.

More recently, with the accumulation of knowledge, the proliferation of disciplines, and the increased importance of having an informed population, schools have taken on further tasks. They have become the logical site for the transmission of rapidly accumulating wisdom as well as for the inculcation of skills that will permit further discoveries to be made and deeper understandings to emerge. In ancient and medieval times, the studies most esteemed were the *trivium*, which featured grammar, rhetoric, and logic, and the complementary *quadrivium*, which encompassed arithmetic, astronomy, geometry, and music. By the nineteenth century, various sciences (physics and chemistry), social sciences (history and geography), and modern languages were added to the standard fare, and in the twentieth century, precollegiate education was expanded further to cover a range from home economics to computer programming.

Just how, and to what extent, each of these topics is covered has varied greatly across schools and across societies. Sometimes teachers are expected to have mastered the subject or skill in question, while at other times they simply introduce specialists (the music teacher) or transmit textbook knowledge about the topic (keeping one chapter ahead of the students). Sometimes the subject is treated as a closed body of information to be covered, while in other cases it is assumed that the students are learning methods of inquiry—how to carry out a scientific experiment, how to research and write a paper, how to pose important and as-yet-unanswered questions within a discipline.

THE THREE ASSIGNMENTS OF MODERN
SECULAR SCHOOLS

Today, the modern secular school is encountered all over the world. In such a school, the religious, moral, and political messages that dominated (and also sustained) earlier schooling have receded in importance. However, such messages may constitute part of a "hidden curriculum" that, while operating in powerful fashion over some students, is not officially mandated and may even be proscribed by law. There may be a ritualistic pledge to the flag or a moment of silent prayer or occasional discussions about kindness or plagiarism, but except in times of national crisis, these noncurricular functions are largely considered the task of home, the church, or some other community organization. The mission of the early years of school is to introduce all students to the basic literacies. Thereafter, there may well begin some form of grouping or tracking of students; the more able students will be directed toward disciplines that they can pursue at secondary and higher institutions, while the less able students will either cease school altogether or enter vocational or remediation tracks.

Whatever its noncognitive responsibilities, the modern secular school seeks to present three kinds of knowledge across the disciplines:

1. *Notational sophistication.* On the assumption that the entering students have already mastered the first-order symbol systems, the task here is to master the major written codes of the culture and to learn to use them effectively. Written language and written numerical systems are almost always featured. In addition, notational sophistication often includes the ability to read charts and graphs, to manipulate scientific symbols and equations, and to learn computer languages; less frequently, schools also provide at least a nodding familiarity with more esoteric notational systems, such as those used for music or dance, sailing or soccer.

2. *Concepts within the discipline.* Every discipline that has undergone appreciable development has accumulated a cluster of important concepts, frameworks, key ideas, and examples. Often these bear some resemblance to concepts employed in lay society, but the definitions and uses are explicitly prescribed within the discipline. The young biology student needs to understand evolution, the gene, and taxonomic classifications; the physics student must master gravity, mag-

netism, and the laws of thermodynamics; the social studies student requires a technical grasp of political revolutions, constitutional government, and the balance of payments or of power. Ideally, these concepts are presented so that students will be able to apply them in new contexts; all too frequently, however, they are treated simply as lists of words to be memorized—instances of inert knowledge.

3. *Forms of exposition and reasoning within the discipline.* Disciplines differ from one another not only in overt subject matter and pivotal concepts but also in terms of the ways in which disciplinary experts formulate and tackle problems. Historians and physicists both collect evidence and reach conclusions, but the kinds of evidence that are relevant, the ways in which the evidence is culled and assessed, and the manner in which a study proceeds, arguments are made, and conclusions are established are radically different. While instruction in such "epistemic forms" is rarely explicit and the modeling of procedures may be only approximate, it is crucial for students to appreciate the different kinds and status of knowledge across the various disciplines.

ASSESSING LEARNING

No less so than masters in an apprentice system, those who operate schools need to determine whether students under their charge are learning anything. So long as the school is informal and all students are learning precisely the same materials, there need be little formal screening; the group helps out the lagging pupils, who are rarely assessed individually. When the school is inculcating a desired performance, like the writing of script or the memorization of prayers, it is possible to observe students directly and to determine their progress. When the class is reasonably small and the required knowledge sufficiently spelled out, student learning can be reliably monitored on the basis of daily recitation; it is clear which students have learned their times tables, have memorized twenty lines of poetry, and can list the kings, presidents, or dynasties in order.

As disciplines proliferate and the burdens imposed upon the school increase, however, pressures mount to shift to more efficient forms of determining student progress. Enter the test. The test is the ultimate scholastic invention, a "decontextualized measure" to be employed in a setting that is itself decontextualized. Students learn about scientific principles or distant lands while sitting at their desks reading a book or listening to a lecture; then, at the end of the week, the month, the year, or their school careers, the same students enter a room and, without benefit of texts or notes, answer questions about the material that they are supposed to have mastered. Some of these measures, such as the weekly quiz, are brief and informal; others, like the Chinese examinations for entry to the officialdom or the British examinations for university matriculation or enrollment in the Civil Service, may last for days.

In a modern secular society, tests have taken on profound importance. They are often the chief vehicle for determining who will receive the awards that the society can mete out. Examinations like those at the end of secondary school are indeed high stakes; anxieties and skullduggery frequently surround them. Over the years, tests have undergone blistering attacks from many quarters, and yet they seem to survive and even to gain in potency. Partly in response to criticism, appreciable efforts are now made to ensure that the examinations are fair, in several senses; that the questions represent a reasonable sampling of what one wants students to know; that no student can get the questions (or answers) beforehand; and that the test items are not biased in favor of or against any particular social or ethnic group.

In the United States, so-called "standardized tests" have been developed to the greatest extent. The tests typically feature multiple-choice items or very short answers; insofar as possible, the examinations are scored by machine, and the results locate students within various target groups with statistical precision (for example, the 67th percentile for suburban middle-class tenth-graders attending public schools). The "subjective" element of testing is virtually eliminated, leading to the honorific epithet "objective testing." Whether these instruments also provide a good sampling of the skills and understandings that one wants students to acquire is much less clear. As psychologist Ulric Neisser suggests, academic knowledge is typically assessed with arbitrary problems that a student has little intrinsic interest in or motivation to answer, and performances on such instruments have little predictive power for performances outside of a scholastic environment.

There are answers to this critique. It could be maintained that the ability to perform on decontextualized measures is worth ascertaining; after all, in at least some vocational positions, it is important to be able to "bone up" quickly and work effectively with novel materials in unfamiliar surroundings. It could be maintained that the purpose of tests is to predict future performances in school, rather than outside of school; of course, such prediction is helpful mostly for those cases where a person actually remains in school—as do professors! Finally, it could be argued that school is itself a context of importance, decontextualized only in comparison to milieus that are no longer relevant, such as the farm or the craft shop. While each of these arguments has its merits, I still conclude that formal testing has moved much too far in the direction of assessing knowledge of questionable importance in ways that show little transportability. The understanding that schools ought to inculcate is virtually invisible on such instruments; quite different forms of assessment need to be implemented if we are to document student understandings.

THE EFFECTS OF SCHOOL

Even though testing may not provide the most crucial information on the progress of each individual student, it seems highly likely that a steady regimen of school yields a cohort of people who are different from those who have not attended school. After all, how could it *not* matter when students spend hours each day throughout their childhood sitting quietly in a room, listening to an adult to whom they have no familial relation, reading books on exotic topics, and doing considerable writing on command and for examinations on which their future is believed to hinge?

Consider, as one example, the kind of talking and thinking that occurs in school, in comparison with talk typically encountered at home or on the streets. Young pupils are exposed in class to talk about personages and events that they cannot see and may never encounter in the flesh. Older pupils hear discussion about abstract concepts that have been devised to make sense of data or facts that have been collected by scholars for their own disciplinary ends. Children of all ages are asked questions about remote topics, required to respond individually, and evaluated on the basis of the content and form of their responses.

David Olson has pointed out that, as one moves toward the older grades, discussion in school contains not just assertions about the topic in question but also assertions about what one or another scholar or cadre of specialists believes or *claims* is true of the topic in question. No longer is it enough to list the four principal causes of the French Revolution; instead, one learns why one school of historians has invoked one set of claims and how other schools counter these arguments and put forth rival sets of claims, which themselves demand scrutiny. To be sure, such a distinction is not honored in every schoolroom, yet a student who does not appreciate the difference between a factual assertion and the claim put forth by a disciplinary expert will miss much of the import of scholarly discussion.

In a number of respects, then, the talk in school is qualitatively different from language as it is customarily deployed on the streets. The language of school is remote from daily experience, favoring abstract terms and concepts and entailing formulaic exchanges between teacher and student. Meanings are often defined in technical ways, and there is considerable metalanguage—talk about talk. These tendencies are all heightened in the case of written language, which allows more precision, features less redundancy, and is replete with assertions, claims, inferences, judgments, and a raft of other metalinguistic devices. (Consider, for example, my own claims as expressed in this and the next sentence—easy enough to read in a book, but not the sorts of utterance that one is likely to encounter in casual conversation.) As Olson points out, sometimes these uses of language are stated explicitly, but more often than not, it is simply assumed that readers will appreciate the particular uses of language embedded in a written argument. This assumption may not cause difficulty for students who are excellent readers or for those who come from a community where language is customarily used in a scholarly way, but for students whose primary reference point remains the informal language of the street, written texts may be impenetrable.

The Soviet psychologist Lev Vygotsky has helped to convey the special features of school in his discussion of the differences between "spontaneous" concepts, on the one hand, and "scientific," "nonspontaneous," or "systematically learned concepts" on the other. Spontaneous concepts (like *brother* or *animal*) are picked up in everyday life, whereas scientific concepts (like *gravity* or *mammal*) are learned primarily in a school setting. Even though the definitions of scientific concepts are often quite technical, they are typically mastered more readily than spontaneous concepts, for several reasons. The scientific concepts are the explicit regimen of school; they are taught verbally by teachers; their definitions have a crispness that cannot be readily applied to spontaneous concepts; and they belong to a system of concepts whose interrelations can be explored. Thus, even though his intuitions about family matters might be quite well developed, a child may well have an easier time defining Archimedes' principle than in explaining what a family is. Vygotsky is no doubt correct in his claim that children *appear* to master scientific concepts more readily than spontaneous concepts; yet, if the claims of this book are correct, the scientific knowledge may often be quite fragile and readily overridden by more deeply entrenched spontaneous concepts.

So far, my description makes it sound as if the student is alone in school, having to learn concepts, draw inferences, or make claims without the help of other people or of reassuring props in the environment. Probably every reader of this book can recall times—for example, during a difficult examination—when he or she felt just this way. It may be more appropriate, however, to think of the student in school not as being inherently isolated but rather as having to learn to make new, different, and strategic uses of the sources of information around her. The successful student is one who learns how to use research materials, libraries, notecards, and computer files, as well as knowledgeable parents, teachers, older students, and classmates, in order to master those tasks of schools that are not transparently clear. In a terminology that has recently become fashionable, intelligence is "distributed" in the environment as well as in the head, and the "intelligent student" makes use of the intelligence distributed throughout his environment.

Though few observers would argue that school achieves *no* effect, it has not been a simple or straightforward task to determine just what are the effects of spending half of one's waking hours in these odd institutions. Careful studies by Michael Cole and Sylvia Scribner have demonstrated that literacy per se makes little if any discernible difference; mastery of scripts for certain religious or ritualistic purposes proves to be as isolated (and nontransferable) a skill as learning a particular board game or nonsense verse. Literacy as part of general schooling does seem to make a difference, but under such circumstances it is not possible to determine the effects of the literacy portion of the amalgam as distinct from other scholastic accoutrements.

Not surprisingly, regular attendance at school helps students to demonstrate those cognitive skills that are directly or indirectly the mission of the school. Schoolchildren are better able to handle tasks for which no context has been explicitly introduced; to assume that new problems are instances of a class of problems that can be solved by a general rule; to memorize apparently arbitrary sorts of materials and to impose an organizational structure upon them; to reason in specific ways (for example, syllogistically); to engage in dialogue with an older person about remote topics, including their own performances on tasks; and to succeed on tests and testlike procedures. As noted earlier, the disparity in performance between schooled and unschooled children can be reduced substantially when the unschooled children have been familiarized with the procedures that typify a school experience or when performances feature materials or practices that are already well known to the unschooled population.

To my mind there is little question that, when the training is of good quality and has been carried out over an extended period of time, schools fashion a specific kind of person: a young adult who thinks about many aspects of the world in ways that are qualitatively different from those exhibited by most people who have not had the opportunity to attend school. Scholars and societies have over the millennia devised impressive schemes of knowledge (such as the laws of physics) and potent approaches to the acquisition of further knowledge (such as procedures of laboratory experimentation). By far the most efficient way to gain familiarity with them is to attend school and to master its curricula and its practices. And, of course, the effects of schools are most likely to be pronounced in those instances where the graduate actually continues to use the knowledge, skills, and understandings acquired in school. On the other hand, in those instances where the schooling is uninspired, where the masters are such in name only, or where the graduates go on to pursue vocations unrelated to the curriculum of the school, one may question whether the knowledge and skills attained will prove of value to the students or to the society that has entrusted them to the institution called school.

INSTITUTIONAL CONSTRAINTS

I have argued that human beings are constrained by their species membership to learn in certain ways. Although schools harbor no genetic limitations, these institutions may also be thought of as peculiar kinds of organisms, with their own kinds of constraints. Some of these constraints probably characterize schools all over the world, while others prove specific to certain times, locales, and/or populations.

Beginning with those constraints that are likely to be encountered everywhere, schools are institutions that place together individuals who have not known one another, to work on tasks that appear more or less remote from the operation of the remainder of the society. It is therefore necessary to set up procedures by which the institution can run smoothly and to have rewards and punishments that are appropriate to its purposes. It is hardly ideal to have to transmit knowledge in mass form, with tens or scores of students in the same room, each with his own strengths and weaknesses, approaches to learning, goals, and aspirations. Teachers must also deal with noncognitive problems that beset their students, problems that are seemingly unrelated to the overt mission of schools yet that can cripple a class as effectively as would a plague or a fire.

Journalist Tracy Kidder has put it whimsically:

> The problem is fundamental. Put twenty or more children of roughly the same age in a little room, confine them to desks, make them wait in lines, make them behave. It is as if a secret committee, now lost to history, had made a study of children and, having figured out what the greatest number were least disposed to do, declared that all of them should do it.

The best teachers prove able to cope with these limitations, perhaps using some students to help others, presenting lessons that can speak to the range of students, or grouping students so that their nonacademic problems are less disruptive. But even these teachers are hindered in ways that a master or tutor working in a one-on-one situation would not be.

As institutions set apart from the rest of society, schools must confront their relation to their community. At various times and in various ways, schools have sought to build or maintain bridges with the family, the home, or other community institutions. For the most part, however, schools have found it more efficient to operate independently of other institutions. This practice proves particularly problematic in the contemporary society, where powerful educational (and noneducational) forces are constantly at work in the media, in the commercial sector, and on the streets. The decision to ignore these forces can be understood, and yet, precisely because they are so powerful and ubiquitous, these forces may well overwhelm the lessons and themes of school.

Just as the mind of the five-year-old endures in the school-age pupil, so too the values and practices of the wider community do not disappear just because the student happens to be sitting in class and listening to the teacher talk. Once the student departs from class at the end of the day, or at the end of her school career, the messages and practices featured on television, the objects prized by the consuming society, the games played in arcades or on the floor of the stock exchange achieve enormous salience. Just how to balance and integrate the mission of school with the practices of the wider community is a problem that few educational institutions have solved.

Schools are also bureaucratic institutions within communities and have additional constraints imposed by that factor. Inasmuch as schools always require support from the outside world, teachers and administrators must prove sensitive over the long run to the goals of those who pay for their operation. Particular goals will of course vary across communities and cultures. In modern Western industrialized society, extremes of bureaucratic constraints have been represented by France, on the one hand, and the United States, on the other. In the case of France, there is such tight control over the curriculum and syllabus that students all over the country (and in colonies and former colonies) study the same topics in the same way and are tested on them with the same examinations. Underlying the syllabi and the practices is the most important topic of all: a strong image of what it means to be an educated Frenchman or Frenchwoman. Interest in the annual baccalaureate examination is sufficiently high that the questions are published in the newspaper and reported on the television news. In the United States, by contrast, each of the more than fifteen thousand school districts has considerable autonomy over what is taught and how it is assessed. Talk of a national curriculum or a national examination system used to be out of the question, and even today such topics must be mentioned in very tentative terms.

Despite (or perhaps because of) local control, schools in the United States are subjected to many powerful pressures, from such bodies as teachers' and administrators' unions, school boards, state legislatures, and the voting public. (It should be noted that those in position of most power often know little or nothing about the daily practices of education.) These combined pressures make it very difficult for individual teachers to operate with much autonomy or sense of empowerment. Perhaps as a reaction to the fact that external agencies so often attempt to institute far-reaching reforms "from the top," schools—like other bureaucratic institutions—have developed strong protective mechanisms that often preclude any meaningful kind of reform or strangle it before it has a chance to take hold.

Mechanisms mediating against change range from teachers' pressuring their peers not to work longer hours on an experimental program to the adoption of mandated textbooks that call for precisely the kind of fact-recollecting performances that educators are trying to reject. Paradoxically, if genuine change is actually to come about, it may be necessary *not* to impose change.

Even though educational systems may pay lip service to goals like "understanding" or "deep knowledge," they in fact prove inimical to the pursuit of these goals. Sometimes these goals are considered to be hopelessly idealistic or unrealistic; at most, in the view of educational bureaucrats, schools ought to produce citizens who exhibit some basic literacies and can hold a job. But even in cases where these goals are taken seriously, events conspire to undermine their pursuit. Particularly when systems are expected to produce hard evidence of their success, the focus sooner or later comes to fall on indices that are readily quantified, such as scores on objective tests. Measures of understanding must be postponed for another day or restricted to a few experimental schools, which are allowed to operate under waivers.

Educational researcher Linda McNeil has helped to elucidate the conflicts engendered by such a system. In the interests of efficiency and accountability, school systems tend to mandate large sets of rules and procedures. Many of these have only questionable relevance to the daily operation of classes and to the learning of students, and yet all teachers and administrators must adhere to them. At the same time, teachers are often encouraged—at least at the rhetorical level—to take the initiative and to be forceful and imaginative in their teaching. In fact, however, they feel caught in a bind, for adhering to the regulations is so time-consuming and exhausting that little time or energy remains for innovation. Risking censure or worse, a few teachers will ignore the regulations in order to pursue a more individualized program of instruction. Most teachers, however, will achieve an uneasy truce, with both their superiors and their students, by adopting "defensive teaching." Adhering to the rules, not making excessive demands on anyone (including themselves), asking students mostly to memorize definitions and lists rather than to tackle challenging problems, they will maintain control over their classrooms, but at the cost of educational inspiration. As McNeil phrases it, "When the school's organization becomes centered on managing and controlling, teachers and students take school less seriously. They fall into a ritual of teaching and learning that tends toward minimal standards and minimum effort." In terminology on which I elaborate in the next chapter, schools everywhere have embraced "correct-answer compromises" instead of undertaking "risks for understanding."

Nearly all the problems and constraints routinely encountered in schools are exacerbated in the urban American schools of today. Problems are almost always magnified in large bureaucratic settings, where many thousands of teachers, administrators, and students must be "served" and the pressures for uniform treatment of diverse "customers" are profound. Classes are larger and more difficult to control; students are often unmotivated, and they may be frightened, agitated, hungry, or ill as well; regulations proliferate with little rhyme or reason. Teachers feel buffeted about by contradictory messages: Students should learn cooperatively, and yet separate evaluation must be performed each individual student; children with problems should be "mainstreamed," and yet it is important to track the talented students so that they can gain college admission; teachers are expected to act in a professional manner, and yet their every move is scrutinized by various monitoring bodies. The result is a virtual logjam in many of our nation's public schools.

Even when classes are small and students are motivated, it is necessary for teachers both to be truly knowledgeable and to know how to transmit the desired or required knowledge to students. In some societies, teachers are selected with great care, well trained by master teachers, ultimately given considerable autonomy, and encouraged to remain in the classroom rather than to assume administrative posts. Education—indeed, even education for understanding—can flourish under such circumstances. In most cases, however, school teaching, at least below the secondary or higher levels, is considered a low-prestige occupation, and those charged with the education of the young may have only modest intellectual abilities and pedagogical skills. The gifted women who might have gone (or perhaps would have been forced to go) into teaching two generations ago are now attracted to higher-paying, more prestigious positions, depriving the schools of a cohort that was of enormous value in the past.

As a final institutional feature, schools must be accountable for the progress of their students. To ensure that the education has been successful, it is important to be able to "debrief" students. In the past, because teachers often remained with the same students for several years and because the demands of the curricula were less burdensome, much of this assessment could be handled in the course of daily interchanges. Today, however, schools throughout the world have moved toward less personalized forms of assessment. Certain economic and meritocratic advantages are associated with the adoption of standardized instruments and with regular calculations of "seat time," "time on task," and dropout and promotion rates. Yet the kinds of instruments increasingly favored often prove remote from the deeper kinds of understanding that many educators would like students to acquire.

Because of such pervasive constraints on human learning and a parallel set of constraints operating on community institutions, it is difficult to mount an effective school and even more difficult to demonstrate that it has been effective. We run the risk of investing incalculable resources in institutions that do not operate very well and that may never approach the effectiveness that their supporters—and, for that matter their detractors—would desire. Moreover, it is my own belief that until now, we have not fully appreciated just how difficult it is for schools to succeed in their chosen (or appointed) task. Reflecting the argument of this book, we have not been cognizant of the ways in which basic inclinations of human learning turn out to be ill-matched to the agenda of the modern secular school.

CHAPTER 8

The Difficulties Posed by School:
Misconceptions in the Sciences

F or some readers of this book, the very notion that school poses
difficulties for children may seem odd. After all, such readers
may well have breezed through school with few problems, and, if
they are fortunate, their children or other young people of their acquaintance may also have experienced little overt difficulty in school.
To be sure, they read of poor test performances or of school dropouts,
but surely, they think, these problems are related to conditions extrinsic to schools (or to The School). If we could simply roll back the
clock to earlier days, avoiding the temptation to "spare the rod, spoil
the child," all would be well in the schools of America and the world
today.

According to my contrasting view, much of what we have discovered about the principles of human learning and development conflicts sharply with the customary practices of schools, as they have
grown up around the world. Until recently, these conflicts and contradictions have been largely hidden from view, for several reasons.
Not only have schools been concerned with a small (and privileged)
minority of the population, but the materials to be mastered in school

have been relatively unchallenging, and the performances counted as evidence of success have been limited in scope. Even a century ago, fewer than 10 percent of American students entered secondary school, and most schools around the world were satisfied if, at the end of five or eight years, students could read, write, and reckon with a modest degree of competence. Inasmuch as the students had been working on these literacy skills for up to eight years, it was not unreasonable to expect such skills to have coalesced reasonably well in even the weaker pupils. Only a few students—presumably the most gifted or the most privileged—would continue their schooling and perhaps eventually join the ranks of teaching or of other professions.

Once the clientele of schools became more universal, and once the sweep of schooling extended beyond the literacies to encompass a range of disciplines, the burden placed upon the school became much heavier. Larger numbers of students had to be trained on a greater body of materials. By the turn of the century, universal schooling had been mandated in the United States; at the time of completion of secondary school, students would be expected to have mastered at least ten disciplines ranging from Latin to modern languages, from mathematics to history. The powerful Committee of Ten on Secondary School Studies, a group of educational leaders who recommended policy for the nation's schools, minced no words:

> Every subject which is taught at all in a secondary school should be taught in the same way and to the same extent to every pupil so long as he pursues it, no matter what the probable destination of the pupil may be, or at what point his education is to cease.

Although few would have any reason to recognize it, a collision course was virtually inevitable. On the one hand, the demands being made on the school were increasing in virtually exponential fashion. On the other, the ways in which students learn and the kinds of conceptions and skills they bring to school were largely invisible to pedagogues, and even more unknown to those who set educational policy. Only the most optimistic assumption of a preestablished harmony between the student mind and the school curriculum would justify the prediction that the schools as constituted could succeed in their ambitious and ever expanding mission.

By reviewing the arguments presented in earlier pages, I hope to provide some perspective on the vexed mission of the school. Then, in light of these general considerations, I shall turn in this chapter and the next to recently gathered evidence from a range of disciplines and content areas that provides further documentation of the manifold difficulties inherent in achieving effective education. My own recommendations about how best to deal with difficulties will be presented in chapters 11 and 12.

First, however, it is important to underscore one point. One cannot begin to evaluate the effectiveness of schools unless one makes clear one's ambitions for the school. In what follows, I highlight a single criterion for effective education—*an education that yields greater understanding in students.* Whereas short-answer tests and oral responses in classes can provide clues to student understanding, it is generally necessary to look more deeply if one desires firm evidence that understandings of significance have been obtained. For these purposes, new and unfamiliar problems, followed by open-ended clinical interviews or careful observations, provide the best way of establishing the degree of understanding that students have attained.

VARIETIES OF UNDERSTANDING

According to the analysis put forth in Part I, all normal young children raised in a reasonable environment can be expected to attain two ways of representing knowledge:

1. A sensorimotor way of knowing, dating from infancy, in which one comes to know the world primarily through the operation of one's sense organs and one's actions upon the world. Piaget's portrait of the competent infant, with his incipient understandings of matter and of other people, provides a reasonable capsule account of such a young child.
2. A symbolic form of knowing, dating from early childhood, in which one comes to know the world through the use of various symbol systems, chiefly those that have evolved over the millennia in the culture in which one happens to live. Our portrait of the competent symbol user is an attempt to capture the mind of this somewhat older child, who has still not entered the formal scholastic system.

Through a combination of these forms of knowing, and by virtue of the various proclivities and constraints under which knowing humans operate, children by the age of five or six have evolved a quite robust and serviceable set of theories: about mind, about matter, about life, about self. In addition they have mastered a series of performances and acquired a set of scripts that constitute a prominent part of their cognitive repertoire. Finally, by the time of their entry to formal schooling, children have also developed more specific intellectual strengths and styles, which are part and parcel of the ways in which they will interact with the world beyond home. These ways of knowing may well not be consistent with one another, but latent contradictions rarely prove problematic outside the setting of school. In general, youngsters simply draw on these capacities and understandings in the contexts in which they have been observed as well as in the workaday settings in which they seem to be appropriate.

Should children remain in an unschooled environment, their skills and learning will continue to increase at a moderate rate. Some enhancement will occur simply as a consequence of their observations of more competent individuals at work in their environment; other increments in competence will be attendant upon their inclusion in an apprenticeship or some other variant of informal education.

Earlier, I conceptualized understanding in terms of the way that an expert handles the materials, problems, and challenges posed within his domain. I must now stress that, under the circumstances just described, the issue of understanding rarely proves problematic. So long as performances are acquired in the contexts in which they are customarily employed, understandings should arise in a natural fashion. The reasons for carrying out actions or for offering explanations are patent and noncontroversial, and learners acquire them as a matter of course. The ways of acquiring skills are simply an amalgam of sensorimotor and symbolic knowledge; the competent individual learns readily how to commute back and forth between these ways of knowing and how to integrate them in order to execute the task at hand. What one says about sewing or skating or singing fits in with how one sews, skates, or sings, even as accompanying gestures or depictions further support the mastery of these skills.

Of course, there can be disjunctions between sensorimotor knowledge and first-order symbolic knowledge. Take, for example, Piaget's classic demonstrations of conservation. Preschool children believe that a beaker in which water reaches a higher level must contain more water than a beaker in which the water attains a lower level, even if the latter vessel is considerably wider. In the dozens of studies of conservation of liquids carried out over the decades, it has been established that such apparent nonconservers are less likely to render a mistaken judgment if they themselves carry out the pouring or if the beakers in which the water has attained different heights are hidden from view and the subject knows only the fact that water has been poured from one beaker to another. It is also the case that subjects are sometimes confused by words, and particularly by the ambiguity in the terms *more* and *less* (*more* or *less* than what?); if subjects are simply allowed to choose which of two glasses of juice or two piles of chocolates they would prefer, they may emerge earlier as genuine conservers.

The key point here is not the usual absence of conflict between sensorimotor and symbolic representations; rather what should be noted is that, even in the absence of formal scholastic training, youngsters soon reconcile these contrasting conceptualizations of a situation. There may well be neural mechanisms that facilitate the reconciliation between the older forms of knowing involved in sensory discrimination and motoric activity, and the use of familiar, well-entrenched first-order symbol systems. Or possibly parents and other inhabitants of the community facilitate a reconciliation between apparently contradictory conceptions that arise from sensorimotor and symbolic forms of representation. If the child is ready for a reconciliation, it may help to hear an older sibling remark, "It *looks* like there's more there, but *actually* if you pour the water into that empty beaker, you'll see that the water levels are really the same."

I do not wish to imply that all highly contextualized learning is free of problems. Certainly, some students will learn much more readily than others in an apprenticeship situation, either because they have a more appropriate blend of intelligences or because their style of learning happens to be more compatible with the teaching style of the master. Nor do I want to contend that deep understandings will necessarily or automatically emerge; no doubt some masters are happy to accept derivative performances, and some students are content simply to mimic what they see before their eyes. In such a situation, however, it is less likely that a student will radically misconstrue the nature of the desired behaviors, and in general the model is presented in enough different ways, over a sufficiently long period of time, that the learner eventually comes to master the desired skill with some degree of flexibility. The learner may still be unable to reflect upon, or explain, the mastered activity, but these failures are unimportant for most purposes.

Schooling introduces several other forms of knowing the world. The initial impulse giving rise to the establishment of school is the need for young individuals to master various kinds of notational systems. While there are legitimate reasons for the acquisition of these literacies, their rationale will typically prove obscure to young children, even as the ways in which they have to learn them will prove unfamiliar to most beginning students. Nonetheless, particularly if students attend regularly and the regimen continues long enough, most children will acquire serviceable literacies and thus justify the investment of time and money in their education.

Just how and where to apply these literacy skills proves far less evident. For ritualistic or religious reasons, the mastery of a sacred language may be essential. Otherwise, the capacity to read a religious text in a foreign or dead tongue has scant pragmatic value, unless (like a medieval physician) one is learning a trade whose texts exist only in this tongue. Unless teachers, parents, or other respected elders make use of these skills in their daily lives, the manifest purposes of these literacies will remain obscure. During the pre-Revolutionary era in America, a great many adult colonists learned to read in order to be able to keep informed about the possibility of political revolution in their own communities. Latin American educators like Paolo Freire have trusted that a similar political impulse would ease the task of learning Spanish or Portuguese for masses of uneducated citizens.

Going beyond simple literacy, a further mission of the schools is to transmit concepts, networks of concepts, conceptual frameworks, and disciplinary forms of reasoning to their students. These topics generally bear some relation to the areas in which students are ordinarily interested and about which they have already developed intuitive theories, schemes, and kindred explanatory constructs; after all, science treats the natural world, even as history relates the story of one's group and of other relevant friendly or hostile groups.

To the extent that these materials are presented simply as lists or definitions to be memorized, they can usually be mastered by students who apply themselves to the task at hand. The curriculum of school ought to go beyond a rehearsal of facts, however, and introduce students to the ways of thinking used in different disciplines. Such an introduction would involve exposing students to new ways of conceptualizing familiar or unfamiliar entities, be they the laws that govern objects in the physical world or the ways in which events are conceptualized by historians.

The content of the various disciplines is typically encountered in forms quite remote from the conceptions the student brings to the class. The student learns about the laws of physics or the causes of war by reading a textbook or by hearing the teacher lecture. Hence the challenge for the educator is threefold: (1) to introduce these often-difficult or counterintuitive notions to the students; (2) to make sure that this new knowledge is ultimately synthesized with earlier ideas, if they are congruent with one another; (3) to ensure that the newer disciplinary content supplants previously held conceptions or stereotypes that would in some way collide with or undermine the new forms of knowledge.

At last we can confront directly the primary reasons why school is difficult. It is difficult, first, because much of the material presented in school strikes many students as alien, if not pointless, and the kinds of supporting context provided for pupils in earlier generations has become weakened. It is difficult, second, because some of these notational systems, concepts, frameworks, and epistemic forms are not readily mastered, particularly by students whose intellectual strengths may lie in other areas or approaches. Thus, for example, students with strengths in the spatial, musical, or personal spheres may find school far more demanding than students who happen to possess the "text-friendly" blend of linguistic and logical intelligences. And it is difficult, in a more profound sense, because these scholastic forms of knowing may actually collide with the earlier, extremely robust forms of sensorimotor and symbolic knowing, which have already evolved to a high degree even before a child enters school.

Education for understanding can come about only if students somehow become able to integrate the prescholastic with the scholastic and disciplinary ways of knowing and, when such integration does not prove possible, to suspend or replace the prescholastic ways of knowing in favor of the scholastic forms of knowing. Finally, students need to be able to appreciate when a prescholastic form of knowing may harbor a different or even a deeper form of understanding than the discipline-related form of knowing learned in school.

Up to this point I have spoken of the difficulties of school primarily in terms of the problems experienced by students as they are asked to think in new kinds of ways about new kinds of concepts and forms. Even in the happiest scholastic environment, such a regimen may pose problems. Yet, as I have shown in the previous chapter, human constraints on learning are magnified by the equally burdensome constraints under which schools themselves must operate. Although it would be desirable for teachers to work directly with small and well-motivated groups of students, most schools are burdened with

149

large classes, onerous rules and regulations, disruptive demands for accountability, and students who have many personal problems. It is not surprising that an education geared toward understanding is a low priority in such schools; by their nature, bureaucratized institutions have difficulty in dealing with ends that cannot be readily quantified.

In fact, what seems to have evolved in most parts of the scholastic world is an uneasy kind of detente. Teachers require students to answer preset kinds of problems, to master lists of terms, and to memorize and then feed back definitions upon request. They do not ask students to try to reconcile their earlier, partial forms of understanding with the notations and concepts of school; instead they deal only with the latter forms of knowing, hoping that students can later develop the reconciliations on their own. Nor do teachers pose challenging problems that will force their students to stretch in new ways and that will risk failures that might make both students and teacher look bad.

As I have come to express it, neither teachers nor students are willing to undertake "risks for understanding"; instead, they content themselves with safer "correct-answer compromises." Under such compromises, both teachers and students consider the education to be a success if students are able to provide answers that have been sanctioned as correct. Of course, in the long run, such a compromise is not a happy one, for genuine understandings cannot come about so long as one accepts ritualized, rote, or conventionalized performances.

No doubt educators have arrived at this compromise for many reasons, not least because the distance between students' intuitive understandings and the understandings exhibited by disciplinary experts is so vast. Scholastic responses—correct-answer compromises—seem a viable midpoint between these disparate forms of understanding. But just how great is the disjunction between scholastic and nonscholastic forms of understanding has become apparent only in recent years. This area has been the major concern of a number of scholars who call themselves "cognitive scientists interested in education" or "educators interested in cognitive-scientific research." The names of many of these researchers are found in the notes keyed to the relevant studies, but it is appropriate to pay special tribute to the work of Michael Cole, Jean Lave, Lauren Resnick, Sylvia Scribner, and their associates. Their work has much influenced my own thinking and informs much of the ensuing discussion.

As I have already suggested, each discipline, and perhaps each subdiscipline, poses its own peculiar forms of difficulties, its own constraints that must be tackled. The disjunctions between intuitive understandings of history and the formal versions encountered in school are not directly comparable to the disjunctions encountered in physics, mathematics, or the arts. These distinctions should not be in any way minimized but it will be useful from here on to group these disjunctions under three principal headings. In the case of science and science-related areas, I will speak of *misconceptions* that students bring to their studies. In the case of mathematics, I will speak of *rigidly applied algorithms*. Finally, in the case of nonscientific studies, particularly those in the humanities and arts, I will speak of *stereotypes* and *simplifications*.

In this and the following chapters, I lay out these difficulties in some detail. Each of these kinds of difficulties can be dealt with, I believe. Accordingly, in chapters 11 and 12 I argue that misconceptions are most effectively addressed in "Christopherian encounters"; that rigidly applied algorithms require explorations of the relevant semantic domains; and that stereotypes and simplifications call for the adoption of multiple perspectives.

Before turning to specific lines of research, I must underscore two points. First, I must stress that there exists no sharp line between misconceptions and stereotypes. Indeed, difficulties in mathematics and in certain of the social sciences seem to fall about midway between the prototypical misconception in physics and the prototypical stereotype in history or the arts. It is mostly for pragmatic reasons that I have divided the evidence on these difficulties into two large chunks. Scientific and mathematical misconceptions will be discussed in the remainder of the present chapter, and stereotypes encountered in the remaining areas of the curricula will form the subject matter for chapter 9.

I must also concede that use of the terms "misconceptions" and "stereotypes" entails a risk; these terms may imply that the views of young students are completely inadequate and that the views of older children or disciplinary experts are entirely superior. In fact, however, the situation proves far more complex. There are positive rationales underlying the views held by young children, and often these perspectives harbor important insights, which may be lost by older children and may seem obscure or remote to beginning students. By the same token, there is no smooth road from misconceptions to correct conceptions, from rigidly applied algorithms to flexible trafficking between formalisms and their referents, from stereo-types to rounded, multiply nuanced views. All understandings are partial and subject to change; far more important than arrival at a "correct view" is an understanding of the processes whereby mis-conceptions are reformulated or stereotypes dissolved. Because of their vividness and suggestiveness, I continue to use the terms "mis-conceptions" and "stereotypes" here; however, it would be more ac-curate to speak of "earlier understandings" and "more elaborated forms of understanding."

MISCONCEPTIONS IN PHYSICS

Perhaps the most dramatic instances of student misconceptions are those taken from physics. American students headed for elite tech-nologically oriented colleges have taken a number of years of general or natural science, and many have studied at least one year of physics. Thus by the time they pursue physics at the college level, they should have acquired at least a reasonable familiarity with the concepts and frameworks of Newtonian mechanics. Such students in fact get high scores on standardized tests of physics knowledge, and they are likely to earn honor grades when they are tested at the conclusion of a semester or year of college physics.

What happens when these students are probed or tested on their knowledge of physics in a context outside of their classroom? What happens when they have to draw on the knowledge they have osten-sibly obtained through several semesters over the years, in order to explain a demonstration or account for a new phenomenon outside the laboratory? Let us see.

Researcher Andrea DiSessa devised a game called Target, which is played in a computerized environment with a simulated object called a dynaturtle. The dynaturtle can be moved around a computer screen by means of commands like FORWARD, RIGHT, LEFT, or KICK, the latter command giving the dynaturtle an impulse in the direction that the simulated object is currently facing. Typically the dynaturtle is given commands like RIGHT 30 (degrees) or FORWARD 100 (steps).

The goal of the game is to give instructions to the dynaturtle such that it will hit a target and do so with minimum speed at impact. Participants are introduced to the game with a brief description of the commands and a hands-on trial, in which they have the opportunity to apply a few kicks with a small wooden mallet to a tennis ball on a table.

So described, the game sounds simple enough, and, indeed, both naive elementary school children and college physics students approach it with enthusiasm and confidence. Yet nearly everyone at both levels of expertise fails dismally. The reason, briefly, is that success at the game requires an understanding and application of Newton's laws of motion. To succeed, the player must be able to take into account the direction in which and the speed with which the dynaturtle has already been moving. Whatever their formal training, however, players of this game reveal themselves to be dyed-in-the-wool Aristotelians. They assume that, so long as they aim the dynaturtle directly at the target, they will succeed, and they are mystified when the KICK does not result in the desired collision.

Consider what happened to an MIT student named Jane, who was studied intensively by DiSessa. Jane knew all the formalisms taught in freshman physics. She could trot out the equation $F = ma$ under appropriate textbook circumstances, she could faithfully recite Newton's laws of motion, and she could employ the principles of vector summation when asked to do so in problem sets. Yet as soon as she began the game, she adopted the same practices as the naive elementary school students, assuming that the turtle would travel in the direction of the kick. For half an hour she stuck to this inappropriate strategy. Only when she was convinced that this strategy would not work did she make the crucial observation that an object will not lose its prekick motion just because one applies a kick in a certain direction. This realization finally led to experimentation in which the velocity (or speed in a particular direction) of the dynaturtle was at last taken into account.

DiSessa explains Jane's behavior as follows:

> We have already discussed the remarkable similarity of [Jane's] cluster of strategies to those exhibited by 11- and 12-year-old children. But what is equally remarkable is the fact that she did not, indeed for a time could not, relate the task to all the classroom physics she had had. It was not that she could not make the classroom analyses; her vector addition was, by itself, faultless. It is more that her naive physics and classroom physics stood unrelated and in this instance, she exercised her naive physics. . . . One might imagine classroom physics operating within a conscious symbolic scheme typified by discrete entities with well-defined and explicit relations, whereas naive physics might operate in a less integrated way— more like Piagetian action schemes.

Of course, it would be wrong to draw excessive conclusions from the simple failure of one student to draw upon her formal training when confronted by a computer game. But Jane's behavior turns out to be quite typical of what is found when students with training in physics or engineering are posed problems outside the strict confines of class—that is, outside what might be called the text-test context. Here are some further examples drawn from the large literature on the topic:

- Classical physics teaches that objects move in a straight line when no external force acts on them. Students are shown a diagram or an apparatus of a certain shape—say, a curvilinear tube—and asked to predict the trajectory of an object that has been propelled through the apparatus and is then shot out from it. Nearly half the subjects who have studied physics indicate their belief that the object will continue to move in a curvilinear fashion even after it has been released from the tube.

    Interestingly, the students do not even express ignorance of the laws of motion; rather they articulate laws at variance with formal physical laws. As they express it, an object that moves through a curved tube acquires a "force" or "momentum" that causes it to continue in curvilinear motion after it emerges from the tube. After a while, this force dissipates and the trajectory eventually becomes straight.

- Students are asked to designate the forces acting on a coin that is tossed straight up in the air and has reached the midpoint of its trajectory. In one study, mentioned briefly in chapter 1, 90 percent of the engineering students who had not yet taken their mechanics course and 70 percent of those who had answered incorrectly. In general, they indicated two forces, a downward-pointing one representing gravity and an upward-pointing one representing "the original upward force of the hand." In fact, however, once the coin has been tossed, only the gravitational force is present (except for an insignificant amount of air resistance). Researcher John Clement explains that most people, whether or not they have survived a mechanics course, are not able to comprehend that an object can continue to move in a given direction even though the only force apparently operating on it is exerted in the opposite direction.

- More advanced students who have taken a course in the theory of special relativity are asked to reason aloud as they work toward the solution of problems posed by cognitive researchers. One problem considers the workings of a light clock; the second involves the synchronization of distant clocks. Students are able to repeat back accurately the principal claims of relativity theory, according to which temporal and physical properties must be considered in light of a particular frame of reference. And yet students reveal in their responses that they in fact adhere to a belief in absolute space and time. Even a tutor in the course "shows a firm Newtonian commitment to a mechanistic view of the world, which requires that objects have fixed properties such as length, mass, etc. and that explanations of phenomena should be given in terms of these objects and their interactions." Only when students and the tutor are made to confront the inconsistencies between the claims of Newtonian and Einsteinian models of the universe do they begin to engage the problems in the proper fashion.

- Elementary and middle school students receive instruction in the fact that the differences in seasons are caused not by the earth's physical distance from the sun but rather by the angle at which the sun's rays pass through the earth's atmosphere. Students learn to parrot back this response when directly questioned about the matter. Yet it is apparent that they do not really believe the scientific evidence, because as soon as the question is posed to them in an altered form, they revert to an explanation in terms of physical distance. Even belief in a flat world proves robust. Having conceded that the world is round, students regress to a compromise: Like a grapefruit that has been cut in half, the earth is rounded on the bottom but remains comfortably flat on top.

This list of surprising misconceptions and failed performances could easily be extended, but the general point should be clear. Nearly all students without formal science training and a disconcertingly high percentage of those with such training offer explanations that are at variance with simple and well-established laws of motion and mechanics. This is not a case of simple ignorance of the principle under investigation; many of the students know—and can state—the laws on which they should be drawing. Nor is it a case of factual errors; the students are not being asked whether the sun is a star, or a dolphin is a fish. To be sure, some students do respond correctly, and in many cases the group to whom the college students are being compared is aged ten or twelve rather than our proverbial five years of age. Still, the consistent misconceptions exhibited by well-trained science students are disconcerting.

We begin to understand what is going on here when we think back to the robust theories of matter that children develop during the first years of life. Researchers in science education refer to the core ideas that undergird these theories as "primitives." By virtue of their sensorimotor and symbolic interactions with the world, young children develop primitives of the following sort: Agents apply forces to objects, and these forces are transferred to those objects, allowing them to proceed for a while before they "die away"; one can tell how much of each force has been imposed on objects by observing their trajectories; if one wants something to go in a certain direction, one should just propel it in that direction and it will proceed on the desired course; all things fall down, but heavier things fall faster; friction occurs only when things are moving; perceived warmth is determined by distance from a source of heat; and so forth.

The point about these primitives is not that they are completely wrong or completely useless. Indeed, they develop and endure precisely because they prove sufficiently functional in the world of the young child and can be drawn upon with some utility even in the adult world. What is striking is that even students with formal training fall back upon these primitives so readily when they are confronted with a problem, puzzle, or phenomenon outside of the constrained environment of a science class or test.

We can move toward an explanation of these astounding results by analyzing the problem in the following way. On the one hand, the lessons in physics class are learned in such a way that they can be produced in certain debriefing contexts, specifically on homework assignments and in classroom tests. Memorization of certain key demonstrations, definitions, and equations suffices, particularly when the students know in advance the form that such debriefing will take place. So long as the questions are put in a certain expected framework, the students will appear to understand, and the essential bargain of science teaching will have been honored. The correct-answer compromise prevails.

When, however, the student is not primed to expect a certain element of physics knowledge to be invoked, a second, more powerful set of mechanisms is readily invoked. These are the long-entrenched theories of matter that are based on the phenomenological primitives that were formed early in life. Never overtly examined, never brought into direct confrontation with laws of physics that turn out to invalidate or limit them in various contexts, these principles emerge spontaneously as soon as a new problem comes across the horizon. And this is why the apparently competent eighteen-year-old performs little differently from a seven-year-old.

It would be misleading to suggest that the correct explanations or conceptions are necessarily more sophisticated or complex than the misconceptions, although in the case of relativity that might well be the case. (Indeed, in some cases, the correct explanations can be thought of as simpler, because they have been designed to explain idealized worlds, such as worlds without friction.) The following account may be closer to the mark.

By virtue of living as a human being in a world with certain expectable physical and social dimensions, every person develops a whole collection of concepts, schemas, and frames that he brings to bear in attempting to play games, explain phenomena, or simply make his way around the world. Certain of these schemas are most readily elicited in a given context, although others may well be evoked, depending upon particular circumstances, hints, or special efforts.

To take an example, in trying to understand a phenomenon like electricity, students draw on available mental models like "flowing water" or "teeming crowds"; whether they invoke the water model or the crowd model will depend on such factors as the wording used in a textbook, their prior preference for one of the models, their own experience with electrical cords, thunderstorms, batteries, and other electrical devices and phenomena. In principle this procedure of searching for the most appropriate and illuminating model is not different from that confronted by physicists who struggled for centuries to determine whether light is better thought of as composed of particles or of waves or of some strange amalgam of these two analogues. The goal of effective science education is to help students to understand why certain analogies, mental models, or schemas are now considered to be the most appropriate for understanding a given phenomenon or set of phenomena. This state of affairs—an enhanced understanding—can come to pass only if the students become familiar with the new models, understand the reasons for them, perceive why they are more appropriate than the older, competing ones, which may well have retained their attractiveness, and are then able to draw upon them when they encounter a new problem, puzzle, or phenomenon. No small task—even for physicists! In chapter 11 I suggest that one promising route toward such enhanced understanding is the creation of Christopherian encounters: situations where students' earlier models or misconceptions are brought into sharp focus because of an experience that directly challenges the viability of the model they have been favoring.

MISCONCEPTIONS IN BIOLOGY

Physics, of course, is the "hardest" of the sciences (except, perhaps, for physicists!) and one might speculate that comparable misconceptions might be less frequently encountered in other disciplines such as biology. It is true that certain misconceptions of early childhood do get resolved by the years of middle childhood, perhaps even in the absence of explicit tutelage. As Susan Carey has shown, ten-year-olds have abandoned the conceptions that only moving objects are alive, that human beings are prototypes of all animals, and that all biological functions are under voluntary control. For this ensemble of "folk" biological conceptions, they substitute a lay theory of biology that is at least roughly serviceable. According to this theory, biological organisms are characterized by a certain physical structure and by the capacity to carry out such functions as eating, breathing, growing, and dying; plants and animals, but not inanimate objects, are seen as alive; humans lack special status in the animal kingdom; and membership in a species category is determined by underlying constitution, rather than by surface appearances.

Yet once one probes more thoroughly into the subject matter of biology, one finds primitives and misconceptions that align quite closely to those encountered in physics. The understanding of evolutionary theory seems to harbor as many landmines as the understanding of Newton's laws of motion; even students with two years of training in biology continue to exhibit elementary misunderstandings. Thus, while abandoning Biblical creationism, students continue to adhere to Lamarckian accounts in which characteristics acquired in one generation (the giraffe who stretches its neck further to reach more distant food) can be passed on to the next generation. They fail to distinguish between changes that can be observed at a given historical moment and the chances that these changes may be manifest in future generations, attributing changes to environmental alterations rather than to random processes of mutation and natural selection. Students also show a proclivity for invoking teleological explanations, in which evolution is directed along a preconceived path toward certain extrinsic goals. It is difficult for students to understand the undirected nature of evolution; they prefer to see later-evolving species as in some way better, more closely approximating an ideal of perfection.

Misconceptions and naive theories abound across the biological terrain. The processes whereby plants make food are widely misconstrued. Students report a mix of impressions: that soil loses weight as plants grow on it, that the soil is the plant's food, that roots absorb soil, that chlorophyll is the blood of the plant, and that chlorophyll is unavailable to plants during the autumn and winter so the leaves cannot get food. Invocation of purpose and intention is rife; chameleons change colors when they want to in order to avoid their predators. The laws governing heredity are also misinterpreted; for instance, in place of a thorough understanding of the concepts of heterozygosity and homozygosity, students simply assume that heterozygosity is in effect whenever they observe a trait distributed in the ratio of 3:1, and they assume that these ratios are precise rather than just averages that emerge over large numbers of observations. Nor are such processes as meiosis and mitosis well understood; even some "expert-level" biology students mistakenly attribute the structure of chromosomes to the number (technically, the ploidy) of chromosomes.

Although the sources of these biological misconceptions have not been studied in the same degree of detail as have the misconceptions in physics, the same kinds of principles seem to be at work. The earliest tendencies to view everything that moves as alive may be abandoned, but students are still prone to believe that biological processes reflect the intentions of a living substance (parasites are trying to destroy their hosts) or the teleological tendencies of an overriding principle like evolution (human perfection is the goal of evolution). Processes that cannot be seen are assumed not to exist, while those that can be seen are assumed to have direct, unmediated effects on their surroundings. Finally, in lieu of a deeper understanding, students turn to certain key markers (like a given numerical ratio) as an indication of a principle like heterozygosity.

PROBLEMS IN MATHEMATICS: RIGIDLY APPLIED ALGORITHMS

Perhaps, one might argue, it is the disjunction between the world as described by recondite scientists on the one hand and the world of practical experiences on the other that leads to these frustratingly poor performances in sciences like physics and biology. Or perhaps it is the fact that textbooks rarely follow an orderly progression but instead shift abruptly across from one chapter topic to another. Maybe when one turns to mathematics, where students have studied topics for up to a decade, where the order of presentation is presumably logical, and where it is "simply" a case of manipulating notational schemes, one will encounter a happier picture.

Alas, one does not. Indeed, the performance on mathematical problems reveals strikingly analogous kinds of deficiencies. Once again, the students typically fail as soon as the problem is expressed in a slightly different way or an unexpected example is encountered or described.

A fascinating set of studies by Jack Lochhead, John Clement, and their colleagues at the University of Massachusetts at Amherst has documented the surprising fragility of mathematical understanding. If one is told that there are six times as many students as professors and that there are ten professors, nearly everyone can immediately compute the number of students. When one is told that there are sixty students and asked for the number of professors, the performance is virtually as good. But when students are asked to write out a formula that captures the relevant proportion, using S for students, and P for professors, the majority of college students fail. (The reader might try this exercise before reading the next paragraph.)

What happens with this apparently simple assignment? The majority of college students write the formula $6S = P$. It seems correct to them. Yet this formula would yield the astonishing conclusion that, if there are 60 students, there would be 360 professors ($6 \times 60 = 360$)!

It might seem that this is a trick question, and it is true that the occurrence of the word *six* near the word *students* may entice some problem solvers to fall into the $6S$ trap. The more fundamental problem, however, is that students at the college level do not understand the basic algebraic principle that a letter like S stands for "number of students," that P stands for "number of professors," and that equations must be worked out on the basis of those stipulations. Instead, they seem to believe that the letters in equations label concrete entities, like the actual professors or students themselves. Even more disconcertingly, the University of Massachusetts research team has discovered that this assumption proves extremely robust and is accordingly very difficult to eradicate. Reflecting the line of analysis that I have introduced here, students can learn to memorize the phrase *X refers to the number of some entity* . . . , but they revert to their earlier inadequate approaches once they have departed from the instructional setting.

An insufficient understanding of algebraic notation leads to an unhappy situation: Whenever students have to use it in a situation described in certain ways, they are prone to err. Clearly, one can make students perform better by expressing the problem in a way that allows them to succeed, even when they do not understand the operation of the notation. For example, one could improve performance on the above problem by saying "the number of students is six times the number of professors," thereby encouraging the student to write $S = 6P$ and leading to the correct equation $60 = 6 \times 10$. But just as surely, such a crutch is exactly what understanding should *not* require.

In some ways, it is legitimate to think of these algebra students as harboring misconceptions—for example, the belief that S stands for students rather than for "number of students." But these algebra students exemplify a more fundamental problem in mathematics, the practice of *rigid application of algorithms*. The ways in which mathematics is customarily taught and the ways in which students learn conspire to bring about a situation where students perform adequately so long as a problem is stated in a certain way and they can therefore "plug numbers" into an equation or formula without worrying about what the numbers or symbols mean. In such an approach, the student pays attention to syntactic considerations: When one hears that there are six times as many students as professors, the response to write $6S = P$ is reliably triggered and an algorithm is automatically invoked. True understanding goes well beyond such a syntactic approach. Students are most likely to succeed over a wide variety of problems if they have explored the relevant semantic domain—in this case, the relation of students to teachers, or of one population to another—and have come to understand the ways in which algebraic expressions can capture that situation.

Mathematical misunderstandings emerge across the age spectrum and in diverse areas of mathematics. A rule of thumb measure of lack of mathematical understanding, indeed, is the extent to which, when given a string of numbers, students immediately and reflexively begin to perform certain operations upon them. We have already witnessed the compulsive desire on the part of preschoolers and early school-children to sum up any collection of spoken or written numbers they happen to encounter. For an analogous reason, most students encounter difficulty when they are first asked to add fractions, because they simply proceed to add together the two numerators and the two denominators. (Thus ½ and ½ are seen as summing to $^2/_4$.) One can safely assume that the *wrong* answers on many items on a College Board aptitude or achievement examination will be the sum or the product of two numbers in the problem; test makers know that students who are stumped will simply add or multiply, rigidly applying the most relevant algorithm, and hope for the best.

Notations occasion much confusion. The similarities in symbolic notation between decimals and whole numbers mask crucial differences in their meanings. For example, in whole numbers, the units or ones position is held by the rightmost digit, while in decimal fractions, the ones position is marked by a decimal point (or, alternatively, it may be thought of as immediately to the left of the decimal point). The whole numbers build up from one through grouping by ten; in contrast, decimal fractions build up by tens when moving to the left and break down by tens to the right of the decimal point. (These ideas prove difficult to express in words, a fact that may contribute to student confusion.) Students must come to understand that the decimal system uses numerical notations and rules of the sort that govern whole numbers to represent quantities that are like fractions. It is no easy task to appreciate that .6 is greater than .5999, yet less than .60001.

One stumbling block of a profound nature in mathematics learning involves the precise meaning of words. In normal conversation, one is given considerable latitude in how one uses the lexicon, and this freedom adds to the humor and spice of daily intercourse. But such imprecision can be fatal in the area of mathematics. Researcher Pearla Nesher points out that the simple word *is* can assume at least four different symbolic expressions, denoting equals, class membership, existence, and entailment. Failure to appreciate these subtle differences can lead to a complete misconstruction of a problem.

It has been proposed that, on occasion, the linguistic practices embraced by particular cultural groups may render certain subject matter, as currently taught, especially difficult. Educator Eleanor Wilson Orr has documented the grave difficulties experienced by inner-city black youngsters whose use of language often does not align closely with the precise uses prescribed in mathematics textbooks. For example, such students often say "twice as less," which cannot simply be equated with "half as much"; some students do not distinguish between a location (as customarily represented by a point) and a distance (represented as a line segment) and therefore will say things like "(The town of) Aurora equals the distance from Cleveland to Washington"; some conflate the words *any* and *some* as well as *at* and *to*, or *for* and *of*. Although these distinctions may not matter in ordinary, context-rich discussion, they can collide with usages in textbooks where a single denotation—and no other—has been intended.

If mathematics textbooks tend to be unforgiving, programmed computers are even less flexible. A word or expression in a computational language has one and only one meaning. Sometimes, in an effort to make such languages "user-friendly," inventors of the languages employ the words of natural language. Although this gesture may help the novice approach and enter the general realm of the intended meaning, it can ultimately be confusing rather than helpful, because students—and here the problem proves pervasive across racial and ethnic lines—fall back on the vernacular rather than on the technical definition of the term. My colleagues David Perkins and Rebecca Simmons report students' assumption that if they give a variable in a Pascal program the name LARGEST, the computer will "know" that it should store the largest of a series of numbers it reads into that variable, because it "knows" the meaning of the word *largest*.

One can see at work the disjunction between intuitive or commonsense knowledge on the one hand and emerging notational sophistication on the other. I recently observed an eight-year-old who was learning how to measure with a ruler. His goal was to measure a Y-shaped cardboard cutout. Apparently grasping the requisite procedures, he would align one of the arms of the Y flush against the ruler and then read off the number at the other end— "four inches," "five inches," even "between five and six inches." Then, however, he decided to measure the short segment (or tip) that forms the end of the arm. In this instance, he placed the segment at the middle of the ruler and announced that it was "seven inches." Obviously he did not appreciate that all measures need to take place at a point of origin (or its equivalent) and that the measure represents extent of deviation from an origin. Instead he simply applied the algorithm of reading off the number that coincided with his current focus of attention.

Of course this eight-year-old child knew in a sensorimotor way that the tip was much shorter than the arm of the Y, and when I asked directly "Which is longer?" he readily acknowledged that the arm was longer. His failure came about because, in our terms, he did not appreciate the relationship between the sensorimotor information (which segment is longer) and the operation of the measuring system. He resembled the child asked the temperature of two recently merged containers, each containing water at 10 degrees, who blithely sums the amounts and reports that the new blend is 20 degrees. Instead of integrating the algorithm with intuitive knowledge, the child allows the algorithm to dictate what the answer is.

Even as disjunctions occur between intuitive and notational knowledge, there can also be curious separations between putatively related forms of notational knowledge per se. Paul Cobb has told the story of a little girl who added 16 and 9 correctly by counting on (simply adding on each of nine units beyond 16). Given the identical problem in written form, she failed to carry the 1 and obtained 15. She considered both to be correct, 15 for the worksheet problem and 25 when the problem represented 16 cookies and 9 more. In Cobb's words, "For her, school arithmetic seemed to be an isolated, self-contained context in which the possibility of doing anything other than attempting to recall prescribed methods did not arise."

In a related example, Robert Lawler described his six-year-old daughter, who could do mental calculation with numbers and also with money but was unable to connect the two realms. She could add 75 cents and 26 cents, using her knowledge of quarters, and come up with the right total in terms of coins; when given the numbers, she was able to add by tens and count the remainders. But only some months later did a moment of insight occur when she was first able to appreciate the relation between a coins microworld and a numerical microworld.

I do not wish to suggest that these errors and disjunctions are a shocking matter; indeed they are a natural human phenomenon, one that can be instructive. I recommend that parents and teachers be alert for such difficulties and encourage students to examine them critically. The point is that the errors or misconceptions are a warning sign, a signal of incomplete understanding. The teacher should not simply indicate the correct procedures (no, you find a common denominator and convert both fractions to it); if this is done, the child is likely to revert to her old habits as soon as she fails to recognize an instance that calls for the memorized procedure. Rather, the teacher needs to work with the student on three dimensions: (1) an understanding of what is involved (why one cannot simply add numerators and denominators); (2) an exploration of the particular semantic domain being investigated (whether it be pieces of a pizza or portions of a lot); (3) how best to relate the formal algorithmic rules to the particulars of a given semantic world. If such a procedure is followed, there is a reasonable chance that understanding will be achieved and that comparable errors will be much less likely to occur in the future. In fact, according to this analysis, if an understanding student were left on a desert island, she could even reinvent a procedure such as the addition of fractions that she had long since forgotten.

Perhaps the greatest difficulty in the whole area of mathematics concerns students' misapprehension of what is actually at stake when they are posed a problem. Mathematics teachers report that students are nearly always searching for the steps to take in solving the problem—"how to plug the numbers" into the equation, how to follow the algorithm. The more closely the ordering of words in a problem parallels the order of symbols in the equation, the easier the problem is to solve and the more students will like it. Seeing mathematics as a way of understanding the world, of illuminating a phenomenon, as a kind of conversation or enterprise into which even a young person can become meaningfully involved is a rare occurrence. And yet, how can genuine understanding ever begin to come about without such an attitude?

It should be evident that erroneous conceptions and misunderstandings are as rife in mathematics as in the natural sciences. When they are still young, children develop a strong intuition about number, about what is more numerous or less numerous; their understanding is often conceptualized in terms of a number line, running from little or nothing (0) to a very large number (or infinity). Also intuitive are the notions of adding and taking away and dividing up into equal amounts. As much as possible, students attempt to align mathematical problems encountered in the world to such a simple numerical scheme, and in many cases it is at least approximately accurate.

The formal subject of mathematics, however, involves the use of new kinds of symbolic notations, as well as more explicit (and less casual) definitions of familiar words and pictures. Most children do not find it easy to map their intuitions onto these formal mathematical expressions. The world of numbers and numerical operations, as captured in sensorimotor operations, and the world of spoken numbers, written numerical expressions, and textbook formulae never come together in a synergistic way. And therefore, just as they fail to align their physical and biological intuitions with the textbook matter presented in courses in physics and biology, students do not seek to match their numerical intuitions about domains of objects with the demands of arithmetic or mathematics classes. A correct-answer compromise is achieved, in which students learn to follow certain procedures and to plug in certain numbers and symbols, in order to complete the homework and pass the test. Once removed from the test-text context, however, students do not know how to employ these formalisms, and they fall back on the rough-and-ready intuitions of early childhood.

When speaking of the problems encountered by students in the area of arithmetic, the term "misconception" is no longer optimal and may not even be appropriate. In the natural sciences, students have well-developed theories of matter and of life that turn out in some cases to be inconsistent with the principles of physics and biology. In the area of mathematics, however, it is not quite accurate to say that students have misconceptions that fly in the face of the formal disciplinary knowledge. Rather, I have suggested that most students suppress their intuitive knowledge about numbers and domains (like time or money or pieces of pizza) and instead try to follow rigidly applied sets of rules for solving problems. Only when the problem as set actually triggers the algorithm that has been mastered will students get the correct answer; as soon as there is any alteration in the formulation of the problem, the student is likely to get completely lost.

As one moves further away from the natural sciences, the notion of misconceptions proves even less adequate. Better terms might be "stereotypes" or "scripts"—strongly held views of the correct way in which to think about human matters. Accordingly, in the next chapter, when we address learning in the social sciences, the humanities, and the arts, we will speak of student stereotypes. Although the terminology changes, however, the kinds of problems will be familiar to anyone who has encountered the materials in this chapter.

CHAPTER

9

More Difficulties Posed by School: Stereotypes in the Social Sciences and the Humanities

I n this chapter I continue to review the kinds of understandings that students bring to formal disciplinary study. I begin with examples from economics and statistics, two areas that can be said to bridge the natural and the social sciences. With some license, student performances in these areas can continue to be discussed in terms of misconceptions, but I believe that "stereotypes" provides a better characterization. Later in this chapter, I introduce examples drawn from history, the humanities, and the arts. These latter areas are clearly better described in terms of the stereotypes, scripts, and simplifications that evolve in early childhood and that students are prone to impose on curricular materials throughout and after their school years.

PROBLEMS IN ECONOMICS AND STATISTICS

Economics presents an interesting bridge area, because it involves mathematical thinking that is ordinarily applied in the social arena.

James Voss and his colleagues at the University of Pittsburgh compared the performances of students who had taken economics at the college level with the performances of students of equivalent background who had not studied economics. Students were posed problems pertaining to situations in the daily world for which formal analyses are customarily offered in economics courses. For instance, they were asked to describe specific economic situations concerning automobile prices, the federal deficit, and interest rates ("If health care costs rise considerably, what effects, if any, do you think this would have on the size of the federal deficit and why?").

Results were unexpected (although they may not be for readers of this book). College-educated subjects outperformed those without a college education, but there was little difference between those college students who had studied economics and those who had not; despite training, those students who had taken at least one course in economics approached and answered questions with essentially the same degree of success as students who had never studied economics formally. Misconceptions or stereotypes were found across both groups. One such stereotype was an overall "halo effect"; good times were associated with low interest rates. Another misconception was a statement inconsistent with economics theory: "The more they sell, the lower the price should be, because you can still keep the profit the same." A frequent procedure was to develop what was called a "primary rule"—a principle that was drawn on regularly, whether or not it was appropriate (for example, interest rates are determined by the expectation of inflation). Such primary rules seem to occupy a place similar to a rigidly applied algorithm: When in doubt, invoke the rule triggered by a word like "interest" or "inflation."

Even though individual forms of understandings in economics may prove difficult to learn and retain, Voss's finding that college-educated subjects outperformed those without a college education suggests that a college education may lead students to think better or reason in a more powerful fashion. Yet even in this arena one courts disappointment. My colleague David Perkins compared the informal reasoning capacities of students upon entry to college and of students upon their exit from college. Like Voss, he used examples drawn from the sphere of human relations. Sample problems asked students to discuss such social issues as "Would a law requiring a five-cent deposit on bottles and cans reduce litter?" and "Would restoring the military draft significantly increase America's ability to influence world events?" Perkins documented that college has little discernible effect on the reasoning capacities of students. The same kinds of approaches and the same form and number of arguments favored by students as they begin college seem to be favored by students four years later. Perkins wisely shrinks from the conclusion that college has had no effect, but he suggests that if one wants to enhance students' reasoning capacities, one needs to work directly on this mission—for example, by modeling what makes for good or bad argumentation and teaching students how to evaluate their own and others' arguments. Better thinking does not come about for free.

Paralleling the story told by Voss in the area of economics are findings from the area of statistics and probability. In a well-known set of studies, cognitive researchers Amos Tversky, Daniel Kahneman, and their colleagues asked students to answer questions calling for the use of statistical principles. Here are five that typify their collection of dilemmas:

- Subjects were asked to decide whether a particular individual was more likely to be an engineer or a lawyer. Subjects were informed that in the population, 70 percent were engineers and 30 percent were lawyers. As soon as any feature was described that would bias the judgment in one direction (for example, that an individual liked to debate), respondents would completely ignore the base rate and answer only in terms of the representativeness of the hypothetical person ("Oh, then he must be a lawyer").
- Subjects are told about Linda, thirty-one years old, single, outspoken, bright, and very much involved in social issues like disarmament and equal rights. They must then decide which statement is more likely: "Linda is a bank teller" or "Linda is a bank teller and is active in the feminist movement." On any logical analysis, it is more probable that Linda is a bank teller than that she is *both* a bank teller and an active feminist. Yet more than 80 percent of subjects, including those sophisticated in statistics, respond with greater affirmation to the statement that Linda is a bank teller and a feminist.
- Subjects are asked to estimate the number of African nations in the United Nations. Kahneman and Tversky report the astounding finding that the number of the question itself (#10 versus #65), though obviously irrelevant to the answer, nonetheless influences the mean response of subjects. Subjects gave higher estimates of member nations in response to question #65 than in response to an identically worded question #10.

- Subjects are told about the opportunity to purchase a jacket for $125 and a calculator for $15. The purchaser is told that he can buy the same calculator for $10 in a store twenty minutes away. Most people say that they would make the trip. Subjects in another group are told that the jacket costs $15, while the calculator costs $125 in the original store and $120 in the second store. In this case, the majority say that they would not make the extra trip. In the two situations the total purchases add up to the same amount; the choice is always whether to drive twenty minutes to save $5. But respondents apparently evaluate a saving of $5 with reference to the price of the calculators. A one-third reduction from $15 to $10 proves less resistible than a reduction from $125 to $120 (4 percent).

- In one condition, subjects learn of a medical treatment that results in saving the lives of two hundred out of six hundred people. In another condition, subjects learn of a treatment in which four hundred out of six hundred people will die. Though the statistical results are of course identical, people are more attracted to the treatment that is framed in terms of "lives saved."

STEREOTYPES AND SIMPLIFICATIONS IN THE HUMANISTIC DISCIPLINES

What is going on in these studies in the social realm? In addressing this question, we effect a transition from one principal order of scholastic problems to another. Specifically, we move from the order that I have lumped under the label "misconceptions" to a second order, which I term "stereotypes, scripts, and simplifications" and shorten hereafter to "stereotypes."

As I have noted, there is no sharp line between misconceptions and stereotypes, but the latter seems a better characterization of the problems encountered in humanistic studies. Rather than holding a competing theory or a robust misconception that overwhelms the disciplinarily appropriate concept, the subjects in the Tversky-Kahneman experiments exhibit a different phenomenon. Abandoning or bracketing any formal knowledge they have of statistics, probability, or logical analysis, they respond instead on the basis of dominant images, prevalent stereotypes, or favored ways of framing a problem. They ignore information that obviously should be taken into account in making a decision, such as the information about the percentage of lawyers in a population, in favor of assumptions about behavior made on the basis of their daily experience (lawyers like to debate). A stereotype (a lawyer, a feminist) proves more robust than formal disciplinary statistical knowledge or logical thinking. The way in which a problem is framed similarly takes precedence over logic, so that a five-dollar saving seems worth pursuing when it is considered in relation to the cost of an inexpensive calculator but not in relation to the cost of an expensive one, and a cure that is framed as saving the lives of one out of three patients is preferred over one that is framed as leading to the death of two out of three. Even a totally irrelevant number "in the air" compromises rational analysis of geography or politics.

When conceiving of issues in economics, statistics, and other social sciences, one is of course entering the realm of human experiences. Here, it appears, the naive theories of mind constructed during early childhood continue to exert significant power. Consider, for example, the ways in which people judge the causes of actions. It has been found that people attribute their own actions to external causes ("I did this because of a perceived reward, or because of someone else's advice"), whereas observers attribute the very same actions to causes such as personality traits that are internal to the person who took the action ("John did it because he is an ambitious or cruel or insecure person"). It is of course untenable that the very same action could be consistently caused by two different sets of factors in the case of one population (the agents themselves) and a second population (individuals other than the agents). In such cases, researchers document the operation of a "fundamental attribution error": Observers systematically underestimate the importance of situational factors and overestimate the importance of internal dispositional factors. This bias seems to be a residue of a childlike theory in which another person's behavior is attributed to his being a "bad" or a "good" person.

Jonathan Baron, who has studied how people arrive at judgments in the human sphere, has chronicled a whole family of biases that are consistently brought to bear when subjects are questioned about alternative courses of behavior. Among them are the "sunk-cost bias" (people spend more on a project into which they have already sunk resources, even when they are informed that there are better uses for freshly available resources); attention to irrelevant factors (people will continue to focus on a test score, even when they have direct evidence on the trait that the test purports to measure); the "endowment effect" (it takes more money to induce people to give up something than they are willing to pay for it in the first place); the "status quo effect" (people prefer the option they have selected, even when they recognize that another option is superior); the bias to omit rather than to commit (people will spurn a vaccine that can occasionally cause harm, even when the chances of harm are trivial compared with the possibility of harm should the vaccine not be taken). These biases prove very robust and are found with approximately equal frequency throughout life. They tend to disappear only when individuals have gained a great deal of firsthand experience with situations that run counter to the bias or stereotype—for example, by working in a medical setting where decisions about injections are routinely made.

PROBLEMS IN HISTORICAL AND LITERARY STUDIES

Stereotypical assumptions about human nature, along with a ready recourse to the common scripts of human life, contribute to difficulties when one enters the world of the humanities and the "softer" social sciences. These areas have not been so thoroughly investigated as the hard sciences, but the kinds of problems encountered in the other disciplines surface here as well.

What kinds of problems do students exhibit in dealing with literary or historical texts? An initial bias is to assume that one will necessarily encounter some kind of story or dramatic narrative. Understanding proves far easier when the text follows a traditional narrative format, featuring a hero, a crisis, and a happy resolution. Straight expository text proves more difficult, because it does not necessarily furnish markers about who did what to whom; when the assumptions associated with specific genres cannot be involved, the student has to create or revise his own mental models.

The status of facts in expository writing often constitutes a source of difficulty. Students may read *only* for the facts as they are given and utterly fail to appreciate the argument or perspective that has been invoked in stating them in a certain way. The insensitivity of many less-able students to the vocabulary of argument— "contend," "hypothesize," "refute," "contradict"—only magnifies problems of text comprehension. Then, when students do become aware of a realm beyond the factual, a new set of problems may arise. Students now posit a radical disjunction between facts, on the one hand, and opinion, on the other. Such a dichotomy interferes with an appreciation of the far subtler interplay between what is selected as a fact, how it is stated, and which underlying assumptions, goals, and perspectives have governed the selection.

Even when a narrative format is used, the identification of the script in question is not necessarily straightforward. A story about a powerful leader who mistreats his enemies may invoke a scheme for revenge, and indeed, in Hollywood blockbusters or television miniseries, such revenge will predictably ensue. But in historical reality, powerful leaders sometimes continue to be tyrannical without receiving the punishment that is their due. The violation of the standard script, in which injustice is punished or virtue is rewarded, may cause problems here.

In trying to go beyond the narrative and understand the whys of events, students encounter a number of problems. One pervasive tendency is to engage in frank stereotypical thinking—for example, to assume that individuals behave in certain kinds of ways by virtue of class membership ("All Chinese . . . , All Jews . . . , All African Americans . . . ,"). Another is to ignore the author's intentions and biases and assume that the exposition is factual ("This is how things were in Renaissance Florence" or, perhaps, "Machiavelli was telling how things were in Florence" but not "This is Machiavelli's attempt to convince us [or the Medicis or their opponents] about how things were in Florence"). Yet another limitation is to remain mired at the literal interpretation and to fail to appreciate symbolic or allegorical interpretations (*Moby Dick* is a story about a whale hunt departing from Nantucket or about a bitter old man).

Going beyond a single explanation or a literal reading may be difficult, but such a stretch proves essential in the humanistic disciplines. In the human realm, consequences can rarely be attributed to a single event (even in cases as clear-cut as a murder by a deranged individual). The ascent of a political party, the advent of a counterrevolution, the downfall of a character in a tragedy are usually determined by multiple causes. Moreover, it is rarely possible to prove that a particular analysis, no matter how complex, is *the* correct one. Instead one must generally come up with the best among several alternative explanatory schemes, given the amount of time and evidence available to the analyst. Indeed, in the humanities, the raising of questions, rather than the adoption of a single line of argument or the selection of the best among a finite set of alternatives, is often the deep goal of the lesson. The "problem" of Richard II (or of Lenin) can never be "solved"; at most one can understand somewhat more fully the issues that he confronted and the reasons why he dealt with them in the way that he did.

Tom Holt and Dennie Wolf outline the assumptions with which many students enter a history class. Even at the college level, most students view history as the ordering of already-known facts into agreed-upon chronologies. For many of them, in fact, history *is* facts, with issues of interpretation scarcely arising at all. If history is seen as being about people, the people are viewed as generic and remote rather than as particular persons who, like themselves, exhibit an amalgam of sometimes conflicting goals and feelings. It is therefore hardly surprising that students often fail to relate history to the lives of ordinary individuals, let alone to their own; nor can they appreciate how the particulars of everyday life are fashioned (by yet other flesh-and-blood individuals called historians) to form the fabric of history.

Whereas students are sometimes unable to relate a text to their own experiences, at other times students prove unable to distance texts from their own often-idiosyncratic assumptions about human nature. A major biasing factor stems from the simple schemes about human behavior that were developed in early childhood on the basis of interactions with others in the environment. For example, as children they learned to trust certain people like parents and teachers, and in later years they assume that anything told them by a trusted parent or teacher is accurate and exhaustive. The injunctions to "consider the source" or "examine the evidence" seem harsh, but they are important to heed. By the same token, the "conversational postulate" to take individuals at their word, and not to look for more complex explanations when simpler ones will do, biases individuals toward literal readings and interpretations of texts. Students therefore fail to attend to the small but telltale clues that signal symbolic or allegoric meanings.

Pursuing a similar line of analysis, Gaea Leinhardt outlines the complex "moves" made by a competent history teacher. To convey a full explanation of a historical phenomenon, the teacher must present the story or narrative (what happened in a war or a peace settlement); the defining structures (the political and economic forces that were operating); long-term interpretive themes (the tensions that existed across eras or populations); and also the metasystems of history (the kinds of analysis, hypothesis testing, and synthesis in which a competent historian habitually engages). The student must not only abandon a simple fact-script-and-personality view of history but also orchestrate and integrate these different perspectives. For many students, the task proves as formidable as the kinds of integration required in mathematical or physical studies.

Indeed, viewed at sufficient remove, analogous problems in understanding recur across the disciplinary spectrum. Just as people's theories of matter, or of life, bias them toward interpreting natural phenomena in certain ways, so too do their theories of mind, of person, or of self play a major role in the ways in which they interpret texts about human nature. As with the sciences, students may learn to give "proper" interpretations of historical events or proper readings of classic novels or plays when they are under the guidance of a teacher embodying the correct-answer compromise. They can adopt subtle epistemic forms that will help them succeed in formal examinations. But when they are asked about the same types of events or characters some time later, they may well regress to the earlier, more entrenched, and more stereotypical ways of interpretating human behavior.

Perhaps more to the point, when a new political event occurs or a new work of fiction is encountered, such people may have a strong tendency to fall back on assumptions that grow out of intuitive theories of the human realm. Thus, one may have learned as a student that the causes of the First World War went far beyond a single assassination and yet later, in considering the cause of a protest in the streets, attribute it exclusively to the assassination of Martin Luther King, Jr. or the unexpected death of Hu Yaobang. Or one may have been taught that war is seldom due to the behavior of a single evil leader; and yet, once out of class, embrace the "bad man" theory, be he named Muammar al-Qaddafi, Manuel Noriega, or Saddam Hussein. Sophisticated understandings in historical and humanistic studies entail a recognition of the occasions on which naive folk theories are adequate, as well as a recognition of circumstances under which more complex epistemic forms must be invoked.

SIMPLIFICATIONS IN THE ARTS

Although the arts are often seen as quite distinct from formal disciplinary studies, analogous tensions exist among different forms of representation or understanding. A telling set of examples comes from Jeanne Bamberger at the Massachusetts Institute of Technology.

175

Bamberger shows that when subjects are asked to create a notation for a set of clapped patterns, schooled and unschooled music students respond in different ways. In one thoroughly studied example, subjects hear what seems like a set of two claps (grouping A), then a set of three claps more closely bunched together (grouping B), followed by a silence that is as long as the time between the first and second claps in the first grouping or the first and third claps in the second grouping. The pattern is then repeated: a set of two claps and a set of three claps, followed by a pause of the same length as before. The motif, reminiscent of "one, two, pick up shoes; three, four, shut the door," can be repeated indefinitely.

In creating a notation for the pattern, the untrained students group together claps that seem to belong to a group (a set of two claps, followed by a set of three claps), ignoring the length of the intervals between the claps. Their naive renditions look like this:

. .   . .

or like this:

.   .   . .

Thus, a "reader" of their invented notation would reproduce groupings of two and three but would fail to reproduce the intervening intervals in a consistent fashion.

Students with musical training follow metrical patterns, recognizing precisely how much time is taken by each pulse as well as the amount of time between pulses. Their rendering is "literally correct." A typical rendition, which is technically equivalent to standard musical notation, would look like this:

$$. / . / . . / . / . / . / . . / .$$

But the difference between the two responses does not reduce to "right" versus "wrong." The naive students may have failed to produce a metrically accurate rendition, but they have maintained an important sensorimotor form of knowledge—the intuitive or figural feeling for which pulses go together in groupings A and B, in the way that could be indicated by a conventional phrase marking. When reproducing the pattern, they re-create the felt groupings as well. In contrast, the musically trained subjects give a technically flawless response in notating the pattern. But when asked to perform the pattern itself, they may fail to re-create the feeling of common membership that is highlighted in the naive notations and performances. They have produced a correct-answer compromise rather than a fully appropriate rendition. As it were, formal notational knowledge has overwhelmed sensorimotor intuition.

According to Bamberger, the genuinely musical performer is not limited to either the figural/intuitive or the formal/metrical interpretation; instead she honors both the phrasing implied in the figural notation (which is a product of early forms of hearing and producing music) and the metrical regularity captured in the formal notation (which could come about only as a consequence of formal notational instruction). Here, as in certain science explanations, a deeper form of understanding involves a unification of sensorimotor and notational modes of representation.

A classic demonstration of the limitations of understanding in the literary arts was published by the critic I. A. Richards nearly seventy years ago. Richards asked undergraduates at Cambridge University to read pairs of poems and to offer their interpretations and their evaluations of the poems. One would certainly have reason to expect that these students, as highly selected as science and engineering students at M.I.T., would be able to offer convincing interpretations and judgments of literary merit, even when the identities of the poets were not revealed.

No reader of these chapters will be surprised to learn that Richards' study revealed just the reverse. In few if any of the contrasts did the majority of students offer a reasonable précis and interpretation of the poem. Sheer misunderstanding was the rule rather than the exception. In Richards' soft words,

> The most disturbing and impressive fact brought out by this experiment is that a large proportion of average-to-good (and in some cases, certainly devoted) readers of poetry frequently and repeatedly fail to understand [the poem], both as a statement and as an expression. They fail to make out its sense, its plain, overt meaning, as a set of ordinary intelligible English sentences, taken quite apart from any poetic significance.

Moreover, Richards found that the literary judgments were completely at variance with those offered by knowledgeable scholars of English poetry. Poets as eminent as John Donne and Gerard Manley Hopkins fared very poorly at the hands of these youthful (but hardly unsparing) critics, whereas the most popular work was an execrable (and unpublished) poem by one J. C. Pellow.

A look at the grounds on which students based their judgments reveals the kinds of esthetic standards invoked by fairly knowledgeable if not highly trained students. Of most importance to these students were the subject matter (it should be bright and positive, but not too sentimental) and the overt features of form (the poem should rhyme, have regular meter, and avoid words that are too common or too arcane). Studies using other media have indicated analogous kinds of biases among students. Music should be harmonious and have a regular beat; paintings should use pleasant colors and capture the world of beautiful natural phenomena and of attractive human beings. There is little tolerance for work that is abstract, irregular, or experimental, even when it is clear that the artist knew what he or she was doing and the effects are known to be cherished by connoisseurs.

One can locate the sources of these preferences and interpretations in the artistic activities of the young child. Although the artistic productions of young children are often notable for their imagination and subtlety, children's tastes tend to the most elemental and picturesque works. Whether with respect to music, the visual arts, or literary or expository writing—or, for that matter, taste in other areas—young students develop strong prototypes or stereotypes; popular taste and mass culture build directly upon these early predilections. Students and elders move beyond these stereotypes only with difficulty and only following considerable informed experience in exploring the relevant arts, crafts, or other spheres of life.

Just as our earlier discussion of science and history assumes that there are certain more sophisticated performances that signal deeper understandings, this brief discussion of the arts has suggested the existence of more or less comprehensive "readings" of works of art. Such an approach may itself appear to be unsophisticated, inasmuch as it appears to ignore the testimony of the deconstructionists, who claim that there are no authoritative readings of texts, and of extreme relativists, who deny that any works are in an absolute sense better than any others. Although I do not wish to dismiss these critical stances completely, I should indicate my lack of sympathy with them. I find them to be more effective as debating positions than as points of view to which anyone would fully subscribe. Perhaps after one has reached a certain level of sophistication it makes sense to consider these positions, but in the case of precollegiate education it seems sensible to assume that students' readings of a work can be improved and that some works are more worth reading than others. When one observes the leading deconstructionist, Jacques Derrida, trying to explain Nazi tendencies in his master Martin Heidegger and to explain them away in his colleague Paul De Man, it becomes apparent that "straight readings" are sometimes needed even by avant-garde interpreters.

SOME CONCLUDING COMMENTS ABOUT MISCONCEPTIONS AND STEREOTYPES

No doubt in part because it is a delicate matter, researchers have rarely studied teachers, posing them the same problems and reasoning tasks that they have used in probing students. I would not be surprised if, among teachers without explicit training and certification in a discipline, analogous kinds of errors, misconceptions, and primitive approaches were uncovered. Yet even in cases where teachers exhibit deep understandings on such measures—and there are doubtless many examples of such meritorious performances—one cannot assume that their students would necessarily rise to their level. After all, teachers have had many years of familiarity with the material and thus can think about it much more flexibly. Also, teachers have encountered many more kinds of tasks and problems over the years and would be much more likely to recognize the context or clue embedded in a question. But the fact that a teacher herself understands provides no guarantee that her aspiring students will understand equally well—or even well at all. Indeed, the more fully a teacher has assimilated sophisticated understandings, the less she may be able to see into the mind of the child and recognize its tendencies toward misconceptions and stereotypical thinking.

In Part II of the book, I have suggested that understanding is a complex process that is itself not well understood. At the very least, it seems to require teachers and students to move readily from one form of representation to another and back again. Understanding does not and cannot occur unless the relations among different notations and representations come to be appreciated, and unless these formal expressions can be mapped onto more intuitive forms of knowing. At least in most cases, a genuine understanding probably involves some kind of direct confrontation of those habits of the mind that tend to get in the way of a thoroughgoing understanding, the primitives of the physics class or the intuitive representations of the young music student. Because those interfering habits of the mind have not even begun to be understood until recent years, it is optimistic to think that teachers in the past have produced cohorts of students who do understand the material they are studying in the way that convinced readers of this book might desire.

Nonetheless, a good number of teachers and at least some students do come to understand such materials of school as the applicability of laws of physics to a newly encountered phenomenon, the appropriate way to set up and solve an unfamiliar algebra problem, the explanations for a complex historical event, or the optimal interpretation of a line of musical notation or a verse of poetry. In some cases success is due to the student himself, who overcomes indifferent teaching and is able to ferret out the insights on his own. In some cases the success is due to the ingenious teacher who either deliberately or intuitively helps students to advance beyond, or productively draw upon, their earlier ways of thinking and to meet the concepts of school in the terms of the disciplines themselves.

The question naturally arises whether the poor performances of Americans on tests of competence indicate a particularly low degree of understanding in our schools and whether students elsewhere would demonstrate greater success. It is possible that we are dealing here with a problem that is largely American, but I doubt it. Most of the international comparisons of student achievement simply do not assess for understanding but rather for much simpler forms of imitation, rote learning, or well-rehearsed performance. College students or graduate students from other countries who come to the United States still require considerable training before they can evince genuine understanding in their research and writing. I suspect that the correct-answer compromise is prevalent and that education for understanding is a rare commodity everywhere.

Could it be made more common? I have no doubt that it can be. I am optimistic that we—and here I mean to encompass educators from around the globe—can reconfigure our educational environments and alter our pedagogical approaches so that many more students will attain a significant degree of understanding across a wide range of subjects. The key, I believe, is to devise learning environments in which students naturally come to draw upon their earlier ways of knowing and to configure those environments so that students can integrate these earlier forms of knowing with the formats of knowing that are necessarily and appropriately featured in school. Environments that can fuse sensorimotor and symbolic forms of knowing with the notational, conceptual, and epistemic forms of knowing valued in school should engender understanding. In chapter 10 I examine some recent attempts to reform our educational institutions. Then in chapters 11 and 12 I introduce some of the most promising efforts to institute an education that yields understanding.

The surprising thing is that, as a world culture, we have sensed part of the answer all along. The kinds of environments called apprenticeships have for millennia fused the available forms of knowing in a rich and contextualized way. In a preliterate society, it is necessary only to work with sensorimotor and symbolic knowledge. In a literate society, it has become essential to create learning situations in which these earlier forms of knowing come to be utilized in conjunction with the formal ways of knowing that grow out of, and are tied to, specific disciplines. The weaver in a preliterate society just models and adds a few words of explanation; the weaver in a literate society can make use of charts, diagrams, mathematical equations, and books. Unlike the traditional schoolteacher, however, the weaver who teaches for understanding draws upon these epistemic forms when they arise in the course of a genuine problem, a challenging project, a valuable product. A judicious introduction and integration of apprenticeship methods within a scholastic setting should yield students whose potential for understanding is engaged and enhanced.

Toward Education For Understanding

CHAPTER
10

The Search for Solutions: Dead Ends
and Promising Means

Rivaling the topic of weather, the status of education is much talked about in every contemporary society. Whether the discussions take place in Japan, the country generally considered the most successful in educating its young people, or in the United States, whose educational problems have become a virtual obsession among policy makers (though not, at this writing, of the general public), issues of philosophy and practice loom large. As befits a book that has been conceived and written in the wake of countless discussions in America, much of what follows has been written with American issues in mind. I should like to think, however, that my conclusions have more than parochial interest.

So long as discussion focuses exclusively on the need to address certain inadequacies, it is possible to arrive at some consensus. After all, it is not particularly controversial to call for better-prepared teachers, more dedicated administrators, schools with more engaged students and lower dropout rates, and communities that support their educational systems. But when attention turns to the kinds of students one wants at the end, the steps to be taken toward that end,

185

and the priorities among various educational goals, controversies soon surface.

In this book I have sought to be clear about my educational goals. Most important from my vantage point are students who possess genuine understanding of the major disciplines and areas of knowledge. The nature of that understanding will vary across age and discipline; just as a ten-year-old cannot understand science or literature in the same way as a college student can, so too the misconceptions that crop up in scientific discourse are only remotely related to the stereotypes that interfere with the comprehension of historical or literary texts. Moreover, understanding is not an acquisition that clicks into place at a certain developmental juncture. As David Perkins has stressed, processes of understanding involve sets of performances—carrying out analyses, making fine judgments, undertaking syntheses, and creating products that embody principles or concepts central to a discipline. Everyone exhibits fledgling understandings (whether or not these are the ones sought by their teachers), but not even the most distinguished expert ever attains full understanding.

THE LIMITS OF BASIC SKILLS

Seen from this viewpoint, certain putative solutions recede in desirability, and others recommend themselves more assertively. Both educational leaders and members of the wider community have often called for a reemphasis on the basic skills. In large measure, this goal has been invoked in a defensive way. In apparent distinction to the students of earlier eras, our graduates are not able to read, write, or calculate with proficiency, so they cannot hold jobs, let alone be productive citizens in a community.

To declare oneself against the institution of the three Rs in the schools is like being against motherhood or the flag. Beyond question, students ought to be literate and ought to revel in their literacy. Yet the essential emptiness of this goal is dramatized by the fact that young children in the United States are becoming literate in a *literal* sense; that is, they are mastering the rules of reading and writing, even as they are learning their addition and multiplication tables. What is missing are not the decoding skills, but two other facets: the capacity to read for understanding and the desire to read at all. Much the same story can be told for the remaining literacies; it is not the mechanics of writing nor the algorithms for subtraction that are absent, but rather the knowledge about when to invoke these skills and the inclination to do so productively in one's own daily life.

To attain basic skills requires drill and discipline. Yet the imposition of a strict regime clearly does not suffice. What is missing, in my view, are contexts in which the deployment of these skills makes sense. Too many students do not see the three Rs being used productively at home, nor do they witness their utility in school; and too few students are presented with problems, challenges, projects, and opportunities that draw in a natural and productive way on these skills. Hence the three literacies sit like religious icons on the shelf of a tourist shop, reasonably decorative, perhaps, but out of place in this casual context.

Indeed, the pursuit of basic skills may sometimes be counterproductive. In the effort to make sure that students "cover" the curriculum and are prepared for various milestones and tests, teachers may inadvertently be undermining more crucial educational goals. At a conference I recently attended, an educator was defending a focus on the mimetic learning of concepts. She argued that by using such an approach "teachers can cut short the discovery process and save students time." In the current environment, it is understandable that teachers might feel the need to save time, but unless students come to appreciate why the skills and concepts are being inculcated and how to make use of them once they leave school, the entire classroom regimen risks being a waste of time.

Whether the basic skills of American students of today are less well developed than those of students in some golden era of the past cannot be readily determined. Most testing records do not reach back very far, and the relevant instruments have changed over time. Moreover, our population has been shifting rapidly over the decades, with a far greater proportion of our youthful population attending secondary school and college today than, for example, early in this century. Our public school system has rarely served well the less-advantaged student; the difference today is that such students are more likely to remain in school for many years, so their difficulties are more manifest. Finally, school offers a much larger menu of courses than it did a generation or two ago, and therefore less time can be devoted to any particular subject matter or skill.

My own belief is that there has been some slippage in the performance of the student body and that at least one contributing factor has not been sufficiently recognized. In the first half of the century, when women had few alternative professions from which to choose, the ranks of teachers were supplied with many skilled women who read and wrote in a natural and meaningful way in their own lives. Nowadays, highly literate men and women rarely enter the teaching professions below the collegiate level; most people in the profession do not lead a life in which literacy is greatly featured (it has been reported that the average schoolteacher reads a book a year). In fairness, it should also be said that the demands made on nearly every educational professional seem to grow each year.

The phrase "return to basic skills" has come to be invoked as part of the educational agenda of conservative and neo-conservative thinkers. Two American best-sellers of 1987, which are often (although somewhat inappropriately) yoked, reflect two strands of this critique of current educational values and achievements. E. D. Hirsch has sought to heighten "cultural literacy" in this country, whereas Allan Bloom focuses on the great ideas of Western civilization.

CULTURAL LITERACY FOR THE NATION

Hirsch notes that although most countries feature a national curriculum in which specific texts and concepts are central, the United States does not. Perhaps more controversially, he suggests that, in the past, certain textual references were known to most American students, irrespective of the place or manner of their education. Ignorance of such common references, Hirsch argues, proves devastating, particularly for minority students who might wish to be integrated into the historically dominant culture. If one does not appreciate references to important literary figures and characters (Dickens, Huckleberry Finn), pivotal historical events (the battle of Gettysburg), basic scientific principles (the laws of thermodynamics), central cultural icons (Simple Simon, Mother Goose), one not only will feel deficient in reading and in discussion but will not even be able to participate in the cultural conversation. Hirsch would like students to acquire such cultural literacy so that they can have a chance to enter their national community.

Again, if one could simply snap one's fingers and achieve this stock of factual information, few would quarrel with its desirability. Moreover, Hirsch's general analysis of what it takes to be able to read a text in a culturally literate way seems on the mark. But controversy surrounds the issues of how to achieve cultural literacy and what to do once one has in fact achieved it. It is for his recommendations with respect to the attainment of literacy that Hirsch has drawn the most fire. First informally and now with increasing formality and decisiveness, Hirsch has produced lists of cultural references and suggested that they be afforded a central place in the curriculum. Willfully or not, he has provided an almost irresistible plan for many teachers: to teach these lists of terms directly, as they now teach vocabulary lists or mathematical facts, and then to test for them as part of the standard curriculum. Rather than being acquired in the process of a rich diet of reading or through immersion in a culture where such references arise meaningfully in the course of everyday exchanges, cultural literacy becomes the subject matter of rote, ritualized, or conventionalized performances.

To my knowledge, Hirsch did not initially recommend such a rigid educational approach, one that seems destined to deaden, rather than make accessible, the vitality of the culture for most students. Yet his publications and activities in recent years have all pointed toward prepackaging such literacy. Hirsch's initial analysis and recommendations seem well intentioned enough, but an educational policy maker must take responsibility for the uses to which his ideas are put. In this case, it seems to me, the packaged cure is really part of the disease that runs rampant in a sound-bite culture.

What such efforts at sowing cultural literacy seem to skirt are the *reasons* for attaining such knowledge. Unless students have some rationale for wishing to attain this knowledge and regular occasions on which to use it and build upon it, its attainment seems essentially useless. Here an analogy may be drawn to foreign language instruction. Without question, many aspects of foreign language study can—and some must—be acquired by routine drill. Yet in the absence of the opportunity to use the language productively—for reading, writing, or speaking—the instruction seems pointless, and any skill will in all likelihood atrophy.

A TRADITIONAL STRAND IN EDUCATION

Allan Bloom has offered a much more radical critique of American society, as well as a more ambitious nostrum for its educational ills. In his analysis, youngsters growing up in this society have lost their souls. They lack a sense of direction, a sense of community, a sense of value. This state of affairs has been brought about by the reflexive (and unreflective) liberalism of the culture throughout much of this century, a liberalism that has centered in the universities. According to its tenets, students should have virtually unlimited freedom in determining what to study. Teachers should not signal any kinds of grounding values or directions, because, after all, it is wrong to make absolute judgments; relativism, if not nihilism, carries the day.

For Bloom, as for others reared in the tradition of political philosopher Leo Strauss, the cure is dramatic. Students ought to be studying the great texts of the West, those writings dating back to classical times that have furnished the dominant themes of Western civilization. Philosophers (and philosophy) emerge as most important in this regimen; Plato, Aristotle, Locke, and Rousseau become the texts on which one should cut one's teeth. Literary writings by the masters—Shakespeare, Milton, Tolstoy—are also part of this training. These texts should be read, reread, discussed, and absorbed; an atmosphere of philosophical analysis and dialectic must be fostered and, indeed, allowed to prevail. Education becomes a conversation among great minds in which the talented student is encouraged to participate. (There is little place for the student not talented in such activities of exposition and interpretation.)

According to Bloom, it is folly to spend time on the writers—let alone the art and music—of the twentieth century. Writers like Sigmund Freud and Max Weber, fields like sociology, and art forms like rock-and-roll are seen as contributing to the anomie and loss of soul in American youths (and possibly in youth around the world). Only those authors whose work have stood the test of time and those contemporary minds who rail against modernism are worthy of a student's serious attention. Reading and talking—not listening to music or attending films—are the requisite daily practices. If time is well spent, one will emerge as a member of an intellectual elite, a participant in a community of long standing whose culture is the only one worth imbibing and then transmitting to future generations.

It should be evident that the "basic skills" of Bloom have little in common with those called for by advocates of the three Rs or those sought as part of Hirsch's cultural revolution. Bloom is endorsing an explicit political, ideological, and educational agenda, framed according to Western neoconservative values and featuring its own intellectual "hit list." Just as assuredly the education is distinctly elitist—certainly not one for the masses of today, and possibly not one for the masses of any era or culture. (Indeed, mentor Leo Strauss saw the community of the educated as exclusionary, defensive, even hermetic.) I find Bloom's vision to be repellent in its political and sociological aspirations; I need hardly add that, as a practicing social scientist, I also harbor a different set of favorites and villains.

Yet at least one aspect of Bloom's educational utopia is worthy of note. Bloom would not in any way be satisfied with an education in which one simply skims texts, let alone one that substitutes a list of dates and terms for a thorough and critical immersion in challenging ideas themselves. Bloom has a vision of a scholarly, intellectual community in which one enters as an apprentice or novice, reads deeply, discusses widely, and ends up with a nuanced understanding on which one can draw in future reading, discussion, and creation. He even has the required vision of an expert; Bloom is a "Great Books" graduate of the University of Chicago, at which he teaches. In my terms (and I do not presume to speak for Allan Bloom), he seeks an understanding of a specific type, well suited for a certain cultural and historical context but intolerant of rival texts, disciplines, and symbol systems. Suitably broadened and divested of its dubious ethical values, Bloom's version of an educated person has appeal.

THE PROGRESSIVE STRAND IN EDUCATION

So far, the visions of education put forth have a distinctly conservative tinge (although not all proponents of these visions would necessarily accept the unadorned epithet "conservative"; Hirsch sees himself in a liberal tradition, and Bloom shuns labels). From the avowedly liberal region of the educational landscape come other analyses of what is wrong with contemporary education and how best to right its course. I have already revealed my greater sympathy with the vision generally termed "progressive." Here, beginning with a few historical footnotes, I will sketch some aspects of the progressive perspective and indicate some of its attendant problems.

From the time of the settling of the American colonies, education in America has been characterized by two contrasting pulls. On the one hand, those transplanted from Europe or other continents have sought to reestablish the educational traditions of their homeland. This intellectual nostalgia involved a reassertion of not only religious tradition but also the classical curriculum—in this case, the languages of Latin, Greek, and Hebrew. Knowledge was assumed to inhere in (or at least to build upon) the texts of these languages, and any educated person therefore had to be proficient in classical tongues and texts. Less formally, immigrants sought to pass on to their offspring the most valued practices of the cultures from which they came, ranging from crafts and rituals to attitudes and beliefs about the world. To the extent that they possessed any skills of literacy, they also began transmitting these to their youngsters, even before the children entered school.

But America was not the old country; the "city upon the hill" harbored its own educational challenges and opportunities. From early on, there was pressure to create an education that was practical and functional and took cognizance of the manifold possibilities offered by the American continent. Doubt grew about the need to master classical tongues, and a swing began toward the inclusion of modern languages such as German or French, as well as explicit instruction in English, fast becoming the universal tongue of the new land. Also at a premium were those mathematical and scientific skills that could be used in practical fields like mining, surveying, or agriculture. By the time of the Revolution, one could discern two broad educational tendencies: a re-creation of the classical education for an elite headed toward higher education and a much broader-based and more practical education slated for the less privileged as well as for those who would make their mark in the commercial world.

The first half century of the newly created United States saw the appearance of an educational institution called the common school. For possibly the first time in world history, a country of some size made a commitment toward publicly financed education for all its young people. (Unburdened by caution, educational reformer Horace Mann termed the common school the greatest discovery in the history of mankind.) Common schools might not produce students who were fit for college, but they would ensure that every young person had acquired at least the basic literacies, acquaintance of some texts, and a smattering of scientific knowledge. American patriotism and acceptance of core moral, if not strictly religious, beliefs were a significant part of the agenda of common schools as well.

During the half century following the Civil War, American education became far more diversified. There were several forms of elementary education, an emerging public high school, and institutions of teacher education; this period also saw the birth of the university on the one hand and of kindergartens and other forms of early childhood education on the other. Particularly in the large urban centers, bureaucratic efforts were initiated to create a more centralized and more uniform school system. But probably the most important event of the period had less to do with the founding of new institutions or the streamlining of already existing ones and more to do with the articulation of the first full-blown American philosophy of education.

Progressivism is most frequently—and most appropriately—linked with the name of John Dewey. In fact, however, the practices of progressive education had already begun to be implemented in the period before 1896, when Dewey opened the Laboratory School at the University of Chicago, and before he penned the classical texts of progressive education. Crucial, for example, were the efforts of instructional leaders like Francis Parker, first superintendent of the Quincy, Massachusetts Public Schools, later principal of the Cook County Normal School in Chicago, and finally a founding member of the Chicago Institute, which ultimately gave rise to Dewey's educational facility at the University of Chicago.

Such early progressive thinkers placed the child's activities at the center of the educational agenda. The full development of the potential of each child in the community became the watchword of the movement. Toward this end, progressive educators called for more attention to each child as well as for more group activities and co-operative discussion. Spurning a rigidly mandated curriculum with explicit schedules during the day, and calling into question the pervasive systems of rewards, punishments, and regular examinations, progressive educators instead favored rich projects through which children could come to know their world, achieve a fuller understanding of themselves, and begin to secure a feeling for the skills and concepts that lay at the heart of formal disciplines.

Because progressive educators shunned formulas, the schools created in the light of this philosophy were quite varied, in daily procedures as well as in administrative organization and in overall quality. In general, the emphasis fell on practical hands-on activities, on allowing students to proceed at their own pace, and on democratic forms of organization. Grouping by grades, tracking students, and dividing the day according to specific subject matter were all discouraged. Especially in the younger grades, children were led to make careful observations, ask good questions, and carry out relevant experimentation; only after their interest had been aroused was more formal disciplinary instruction introduced.

Consider a typical scenario in a fully functioning progressive program. The children visit stores, factories, forests, and farms and bring the impressions and knowledge they have gained back to their own classroom; sometimes the classrooms come to resemble one or more of these community institutions. With strategic help from adults, the children set up their own laboratories in which they can study nature and carry out small-scale scientific experiments. Again with appropriate assistance, they set up workshops in which they build their own equipment and materials needed for studying different "central subjects," for staging plays, for acting out important historical events, for creating maps and globes, and for decorating their rooms or other parts of the school. Students in such a school are also expected to help one another and to make relevant contributions to the community in which they live (for example, providing goods or services for the poor, the elderly, or the handicapped).

In its most exemplary manifestations, progressive education captured distinctive and enviable aspects of American society. It affirmed the potential of every child to be educated. It embraced the diverse "melting-pot" nature of this land. It spurned learning in the service of some remote philosophical, cultural, or political ideal in favor of an education rooted in practical, clearly significant pursuits. It highlighted activities in and service to the community, insofar as possible blurring the distinction between the school and the community. It sought to make use of the newest scientific discoveries about learning and to convey the most recent findings in the several disciplines. In many ways a progressive school synthesized slices from different educational corners of the whole community. Above all, epitomizing the new American philosophy of pragmatism, progressive education stressed the inherent utility of all genuine knowledge.

Alas, progressive education, along with such offshoots as the "project method," has been so much written about, and so often caricatured, that it is difficult to recapture the initial vision and the most positive manifestations of this great American educational experiment. Yet the fact is that in many places progressive education has worked and has proved successful for its clientele. Two major studies of progressive education—the Eight-Year Study of the 1930s and the New York City Study of the 1960s—documented that, on a broad set of measures, graduates of progressive schools performed as well as or better than those of matched ability and background who had attended traditional institutions.

It is also worth noting, with Lawrence Cremin, that many of the innovations of progressive education ultimately became common coin in America, and perhaps elsewhere in the world as well. Such practices in the early grades as classwide projects, such electives in the high school as shop and home economics, and such activities as field trips to community institutions and classroom visits from local workers or professionals can all be traced to progressive practices. In the same breath it must also be said that it has proved far easier to transplant certain specific practices of the progressive school than to absorb its philosophy or its overall mode of operation.

THE LIMITS OF PROGRESSIVE EDUCATION

The fact is that progressive education, appropriately instituted, is a difficult undertaking, one that ultimately defeated Dewey as well as many of his most dedicated followers. Such an educational regime requires teachers who are well trained, dedicated, and absorbed in their work. It requires parents who not only support the philosophy but are willing to defend it against those (both inside and outside the school) who call for timely achievement of externally mandated curricular goals. It requires a community beyond the walls of the school that is hospitable to students who want to learn from its members and its institutions. And it requires a student body sufficiently motivated and responsible so that it can make the most of the opportunities offered and accept the responsibilities it entails.

Standards are the key to progressive education. In those instances where high standards are instituted and maintained, this form of education can serve as a model for the world. In the absence of such standards, a progressive program can rapidly become an excuse for laziness, laissez-faire procedures, and even anarchy. Yet, as Francis Parker insisted, such standards cannot be imposed from without; they must arise naturally, as students and teachers work together over time in an atmosphere of mutual respect.

When any form of education is practiced in an effective manner, it speaks for itself. There remain today dozens, probably hundreds, of progressive schools that have been carrying on their work quietly and effectively, surviving amid the successive calls for a depression-era curriculum, a World War curriculum, a Cold War curriculum, a post-Sputnik curriculum, a post-Vietnam curriculum, a curriculum founded on basic skills, cultural literacy, or Leo Strauss-style elitism. In fact, in my opinion, progressive education has in recent years received something of a new lease on life as the smug and jingoistic excesses of the Reagan era are being trimmed, as the view of basic skills as a panacea has begun to recede, and as the needs of a heterogeneous American population have once more come to be felt. Some thirty years after the Progressive Education Association officially disbanded, a new Network of Progressive Educators has formed, meetings of progressive educators are proliferating, and new journals and books are being published regularly.

It would be misleading to suggest, however, that progressive education ever captured America. In fact, two trends that emerged at the turn of the century proved far more powerful in quantitative terms. On the one hand there was the trend, associated with a number of school superintendents such as William T. Harris of St. Louis, toward the creation of large bureaucratic school systems; in these monolithic systems, every school under their control hired from the same pool, used the same curriculum, and embraced the same standards of performance. Students and teachers became cogs in a (it was hoped well-oiled) machine. Not surprisingly, schools created in this vein could evince little of the interest in individual growth or sensitivity to the contours of the local community that are virtually synonymous with progressive methods.

Complementing this trend was the mission, associated with major psychologists of education such as Edward L. Thorndike, of punctuating the school experience with aptitude tests (the Stanford-Binet IQ test, for example) and with regular tests of skills and achievement (from reading tests to college admission tests). Historian of education Ellen Lagemann describes the fate of this struggle in graphic terms:

> I have often argued to students, only in part to be perverse, that one cannot understand the history of education in the United States during the twentieth century unless one realizes that Edward L. Thorndike won and John Dewey lost. . . . If Dewey has been revered among some educators, and his thought has had influence across a greater range of scholarly domains, Thorndike's thought has been more influential within education. It helped to sharpen public school practice as well as scholarship about education.

Although I personally lament the hegemony of large-scale bureaucratization and the proliferation of standardized testing, I also feel it is important to point out some of the characteristic weaknesses of the progressive education movement. First, while recognizing each child's individuality and potential for growth, progressive education was insufficiently sensitive to problems that children might encounter in a school setting. Some children will have difficulties in acquiring the basic skills; some children will lack proper motivation; some children will exhibit learning styles that make it difficult to master the disciplines or the discipline of school. It is laudable not to place all these children under the same constraints or labels (or mislabels), and it is exemplary to display patience and flexibility. Yet when this laissez-faire approach is carried too far, as it sometimes has been among progressive educators, one may be left with a large population at sea.

Put another way, progressive education works best with children who come from richly endowed homes, whose parents are deeply interested in their children's education and who arrive at school with motivation and curiosity. (I do not mean to detract from progressive education by noting that *all* education works best with such children.) It is optimistic, however, to expect success with children who come from impoverished backgrounds, who lack the knowledge (or the boldness) that will allow them to explore an environment and learn from their own activities. Progressive education ought to be fused with an approach that can offer more nuanced kinds of help and support to students who are not independent-minded, to students who lack self-discipline, and to students who exhibit distinct learning disabilities as well as to students who have unusual strengths. A large and possibly growing number of students need the kind of help, support, modeling, and/or scaffolding that has often been seen as antithetical to the unstructured atmosphere of progressive education.

Another limitation of progressive education, as it is usually implemented, has been a neglect of assessment. In most traditional forms of education, assessments are common—indeed, all too common. As I have stressed, they are often inappropriate and simplistic, tending to lead away from deeper forms of understanding. Thus it was entirely understandable—indeed praiseworthy—that many progressive educators spurned formal instruments and, where necessary, sought to obtain waivers from the tyranny of standardized tests.

Yet it is legitimate to demand evidence that an educational regimen is working. Too often, progressive educators accepted on faith the effectiveness of their methods; whatever criteria they themselves embraced, they made scant efforts to convince others that students were learning and understanding. Either educators considered such success to be self-evident, or they considered it rude and inappropriate to demand externally imposed indices of accountability, or they insisted on their success being assessed only in terms of their own, possibly idiosyncratic standards. Of course, in cases where such progress was actually made, the absence of documenting instruments was not damaging. But any educational institution must face the possibility that it is *not* effective and must demonstrate a willingness to reflect, evaluate, and change course as often as proves necessary. The reluctance of progressive institutions to allow any kind of evaluation led to the widespread—if often wrongheaded—notion that students were just having a good time and were not mastering anything.

To be sure, the question of what to assess and how to assess it remains extremely problematic, for both traditional and progressive education. My own evolving thoughts on this issue emerge as central in the concluding chapters of this book.

With respect to the achievement of our goal of student understanding, progressive education may well come closer to the mark than its rivals. The progressive focus on meaningful activities, such as broad-scale projects carried out in appropriate contexts in which students have a stake, holds promise of yielding understanding. Progressive education has also recognized the importance of cooperative interactions, a key ingredient in the achievement of richer understandings. It would be anachronistic to condemn progressive education for a failure to deal with student misconceptions and biases; before now, *no* educational philosophy has been sensitive to this problem. Still, it should be recognized among the limitations of progressive education that the faith in students' ability to figure out things on their own may blind educators to the many misconceptions and biases that I have documented.

In any event, the reluctance to assess can open progressive educators to the charge that they have no evidence that understanding is in fact being achieved. My own guess is that the more successful students in such schools acquire rich understandings and are in a favorable position to enhance their understandings. What remains unknown is the size of the population that may have been bypassed in this optimistic, idealistic approach to learning.

In this survey of options of educational reform, I have contrasted two principal orientations. The more traditional "back to basics" stance has been found deficient; the attainment of literacies, whether alphabetic or cultural, assumes little significance in the absence of uses and contexts in which these literacies can be exploited. Allan Bloom's educated community at least harbors an image of engagement and understanding, but this vision is fatally marred by its narrowness and its self-avowed elitism.

More hopeful is the distinctively American brand of progressive education, which may no longer be restricted to North American shores. Not only has this form been molded in a pluralistic and democratic crucible, but the emphasis that it places on richly structured activities and projects, student initiative and "stake," constructive forms of learning, and meaningful involvement with the school and the wider community all point toward an education that seeks and perhaps yields understanding. The limitations of progressive education—its excessive faith in the capacity of students to educate themselves, its reluctance to engage in assessment, and the risk of confusing worthy goals with their successful achievement—are all reparable.

Indeed, it is in the most fully articulated models of progressive education that I find clues toward the construction of an educational environment in which genuine understandings can become a reality. The model is there in the writings of John Dewey and in the practices of Francis Parker and other visionaries of a century ago. It can still be observed at work in many schools today. We now believe that such an education is more difficult to achieve than the optimists of the progressive era may have thought. At the same time we may have available additional tools for approaching this still-alluring educational vision.

CHAPTER
11

Education for Understanding During the Early Years

I magine an educational environment in which youngsters at the age of seven or eight, in addition to—or perhaps instead of—attending a formal school, have the opportunity to enroll in a children's museum, a science museum, or some kind of discovery center or exploratorium. As part of this educational scene, adults are present who actually practice the disciplines or crafts represented by the various exhibitions. Computer programmers are working in the technology center, zookeepers and zoologists are tending the animals, workers from a bicycle factory assemble bicycles in front of the children's eyes, and a Japanese mother prepares a meal and carries out a tea ceremony in the Japanese house. Even the designers and the mounters of the exhibitions ply their trade directly in front of the observing students.

During the course of their schooling, youngsters enter into separate apprenticeships with a number of these adults. Each apprentice group consists of students of different ages and varying degrees of expertise in the domain or discipline. As part of the apprenticeship, the child is drawn into the use of various literacies—numerical and computer languages when enrolled with the computer programmer, the Japanese language in interacting with the Japanese family, the reading of manuals with the bicycle workers, the preparation of wall labels with the designers of the exhibition. The student's apprenticeships deliberately encompass a range of pursuits, including artistic activities, activities requiring exercise and dexterity, and activities of a more scholarly bent. In the aggregate, these activities incorporate the basic literacies required in the culture—reading and writing in the dominant language or languages, mathematical and computational operations, and skill in the notations drawn on in the various vocational or avocational pursuits.

Most of the learning and most of the assessment are done cooperatively; that is, students work together on projects that typically require a team of people having different degrees of and complementary kinds of skills. Thus, the team assembling the bicycle might consist of half a dozen youngsters, whose tasks range from locating and fitting together parts to inspecting the newly assembled systems to revising a manual or preparing advertising copy. The assessment of learning also assumes a variety of forms, ranging from the student's monitoring her own learning by keeping a journal to the "test of the street"—does the bicycle actually operate satisfactorily, and does it find any buyers? Because the older people on the team, or "coaches," are skilled professionals who see themselves as training future members of their trade, the reasons for activities are clear, the standards are high, and satisfaction flows from a job well done. And because the students are enrolled from the first in a meaningful and challenging activity, they come to feel a genuine stake in the outcome of their (and their peers') efforts.

EDUCATIONAL ENVIRONMENTS FOR YOUNG CHILDREN

A reader's first thought on the possibility of youngsters' attending such an intensive museum program rather than or in addition to the public school may be disbelief. The connotations of the two types of institution could scarcely be more different. "Museum" means an occasional, casual, entertaining, enjoyable outing; as Frank Oppenheimer, founder of San Francisco's Exploratorium, was fond of commenting, "No one flunks museum." "School," in contrast, connotes a serious, regular, formal, deliberately decontextualized institution.

Would we not be consigning students to ruination if we enrolled them in museums instead of schools?

I believe we would be doing precisely the opposite. Attendance in most schools today does risk ruining the children. Whatever significance schooling might once have held for the majority of youngsters in our society, it no longer holds significance for many of them. Most students (and, for that matter, many parents and teachers) cannot provide compelling reasons for attending school. The reasons cannot be discerned within the school experience, nor is there faith that what is acquired in school will actually be utilized in the future. Try to justify the quadratic equation or the Napoleonic wars to an inner-city high school student—or his parents! The real world appears elsewhere: in the media, in the marketplace, and all too frequently in the demimonde of drugs, violence, and crime. Much if not most of what happens in schools happens because that is the way it was done in earlier generations, not because we have a convincing rationale for maintaining it today. The often-heard statement that school is basically custodial rather than educational harbors more than a grain of truth.

Certainly there are exemplary schools, and just as certainly there are poorly designed and poorly run museums. Yet as institutions, schools have become increasingly anachronistic, while museums have retained the potential to engage students, to teach them, to stimulate their understanding, and, most important, to help them assume responsibility for their own future learning.

Such a dramatic reversal of institutional significance has come about for two complementary sets of reasons. On the one hand, youngsters live in a time of unparalleled excitement, where even the less privileged are exposed daily to attractive media and technologies, ranging from video games to space exploration, from high-speed transportation to direct and immediate means of communication. In many cases, these media can be used to create compelling products. Activities that might once have engaged youngsters—reading in classrooms or hearing teachers lecture about remote subjects—seem hopelessly tepid and unmotivating to most of them. On the other hand, science museums and children's museums have become the loci for exhibitions, activities, and role models drawn precisely from those domains that do engage youngsters; their customary wares represent the kinds of vocations, skills, and aspirations that legitimately animate and motivate students.

In previous chapters I have documented some of the difficulties exhibited by youngsters in coming to understand the topics of school. It is of course possible that, even if one cannot flunk museum, one might fail to appreciate the meanings and implications of exhibitions encountered there. Indeed, I suspect such non- or miscomprehension often happens on "one-shot" visits to museums. An active and sustained participation in an apprenticeship, however, offers a far greater opportunity for understanding. In such long-term relationships, novices have the opportunity to witness on a daily basis the *reasons* for various skills, procedures, concepts, and symbolic and notational systems. They observe competent adults moving readily and naturally from one external or internal way of representing knowledge to another. They experience firsthand the consequences of a misguided or misconceived analysis, even as they gain pleasure when a well-thought-out procedure works properly. They undergo a transition from a situation in which much of what they do is based on adult models to one in which they are trying out their own approaches, perhaps with some support or criticism from the master. They can discuss alternatives with more accomplished peers, just as they can provide assistance to peers who have recently joined the team. All these options, it seems to me, guide the student toward that state of enablement—exhibiting the capacity to use skills and concepts in an appropriate way—that is the hallmark of an emerging understanding.

If we are to configure an education for understanding, suited for the students of today and for the world of tomorrow, we need to take the lessons of the museum and the relationship of the apprenticeship extremely seriously. Not, perhaps, to convert each school into a museum, nor each teacher into a master, but rather to think of the ways in which the strengths of a museum atmosphere, of apprenticeship learning, and of engaging projects can pervade all educational environments from home to school to workplace. The evocativeness and open-endedness of the children's museum needs to be wedded to the structure, rigor, and discipline of an apprenticeship. The basic features I have just listed may assume a central place in educational environments that span the gamut of ages from preschool through retirement and the full range of disciplines.

In this chapter and the next, I review some promising educational ideas. I begin with instances drawn from early education, from education in the preschool and the primary years. At this age, what is most crucial is the opportunity to work intensively with the materials that nourish the various human intelligences and combinations of intelligences. I stress the impact of encompassing milieus, in which the messages of learning and work are manifest and inviting. Meaningful mastery of the basic literacies is most likely to emerge under these conditions. In the concluding sections of this chapter, I turn to education for children in the middle years. This is a time for intensive involvement in apprenticeships with knowledgeable adults and for the opportunity to heighten basic skills in the context of meaningful and rewarding projects.

In the next chapter, I consider some instances of education of older students, for whom disciplinary mastery is the goal. In these cases, it is vital that students have the opportunity to confront directly the disjunctions among the various ways of knowing and to integrate these into the fullest possible understanding. In the case of misconceptions, I recommend a kind of experience that I term a "Christopherian encounter"; where algorithms are applied rigidly, I suggest explorations of the relevant semantic world; with respect to stereotypes, I urge the adoption of multiple perspectives on a task or project.

As far as I can tell, it is not possible for students to skip the various regimens described here. Students of any age who are novices need a period of exploration and a phase of apprenticeship before they can enter more formal learning environments that deal with disjunctions among ways of knowing. The length of these periods can probably be shortened with older students, but the extent to which they can be truncated is not yet known.

Although I describe contrasting regimens for students of different ages and degrees of expertise, I wish to stress that each of these milieus can be adapted for the range of students. Richly stocked environments, skilled "masters," and lessons that mediate among different modes of representation all have their place *across* the educational firmament. Indeed, even though my descriptions of various projects highlight different facets, a number of themes characterize the range of projects described here and should pervade an education for understanding from start to finish. Among these overarching themes are the recognition that children have different intellectual strengths and learn in different ways; that teachers must serve as role models of the most important skills and attitudes and must in a sense embody the practices that are sought; and that meaningful projects taking place over time and involving various forms of individual and group activity are the most promising vehicles for learning. Perhaps most centrally, all these educational programs feature an explicit concern with assessment. Such assessment should take place, insofar as possible, in the context of normal daily activities of learning; over the course of a youngster's education, assessment in context by others and by oneself should become a regular, increasingly automatic part of the educational experience. The chances that these curricular, pedagogical, and assessment themes will pervade an educational setting is a direct function of the extent to which the genius of the children's museum and the power of the apprenticeship is wedded to the authority and regularity of the school.

I believe that the various experiments and pilot projects described in these concluding chapters can have a beneficial effect on education and that study of these models can be very useful. It is important to stress, however, that it is the incorporation of the ideas, analyses, and understandings on which these projects are based and not the adoption of one or more of their methods that is crucial. Too often, invocation of the label or adoption of the surface practices of an educational innovation is mistakenly taken as evidence that the educational innovation itself has actually taken hold and is achieving its desired effects. A school will not work better simply because it styles itself after a children's museum or institutes reciprocal teaching or mandates the keeping of process-folios. Children will not attain understanding just because they watch masters who exemplify understanding in their own practices. If, however, the reasons underlying such innovations are accepted and teachers and administrators are searching for ways of implementing such innovations, the examples here can prove suggestive.

THE EXAMPLE OF PROJECT SPECTRUM

In our own work with young children, we have devised an educational approach that at its best blends the strengths of the school and the children's museum. The prototype is Project Spectrum, a form of early childhood education spanning the period from preschool through the early primary grades. Spectrum began as a collaborative assessment effort, carried out in conjunction with my longtime colleagues David Feldman of Tufts University and Mara Krechevsky of Harvard Project Zero. At its inception in 1984, our principal goal was to ascertain whether preschoolers already exhibit distinctive profiles of intelligences; we confirmed that even students as young as four years old present quite distinctive sets and configurations of intelligences. In the course of this research, however, we found ourselves developing a more general approach to early education.

In a Spectrum classroom, children are surrounded each day by rich and engaging materials that evoke the use of a range of intelligences. We do not attempt to stimulate intelligences directly using materials that are labeled "spatial" or "logical-mathematical." Rather, we employ materials that embody valued societal roles or "end-states" drawing on relevant combinations of intelligences. So, for example, there is a naturalist's corner, where various biological specimens are brought in for students to examine and to compare with other materials; this area draws on sensory capacities as well as logical analytic power. There is a storytelling area, where students create imaginative tales using an evocative set of props and where they have the opportunity to design their own "storyboards"; this area evokes linguistic, dramatic, and imaginative facility. There is a building corner, where students can construct a model of their classroom and manipulate small-scale photographs of the students and teachers in the room; this area draws on spatial, bodily, and personal intelligences. Numerous other intelligences, and combinations of intelligences, are tapped in the remaining dozen areas and activities in a Spectrum classroom.

It is highly desirable for children to observe competent adults or older peers at work—or at play—in these areas. Provided with the opportunity for such observation, youngsters readily come to appreciate the reasons for the materials as well as the nature of the skills that equip a master to interact with them in a meaningful way. It is not always feasible to provide such an apprentice-master setting, however, and so "learning centers" have been constructed in which children can develop some facility from regular interactions with these materials even by themselves or with only other novice-level peers. In this sense, our "entry-level" environment is a self-sustaining one that harbors potential for cognitive and personal growth.

Over the course of a year or more spent in this nourishing environment, children have ample opportunity to explore the various learning areas, each featuring its respective materials and its unique set of elicited skills and intelligences. Reflecting the resourcefulness and curiosity of the mind of the five-year-old, most children readily explore the majority of these areas, and children who do not cast their nets widely are encouraged to try out alternative materials or approaches. For the most part the teacher can readily observe a child's interests and talents over the course of the year, and no special assessments are needed. For each domain or craft, however, we have also devised specific games or activities that allow a more precise determination of the child's "intelligences" in that area.

At the end of the year, the information gathered about each child is summarized by the research team in a brief essay called a Spectrum Report. This document describes the child's personal profile of strengths and weaknesses and offers specific recommendations about what might be done at home, in school, or in the wider community to build on strengths as well as to bolster areas of relative weakness. Such informal recommendations are important. In my view, psychologists have traditionally been far too concerned with norming or ranking; comparable efforts throughout the school years should help individual students and their families make informed decisions about their future course, based upon a survey of their capacities and options.

Over the last several years, Spectrum has evolved from a means of assessing strengths to a rounded educational environment. In collaboration with classroom teachers, we have developed curricular materials in the form of theme-related kits that draw on the range of intelligences as they may figure in the development of a broad theme such as "Night and Day" or "About Me." With younger children, these curricula are used primarily in an exploratory mode. With older children, they are tied more closely to the traditional goals of school, promoting preliteracy or literacy attitudes, approaches, and skills. Thus children encounter the basics of reading, writing, and calculating in the context of themes and materials in which they have demonstrated interest and an emerging expertise. As they gain proficiency in a board game, for example, children can be introduced to numerical tally systems, and as they create adventures at the storyboard, they can begin to write them down as well as recite or dramatize them.

The adaptability of Spectrum has proved to be one of its most exciting features. Teachers and researchers from several regions of the country have used Spectrum as a point of departure for a variety of educational ends. The Spectrum approach has been adapted with children ranging in age from four to eight, for purposes of diagnosis, classification, or teaching. It has been used with average students, gifted students, handicapped students, and students at risk for school failure, in programs designed for research, for compensatory purposes, and for enrichment. Just recently it has been made the center of a mentoring program, in which young children have the opportunity to work with adults from their neighborhood who exemplify different combinations of intelligences in their jobs. One of my delights as a researcher-turned-implementer has been to sit in on discussions among people who have never met each other but who have adapted Spectrum to their varied needs. It seems clear from such conversations that the Spectrum school-museum blend is appropriate for young children of very different interests, backgrounds, and ages.

In our own work we have made explicit the ties to the children's museum. Working with the Boston Children's Museum, we have transformed our theme-based kits so that they can be used at home and in the museum as well as at school. The home and school furnish regular stimulation, while the museum provides the opportunity to encounter a related display in an awe-inspiring setting, such as the moon and the stars viewed in a planetarium. It is our hope that encountering a similar cluster of themes, materials, and skills in disparate settings will help children to make this cluster their own; we speak of a "resonance" among these milieus that ultimately leads to the child's internalization of important understandings.

Naturally this kind of cross-fertilization works best when children have the opportunity to visit the museum regularly. Thus we are excited by the installation directly in the Washington, D.C. Capital Children's Museum of a Spectrum-inspired Model Early Learning Preschool Classroom—an ambitious melding of school and museum. But even when visits are less frequent, a well-prepared class of students can profit from the opportunity to interact with skilled professionals at a children's museum, particularly if they then have the opportunity to revisit related experiences and lessons on a more leisurely basis at home or at school.

Spectrum has shown particular power in identifying talents and inclinations that are typically missed in the regular school. Donnie (as I'll call him) was a six-year-old who was highly at risk for school failure. The product of a broken home with more than its share of violence and substance abuse, he was having such difficulty in the tasks of first grade that by the second month, his teacher had reluctantly concluded he would have to be retained.

In Project Spectrum, however, Donnie excelled at the assembly tasks. He had greater success in taking apart and putting together common objects, like a food grinder and a doorknob, than any other student his age. (Indeed, most teachers and researchers fail to match Donnie's skilled and seemingly effortless achievements in these mechanical tasks.) We videotaped Donnie's impressive performance and showed it to his teacher. A thoughtful and dedicated person, she was overwhelmed. She had difficulty believing that this youngster, who experienced such trouble with school-related tasks, could do as well as many adults on this real-world endeavor. She told me afterwards that she could not sleep for three nights; she was distraught by her premature dismissal of Donnie and correspondingly eager to find ways to reach him. I am happy to report that Donnie subsequently improved in his school performances, possibly because he had seen that there were areas in which he could excel and that he possessed abilities that were esteemed by older people.

In addition to identifying unexpected strengths in young students, Spectrum can also locate surprising difficulties. Gregory was an excellent student in first grade, apparently destined for a bright scholastic future. In the terms of this book, he displayed skill in the acquisition of notational and conceptual knowledge. He performed poorly, however, across a number of Spectrum areas. His teacher felt that Gregory was able to perform well only in situations where there is a correct answer and where a person in authority had somehow indicated to him what that answer is (an anticipation of the correct-answer compromise). The Spectrum materials posed problems for Gregory because many of the activities are open-ended and do not harbor any evident correct answers; he was thus frustrated and looked to the teacher or to other students for clues about what he should do. As a result of his participation in Spectrum, Gregory's teacher began to look for ways to encourage him to take risks, to try things out in new ways, to acknowledge that there are not always correct answers, and to appreciate that any response entails certain advantages as well as certain costs.

It is important to stress that Spectrum is an emerging approach to early education rather than a finished program. We do not know how successful it can be as a total approach to early education, nor to what extent it can "trickle up" to the older elementary grades. We do know that it is valued by students, parents, and teachers; that its assessments yield quite varied cognitive profiles even among young children; and that its core materials and concepts can be adapted in any number of ways across several populations.

I have described a general approach to education—an amalgam of features of school and museum—and one particular instance of its use with young children, Project Spectrum. When such education has been implemented successfully, young students gain competence and self-assurance in areas where they have potential. At their youthful level of development, it seems appropriate to speak of understanding, for the children are fusing sensorimotor and symbol-using capacities in ways meaningful to the domains in which they are working, and these incipient forms of understanding relate to meaningful adult roles such as mechanic, storyteller, or architect. These understandings build upon intuitive theories; rather than directly challenging them, they temper those theories in the light of practices that are valued in the society.

Anyone familiar with educational practice will appropriately point out that these features are by no means unique to our Spectrum program. Identical or related practices have been observable in sites of good progressive education for the better part of the century. In the case of preschool education, they can be seen in Montessori classrooms, High-Scope classrooms, and other programs influenced by Piaget and Dewey, as well as in their forerunners, such as the classes inspired by Friedrich Froebel and Johann Pestalozzi. I consider this confluence a happy development, one that increases the likelihood that research-based approaches like Spectrum can assume their place in the education of young children.

At the same time, it is important to point out features that make Spectrum distinctive: a theory grounded analysis of student strengths, a concerted effort to relate these strengths to meaningful adult roles, the creation of curricular materials and learning centers that foster these strengths in a natural way, and the development of assessment procedures that can provide reliable information about, and yield pertinent recommendations for, a student's profile of capacities at a given moment in his development. These features not only produce an early education with a distinctive flavor; they also allow children's intuitive theories to be tested out in a comfortable setting, and they encourage a smooth transition to the introduction of basic skills and literacies during the elementary grades.

DEVELOPING LITERACIES IN THE EARLY SCHOOL YEARS

Recently, several approaches that grow out of developmental research have also been applied to the education of young children. Rather than seeking to cover the whole educational landscape, I will focus here on a number of specific areas of the curriculum.

While there are still reasons for introducing youngsters to the world of print through drill and through a focus on phonics, a one-sided stress on this approach makes less sense nowadays. Too many children have little sense of *why* one should read, because they reside in environments where the adults do not read. Notably, a number of programs, typically termed "whole-language" approaches, have proved successful at setting a context for literacy activities while at the same time helping students to acquire the basics that will allow them eventually to read and write on their own.

The fundamental idea of whole-language programs is to immerse children as early as possible in the world of text and to allow them to become meaningful apprentices to competent literate individuals. From the first days of school, students see the elders around them read and write and are drawn into that milieu as expeditiously as possible. They tell stories and have others write them down; they make their own storybooks out of a combination of pictures, invented spelling, and dictated correct spelling; they "read" their stories to others and listen to, comment critically upon, or even "read" the stories written by others; they may type out their own narratives on a computer keyboard. The atmosphere more closely resembles a newspaper or magazine editorial center than an old-fashioned teacher-dominated classroom.

Such a program can work only if teachers embody these approaches and these values in their own lives. It is heartening to report, therefore, that classes filled with student writing and "prewriting" exemplify what is probably the major change in American elementary education over the past quarter century. A whole-language emphasis is far from being a universal practice, but it is being used in many places where it was not seen a decade or two ago.

I believe that this small-scale pedagogical revolution has occurred because teachers themselves have discovered (or rediscovered) not only that they can write but that they actually *like* to write. This spirit is of course infectious, and children are soon drawn into the excitement about letters, words, and meanings. Similar effects are at work in reading. Children read not because they are told—let alone ordered!—to read, but because they see adults around them reading, enjoying their reading, and using that reading productively for their own purposes, ranging from assembling a piece of apparatus to laughing at a tall tale. Fundamental experiences that may in earlier times have been restricted to children reared in highly literate households are now made available to all the youngsters in the school.

Setting an appropriate classroom tone is crucial for other areas of the curriculum as well. Just as American educators have relied too exclusively on phonics while neglecting the *reasons* for reading, there has been a tendency to treat arithmetic as a set of number facts to be memorized. Although this approach may result in somewhat higher scores on tests of basic arithmetical knowledge, it is ultimately self-defeating, because students do not understand the reasons for undertaking these activities that involve numbers.

A fresh approach that echoes "whole language" makes mathematics part of the overall atmosphere of the primary school. Numbers and numerical operations enter the ordinary, meaningful conversation among youngsters and between youngsters and teachers. From the start, children in "whole-math" environments are encouraged to engage in games that involve measuring, counting, and comparing, not merely to rehearse number skills but also to help out in activities that are needed and valued. Kitchen-based experiences like cooking serve as an excellent context, for arithmetical operations constitute a ready and readily understandable part of preparing and then serving a meal to a class. Telling time, going on a trip, buying food and favors for a party, and measuring clothing are but a sampling of the many other activities of consequence that call for the use of numbers. Intriguingly, once children become involved in such apparently pragmatic activities, many of them will go on to acquire—or reacquire— a fascination with the world of numbers and numerical relationships per se.

The same general approach can be used to involve students in the ways of thinking characteristic of science. Unlike the case of verbal and numerical literacy, there has not really been a strong competing vision of science in the early years of school; rather, science has generally been postponed until the years of middle and high school. Such a delay is not necessary, however, and may represent a missed opportunity; as Piaget convincingly demonstrated, scientific habits of mind in many ways fit quite comfortably with the interests and curiosity of young children. The challenge is to mobilize these interests in areas of concern to working scientists, such as the classification of the animal world, the means whereby machines operate, or the paths followed by astronomical bodies.

Perhaps most important for such early science or pre-science training is the serious cultivation of a reflective attitude. Young children very naturally raise questions: "Why do I have a shadow? What makes my shadow long? Why do I sometimes have two shadows?" By the same token, such youngsters are fascinated by the phenomena of growth in plants and animals; by life, death, and illness; by concepts like time and space; by apparatuses like levers, gears, and computers. The scientifically oriented teacher not only encourages such questioning but also reinforces the inclination to observe, to try out small-scale experiments, to note the results of these experiments, and to relate them back to the question that motivated them initially.

For the most part, early science education need not directly address the students' misconceptions. Such a confrontation can occur later on; in fact, it should await the time when the child has been thoroughly immersed in the phenomena that science addresses and has taken her intuitive theories and concepts as far as they can go.

Sometimes, however, it is appropriate to engage children's intuitive conceptions. For example, most young children believe that a sweater contains heat, which it then transfers to the body of its wearer. With such youngsters one can carry out small-scale experiments in which the temperatures of sweaters and persons are independently measured. One can have children leave a thermometer inside a sweater for several days and monitor its changing temperature; one can place the sweater in a sealed bag, or in the sun, and observe its temperature; one can also wear a sweater (or some other garment) for an hour, or place it upon a pet, and observe its changing temperature. In the course of such readily executed investigations, the earliest theories of matter and theories of heat are first articulated, then brought to bear upon the results of appropriate investigations, and finally modified as warranted by the evidence. To be sure, students are unlikely to abandon early theories simply because they have encountered one discrepant demonstration, but the habits of mind developed through such a critical testing of one's intuitive predictions should serve them well in subsequent science education.

Although I have divided these examples into the familiar categories of reading, writing, arithmetic, and science, there is no reason whatsoever for these divisions to be maintained within the classroom. Often, in the style cultivated by progressive education earlier in the century, it makes sense to feature overarching multifaceted thematic units that occupy a dominant physical space in the classroom as well as the better part of the day. A unit on water, for example, provides opportunities for exploration in virtually every area of the curriculum. Students can write about their own beliefs and feelings about water and enjoy classic and humorous texts on the subject. Activities using water can draw on all kinds of counting, measuring, and comparing activities. Historical and geographical issues arise naturally, as students consider the organization of cities around bodies of water and the many disputes that have arisen over the years about access to sources of energy and transportation routes as well as more recent concerns about waste disposal and long-term droughts. Finally, water naturally raises a host of questions that students can investigate in a scientific manner, ranging from the sources and composition of water to the reasons for its flow, its capacity to carry out work, and such phenomena as showers, puddles, evaporation, and conversion to steam or to ice.

While perhaps fun for students, a unit on water does not in and of itself constitute a pedagogical revolution. One cannot assume that students will connect these various facets of water with one another, nor that a multidisciplinary approach is necessarily more exciting or more effective than a univocal perspective. But such a central subject at least makes it possible for teachers to point up the relationships among various facets of a many-sided topic and for students to begin to relate in their own minds the often disparate shards of knowledge encountered in the course of the school day. Students also invest sufficient time in a subject so that they can begin to examine it from several perspectives. While the purpose of these related activities need not be a direct onslaught upon intuitive theories, misconceptions, and stereotypes about the universe of liquids, the by-product is often a more critical stance toward received opinions about various realms of knowledge.

Well executed, a classroom unit on water does more than adding to the child's basic skills in literacy, numeracy, social studies, and science; it constitutes a powerful example of what it is like to use such skills in the prosecution of meaningful activities, activities that can be informative and enjoyable in the manner of an effective exhibit at a children's museum. Moreover, if the school-based activities are integrated sensitively with the more intuitive forms of knowing, it is possible to minimize the unfortunate disjunction between ways of representation that can so cripple subsequent learning.

MIDDLE CHILDHOOD: APPRENTICESHIPS AND PROJECTS

Some of the approaches that have proved effective with younger children can also be drawn upon in middle childhood, when students are encountering the broader range of disciplines in a more systematic way. As before, I begin with examples from our own studies, mentioning other related work as well.

The Key School is an unusual inner-city public elementary school in Indianapolis, Indiana. One of its founding principles is the conviction that each child should have his or her multiple intelligences ("MI") stimulated each day. Thus, every student at the Key School participates on a regular basis in the activities of computing, music, and "bodily-kinesthetics," in addition to theme-centered curricula that embody the standard literacies and subject matter. The school reflects the design and the desires of its faculty; I have been an informal adviser since its initial planning in the middle 1980s.

While an "MI curriculum" is its most overtly innovative aspect, many other facets of the school also suggest an education that strives toward understanding. Three practices are pivotal. First, each student participates each day in an apprenticeship-like "pod," where he works with peers of different ages and a competent teacher to master a craft or discipline of interest. Because the pod includes a range of ages, students have the opportunity to enter into an activity at their own level of expertise and to develop at a comfortable pace. Working alongside a more knowledgeable person, they also have what may be a rare opportunity of seeing an expert engage in productive work. There are a dozen pods, in a variety of areas ranging from architecture to gardening, from cooking to "making money." Because the focus of the pod falls on the acquisition of a real-world skill in an apprenticeship kind of environment, the chances of securing genuine understandings are enhanced.

Complementing the pods are strong ties to the wider community. Once a week, an outside specialist visits the school and demonstrates an occupation or craft to all the students. Often the specialist is a parent, and typically the topic fits into the school theme at that time. (For example, if the current theme is protection of the environment, visitors might talk about sewage disposal, forestry, or the political process of lobbying.) The hope is that students not only will learn about the range of activities that exist in the wider community but in some cases will have the opportunity to follow up a given area, possibly under the guidance of the visiting mentor. One way of achieving this end is through participation in a Center for Exploration at the local Indianapolis Children's Museum; students can enter into an apprenticeship of several months, in which they can engage in such sustained activities as animation, shipbuilding, journalism, or monitoring the weather.

The final, and to my mind most important, avenue for growth at the Key School involves student projects. During any given year, the school features three different themes, introduced at approximately ten-week intervals. The themes can be quite broad (such as "Patterns" or "Connections") or more focussed ("The Renaissance—Then and Now" or "Mexican Heritage"). Curricula focus on these themes; desired literacies and concepts are, whenever possible, introduced as natural adjuncts to an exploration of the theme.

As part of school requirements, each student is asked to carry out a project related to the theme. Thus students execute three new projects each year. These projects are placed on display at the conclusion of the theme period, so that students have an opportunity to examine what everyone else in the school has done (and they are very interested in doing so!). Students present their projects to their classmates, describing the project's genesis, purpose, problems, and future implications; they then answer questions raised by classmates and by the teacher.

Of special importance is the fact that all project presentations are videotaped. Each student thus accumulates a video portfolio in which his succession of projects has been saved. The portfolio may be considered as an evolving cognitive model of the student's development over the course of his life in the Key School. Our research collaboration with the Key School has centered on the uses that might be made of these video portfolios.

In the course of their careers in the American schools of today, most students take hundreds, if not thousands, of tests. They develop skill to a highly calibrated degree in an exercise that will essentially become useless immediately after their last day in school. In contrast, when one examines life outside of school, projects emerge as pervasive. Some projects are assigned to the individual, some are carried out strictly at the individual's initiative, but most projects represent an amalgam of personal and communal needs and ends. Although schools have sponsored projects for many years and the progressive era featured an educational approach called the "project method," such involvement in projects over the years has been virtually invisible in records of a child's progress.

Here our research team has sought to make a contribution. We believe that projects are more likely to be taken seriously by students, teachers, parents, and the wider community if they can be assessed in a reasonable and convenient way. We have therefore sought to construct straightforward ways of evaluating the developmental sophistication as well as the idiosyncratic characteristics of student projects.

According to our analysis, every project can be described in terms of several separate dimensions. Some of these dimensions can be thought of in terms of developmental levels; one would expect beginning students to exhibit the performance of a novice and students with more experience to advance toward the level of journeyman or even master. Assuming such a developmental perspective, one can ask of the project: How well is it conceptualized? How well is it presented? How well has it been executed in terms of technical facility, originality, and accuracy? To what extent, and how accurately, is the student able to assess the project on these criteria? It is possible to secure reasonable consensus on such evaluations, and the fact that projects can be so described and evaluated allows them to be considered seriously by the entire community rather than being dismissed as a frill.

A developmental evaluation of projects is valuable, but other dimensions merit consideration as well. We have focused on two other facets. One is the extent to which the project reveals something about the student himself—his own particular strengths, limitations, idiosyncracies, and overall cognitive profile. The other is the extent to which the project involves cooperation with other students, teachers, and outside experts as well as the judicious use of other kinds of resources, such as libraries or computer data bases.

Students are not graded up or down if projects are more individualistic or more cooperative. Rather we describe projects in this way because we feel that these features represent important aspects of any kind of project in which a person will ever participate, aspects that should be noted rather than ignored. In particular, in working with others, students become sensitive to the varying ways in which a project can be conceived and pursued; moreover, in reflecting upon their own particular styles and contributions, students receive a preview of the kinds of project activities in which they are most likely to become involved following completion of school.

The other form our involvement has taken concerns the preparation of projects. Somewhat naively, researchers and teachers originally thought that students could readily create and present projects on their own. In the absence of help, however, most projects either are executed by parents or, if done by children, are pale imitations of projects already carried out before or observed elsewhere. Particularly common are book reports or television-style presentations in

front of displays resembling weather maps. If students are to conceptualize, carry out, and present their projects effectively, they need
to be guided—"scaffolded" is the term of choice—in the various
phases and aspects of this activity.

Far from undermining the challenge of making one's own projects,
such support actually makes participation in projects possible and
growth in project-execution abilities likely. Just as students benefit
from apprenticeships in literacy or in a craft, discipline, or pod, so
too they benefit from an apprenticeship in the formulation and execution of projects. Some students are fortunate enough to have had
this apprenticeship at home or in some community activity, such as
organized sports or music lessons. But for the vast majority who have
not had such opportunities, elementary school is the most likely place
where they can be apprenticed in a "project" way of life—unless they
happen to go to graduate school fifteen years later!

The course of project construction gives rise to opportunities for
new understanding. A project provides an opportunity for students
to marshal previously mastered concepts and skills in the service of
a new goal or enterprise. The knowledge of how to draw on such
earlier forms of representation or understanding to meet a new challenge is a vital acquisition. Planning the project, taking stock along
the way, rehearsing it, assembling it in at least tentatively final form,
answering questions about it, and viewing the tape critically should
all help to enhance the student's understanding of the topic of her
project, as well as her own contributions to its realization.

These features of the Key School point up some aspects of understanding during the period of middle childhood. To an immersion in
a richly furnished environment one now adds a more or less formal
apprenticeship; skills are acquired in a domain-appropriate form, and
the purposes and uses of these skills remain vivid in the consciousness
of the apprentice. At the same time disciplines are encountered not
in an isolated form that provides little motivation but rather as part
of a continuing involvement in encompassing themes that reverberate
throughout the curriculum of the school. The student's emerging
knowledge and skills are mobilized in the course of executing a project
of her own devising, which has meaning for herself, for her family,
and within the wider community. Such skills and projects are assessed as much as possible within the context of daily school activities, the assessment involving not only the teacher but also peers
and, increasingly, the student herself. The student comes to view the
project from a variety of perspectives, as it speaks to a variety of

audiences and as she observes it evolving, often in unpredictable ways, over the course of time.

I must point out that the picture I have painted is an idealized one. Neither apprenticeships nor projects, in and of themselves, guarantee an education for understanding. Apprenticeships can be occasions for copying or for goofing off; projects can be assembled hurriedly on the last day and can draw heavily on the child's own previous work or the work of a friend or classmate. Some materials must be learned by drill; others are more readily presented by classroom lecture or by textbook reading rather than by hands-on, museum-style activities or by participation in an apprenticeship arrangement. What I call for is not the wholesale abolition of current educational practices but rather the shrewd and judicious introduction of apprenticeships and projects in contexts where their strengths can pay off. When these approaches are pursued over a significant period of time, they should lead to an education that makes sense to the various participants and that leads to more robust and more flexible forms of learning.

Even as the recommended procedures do not constitute a panacea, the Key School and others now being designed along its lines are not utopias. Not all students participate equally in the program, and not all benefit equally from its particular methods. Yet, at its best, this school demonstrates that an education for understanding may be possible even in less favorable settings in America today.

SCHOOLING FOR UNDERSTANDING IN MIDDLE CHILDHOOD

Surveying the country, one encounters numerous other experimental programs that seek to involve the broad range of students in significant projects and aim for an education suffused with understanding. Among those that have recently attracted attention are the schools designed by Henry Levin for accelerated learning and the schools conceived by Stanley Pogrow that seek to develop higher-order thinking skills; both of these programs stress inquiry, discussion, and reflection.

Some of such programs are focused particularly on the acquisition of literacies. Researchers at the University of California at San Diego have for a number of years sponsored an innovative after-school program in which at-risk students work together at microcomputers to carry out various projects, from mastering systems of logic to editing their own newspaper. Among the special features of this program are its satellite linkages to other children all over the world, from Alaska to the Soviet Union. Investigations carried out in class and stories created for the class newspaper have significance not just for the person sitting in the next aisle but for groups located halfway around the world, and computer linkages are the optimal way for such communication to take place. Because the students at both ends of the terminal are strongly motivated to communicate their ideas to others and to comprehend what the others have created, misunderstandings can be nipped in the bud and understandings can arise in the natural course of events. In "Star School" programs, which are similar, students at different sites communicate by satellite with one another and with scientific experts as well, in a joint effort to collect data relevant to global problems, such as the incidence of acid rain or radon in the environment; here language barriers can be readily transcended.

Face-to-face group processes are a major feature of another approach that seeks to enhance literacy in middle childhood. Called "reciprocal teaching" or "reciprocal learning," this approach features a group of students reading a text together, initially under the guidance of a trained teacher. At first the teacher demonstrates the various stances and approaches that one can assume vis-à-vis a text. She articulates the gist of the text, raises questions that occur to her, clarifies possible misunderstandings, and conveys her impression of what might happen next. As rapidly as possible, the teacher relinquishes her central role as a model and the students themselves start to assume the various stances that she has demonstrated. Still, she remains present, ready to provide help to students at their own particular level of competence and to "scaffold" the group to more proficient levels of literacy.

As reciprocal teaching proceeds, each student in turn assumes the roles initially modeled by the teacher, including reading a portion of the text aloud to their peers. In the course of ensuing exchanges, the student assumes a variety of roles: questioner, summarizer, clarifier, skeptic, arguer, thereby having the opportunity—indeed, the obligation—to approach the text in many different ways and to represent it mentally in diverse forms as well. Students learn to work together and to construct meanings together. These roles serve as monitoring devices, indicating which students are beginning to understand and which ones remain confused. Teachers intervene when the students encounter pronounced difficulties and when it is time to introduce new challenges. Rather than seeing a text as a single kind of entity, to be read and absorbed in one way, students now approach it as a congeries of meanings, which emerge as a result of the various interactions among and interpretations provided by students. Most happily, students who participate in reciprocal reading gradually become able to internalize the various roles, so that they can use them even when they are approaching a text on their own, without the benefit of modeling teachers or collaborating peers.

Collaborative procedures like reciprocal teaching have also proved beneficial in other domains of literacy. As early as the first grade, Japanese students are posed arithmetical problems of some complexity and allowed up to a week to solve the problems. They are encouraged to work together, to criticize one another's approaches, and to try out different roles vis-à-vis the problem. Teachers deliberately avoid serving as a source of answers, although they may coach, direct, or probe in various ways. Not only do students come to appreciate early on that mathematics is an active process—what James Greeno calls a "conversation"—but they discover the advantages that can be derived from interacting with their peers, each of whom may have a distinctive contribution to make to the problem-solving process.

One of the most ambitious recent attempts to bolster mathematical understanding at the middle school level has been undertaken by teacher-researcher Magdalene Lampert. Working for a year with fifth-graders in an ordinary American public school, Lampert has sought to transform the students' entire approach to mathematics from a subject where students look for rules, right answers, and teacher approval to a discipline where together they learn to raise questions, put forth hypotheses about underlying principles, and explore the whole arena of mathematical meaning. The teacher's role is to alter the social discourse in the class by initiating and supporting interactions that exemplify mathematical argumentation of the sort carried out by mathematicians and others who use mathematics in their everyday lives. In terms used earlier, a transition occurs from the pursuit of the correct-answer compromise to the undertaking of risks for understanding.

In a representative lesson, students are challenged to discern the patterns that may exist among the squares of numbers ranging from 1 to 100. No specific problem is posed, and no specific answers are given. Students are encouraged to think aloud, to describe any pattern they discover, and to define and argue with one another about the meanings of those patterns. Norms evolve about the proper and improper ways of putting forth ideas and arguing about their plausibility. (An acceptable format would be "I want to question so-and-so's hypothesis"; an unacceptable format would be "That's a stupid idea that doesn't make any sense.") Students are encouraged to spell out and defend their ideas; various graphic or gestural representations vivify their conjectures. When the lesson works well, students arrive with little guidance at key ideas about how exponents work. They make distinctions between exponentiation and multiplication and discover new procedures for solving problems and for discerning fresh relationships. Lampert reports that, in one implementation of this particular lesson, fourteen out of eighteen students expressed at least one mathematically substantial notion about exponents.

Many of these innovations can be implemented using materials that have been available for decades; but increasingly, new technologies are being utilized in conveying middle school curricula. John Bransford and his colleagues at Vanderbilt University have used a well-designed videodisk, linked to a personal computer, to introduce students to the basic ideas of algebra. *Jasper* relates the story of Jasper Woodbury, who, using only a specified amount of money, must purchase a boat, fill its fuel tank, and then return home on the boat before dark. In helping Jasper achieve his goal, students arrive in a natural way at posing and then attempting to answer many of the questions and procedures of elementary algebra. Considerations involving fractions and decimals arise naturally as students deal with volume, time, and distance. In addition, information from related disciplines, including geography and science, crops up as students interact with a medium they enjoy and in which they can come to feel expert.

Working in a similar vein, my colleague Joseph Walters at Harvard provides students with a data base of information about each of the Irish immigrants who arrived on a certain ship in Boston Harbor in 1850. Students adopt a family and make decisions for its welfare, in the process not only utilizing a variety of mathematical operations but also gaining more intimate acquaintance with many historical, economic, and social issues that immigrants confronted during the last century. In related activities, students read journals kept by these families and go on to create at their computer a desktop version of *The Pilot*, the Boston newspaper that served the newly emerging Irish community. As in the case of *Jasper*, the *Immigrant* unit is a child-friendly way of covering large portions of the middle-school curriculum and involving students actively in processes that lead to a more rounded understanding.

Although youngsters typically find such technology-based activities engaging and motivating, their use raises a number of questions. First of all, is one simply making use of the latest gimmick in an effort to capture students' attention? An affirmative answer to this question does not necessarily detract from its utility; after all, gaining the interest of students ought to be a high priority for educators. And if these technologies are more consistent with the students' lives outside of school, then it is simply shortsighted to pretend that the situation does not exist. As I noted in Part II, attempts to insulate the school from the potent effects of the mass media and the consumer society are problematic; it is far better to recognize these factors and attempt to marshal them productively than to ignore them.

A second question has to do with costs. In some cases—*Jasper,* for example—the initial investment in technology is expensive. Until the costs come down, such materials cannot be used widely. The *Immigrant* package, however, is designed to be used on the Apple II-E, the most widely stocked personal computer in American classrooms. The problem with *Immigrant,* then, is not its cost but rather whether teachers feel comfortable using it and whether they can provide the proper support.

The most important question, of course, is whether such technological prosthetics actually improve classroom performance and lead to deeper understandings. The results here are still not definitive, because, not surprisingly, some innovations lead to dramatic effects while others have little or no impact on significant forms of understanding. Even with respect to Logo, the most widely used computer language in American schools, the verdict on educational effectiveness is not in.

My own view is that a well-trained and effective teacher is still preferable to the most advanced technology, and that even excellent hardware and software are to little avail in the absence of appropriate curricula, pedagogy, and assessment. Still, other things being equal, the capacity to immerse oneself in a problem using the latest technology and to be able to manipulate data or events electronically can make a significant contribution to student learning. As with the other educational experiments discussed here, it is not the use of a project like Spectrum or a computer program like *Immigrant* in itself that produces understanding. Rather, such educational interventions are viable to the extent that they can heighten exploration, apprentice-like and cooperative relationships, multiple representations of data, and the assumption of different roles.

Clearly, the kind of school that I am recommending—one filled with apprenticeships, projects, and technologies—differs significantly from the schools of yesterday and of today. In many ways, it more closely resembles a children's museum than the one-room schoolhouse of 1850 or the mass-produced comprehensive school of 1950. It is quite likely that students will prefer this more dynamic and engaging educational environment, but unless that environment yields stronger and more robust understandings, it will not have fulfilled its purpose.

In my view, experiments conducted so far suggest that enhanced understandings may indeed emerge under such circumstances. The kinds of environments for which I am calling encourage students to represent knowledge in a number of different ways, to begin to adopt the roles that are ultimately occupied by skilled adult practitioners, and to engage in the kind of self-assessment that allows one ultimately to take responsibility for one's own learning. Involvement in significant projects and regular discourse with one's peers increase the possibility that one's own stereotypes and misconceptions will be challenged and that a more realistic and comprehensive perspective will begin to emerge. Such a process of reflection on one's own assumptions is crucial if students are to benefit from discipline-centered instruction in secondary school and beyond.

CHAPTER

12

Education for Understanding During the Adolescent Years

I f education has proceeded in satisfactory fashion during the years of elementary school, students should have a solid foundation for the more focused, discipline-based learnings of high school, college, and beyond. During the early years of school, they will have achieved a familiarity with the materials of the physical and social world; their readily absorbing minds should have had ample opportunities to exercise relevant intelligences as these students are immersed in an atmosphere that encourages the emergence of verbal, numerical, and scientific literacy. Projects like Spectrum and institutions like the Key School provide models of how such early education might be carried out.

During the years of middle childhood, according to this desirable scenario, students will have had opportunities to develop more targeted skills—those literacy, numeracy, and scientific skills that will allow them to probe more deeply into the disciplines. Rather than learning these in a rote manner, however, they will have had the opportunity to engage in a number of apprenticeships, where they beheld the most developed versions of these skills being usefully deployed. They will have participated in projects in which they could themselves draw on and cultivate these skills. And they will have had the opportunity to interact with appropriate technologies, which deliver important and intriguing problems to them in an efficient and user-friendly fashion. While an explicit confrontation of earlier misconceptions and stereotypes is rarely indicated, these intuitive understandings should begin to be challenged as students work together on projects, question one another about intriguing problems, and begin to reflect on their own learning processes. Approaches like reciprocal teaching, and technological innovations like *Jasper*, may help in the formation of such learners.

Since few students have had such an ideal education, we cannot judge how successful it might be in preventing or circumventing the difficulties about which I have written in the earlier chapters. My own guess, however, is that even if such difficulties can be reduced or alleviated, even if misconceptions, stereotypes, and rigidly applied algorithms can be attenuated, they are unlikely to be eliminated altogether. The later years of school therefore become the time in which such difficulties must be directly and powerfully confronted.

Many of the innovations described in this chapter are efforts to reduce the likelihood that grave misconceptions and kindred cognitive limitations will become entrenched. I believe that rich environments like children's museums, apprenticeships in and out of school, assessments in context, and teaching that provides diverse entry points and models are all likely to bring about fuller and less misleading forms of understanding. I have noted that progressive schools, when contrasted with traditional learning environments, have often demonstrated significant learning. And I have indicated that the innovative methods described here, when examined in terms of their avowed goals, have typically been quite successful in terms of both impressionistic and quantitative measures. Taken together, it seems fair to contend that these methods represent educational principles of substantial significance and power.

Still, in many cases it will be necessary to go beyond user-friendly environments and confront the difficulties directly. In the following pages, I review a number of efforts, deliberately drawn from diverse areas of the curriculum, where misconceptions and stereotypes have been confronted and more robust understandings have emerged. In the case of misconceptions, I encourage the creation of "Christopherian encounters," where students must directly confront evidence that contradicts their intuitive theories; in the case of rigidly applied algorithms, I call for the exploration of relevant semantic worlds and for an investigation of the ways in which intuitive knowledge of those worlds maps onto formal expressions; in the case of stereotypes, I recommend the adoption of multiple perspectives and stances that stimulate students to examine a phenomenon from a number of different points of view.

INNOVATIONS ACROSS THE CURRICULUM

Kinds of Dynamics in Physics

Roger Osborne, a science educator in Waikato, New Zealand, claims that three kinds of physics can be found in the schools:

1. Children primarily exhibit "gut dynamics." Learned primarily at home, and without language, these represent the child's efforts to learn what happens when, for example, he hurls an object from a high chair or kicks it along the floor. Most of what we have termed a "theory of matter" consists of the child's gut dynamics.
2. "Lay dynamics" are conveyed by the nonspecialist adults with whom the child comes in contact, as well as by the electronic media and the books in his milieu. Children receive much unfiltered information from *Star Wars*, *Space Invaders*, and similar media favorites. They learn about weightless astronauts, they can talk about force fields and time warps, and they appear knowledgeable at a linguistic level about the world of science. In fact, however, this knowledge is superficial, not rooted in experience, and of little practical use; it remains remote from those situations that encourage the taking of "risks for understanding."
3. Finally, there is the "physicist's dynamics," primarily of the Newtonian variety. For beginning students this physics of the expert appears as a strange world of frictionless slopes and pulleys, uniform gravitational fields, point masses, and the like. Having a linguistic and mathematical superstructure of its own, this brand of physics may seem counterintuitive as, for example, when a car moving at a steady speed around a circular path is actually considered to be accelerating. Much of physicist's dynamics either exists in a world quite apart from that of everyday experience or runs counter to it.

According to Osborne's analysis, most students do not appreciate that elementary dynamics courses are designed to provide them with a new conceptualization of dynamics, one that not only is opposed to gut dynamics but uses a language different from that of lay dynamics. Some of the students who do realize that there are two or three discrete worlds learn to operate in the idealized world of the physics laboratory experiment but never allow it to shake their gut or lay dynamics. One then faces the situation chronicled in earlier chapters; once removed from the support of physics classes, students simply revert to gut dynamics, lay dynamics, or some idiosyncratic blend of the two.

In observing elementary school classes, Osborne finds that learning is often a mixture of gut dynamics from the pupils, lay dynamics from the teacher, and simplified physicist's dynamics from the curriculum developer. At the senior high school level, as a consequence, students either appear entrenched in their gut-level dynamics or are simply confused by the amalgam they have previously encountered. Efforts to teach physicist's dynamics directly make physics very hard, and the more reflective students—like my daughter Kerith, described in chapter 1—become painfully aware that they do not genuinely understand the relationships that obtain among naive intuitions, notations, defined terms, and the insights that physicists have painstakingly developed over the centuries.

While not invoking any easy solution, Osborne argues that one must begin to teach dynamics at an early age. Rather than teach physicist's dynamics, however, the teacher should help to develop, challenge, and extend gut and lay dynamics in ways that make better, more comprehensive sense of the world and that lay a groundwork for the formalized conceptions provided by physicists. Gut dynamics can be developed, for example, by affording students opportunities to play with air tracks, air tables, or other near frictionless surfaces; lay dynamics can be developed by learning to use words such as friction (distinguishing force of friction from heat due to friction) and to tease apart aspects of gravity (speed of fall from pull of gravity). Such lessons in the earlier years should place students in a more advantageous position to appreciate lessons about friction or gravity that they encounter in high school or college physics courses.

Christopherian Encounters Between Competing Physical Representations

A number of recent innovations seek to address simultaneously the several ways of representing knowledge. Their aim is to counter the uninspected ensemble of representations that can prove so devastating. Some of the most promising inventions directly pit one way of knowing against the other, thus placing the intuitive but often misleading ideas directly in conflict with forms of conceptualization that are ultimately more fertile. These pedagogical approaches remind me of the case of Christopher Columbus, the first human being to demonstrate unequivocally that the intuitive impression that the earth is flat had to yield to the alternative conception of the earth as spherical; in his honor, I have termed them "Christopherian confrontations" or encounters.

In one such Christopherian confrontation, Jeremy Roschelle (with James Greeno) has created an Envisioning Machine. The computer screen shows two windows, each displaying a different representation of motion. In the "object world" of the lower window, there are balls and a hand; the hand can grasp and carry a ball and can also release it. The motion of the balls is like that in the world, except that the ball leaves a trace, so that its activity over time can be studied.

By contrast, the upper, "Newtonian world" window displays a set of objects that correspond to classical physics theory. The student has available a "pure" Newtonian world, which allows him to manipulate directly the properties of velocity and acceleration, a situation not practical in daily life. Here the objects are depicted as circles that denote point masses, and their motion is shown by arrows that denote velocities and accelerations. The circles can be positioned and the lengths and directions of the arrows can be changed to designate initial velocity and (constant) acceleration. When one or more point masses with associated initial velocity and acceleration arrows are set up, the system moves according to the set parameters and again leaves a trace of all motion.

Students stationed at the Envisioning Machine are given various tasks to perform. For example, they observe motion in the object window and are asked to set the velocity and acceleration of a motion in the Newtonian window so that it matches the observable motion. They can manipulate vectors in the Newtonian world so that they yield models that are qualitatively similar to motions encountered in the observable world. They can also be asked to set up two motions and to compare the effects of different settings—for example, equal initial velocities and unequal accelerations in the same direction.

Finally, it is possible to set up redundant representations of the same property; thus, speed can be represented in terms of length of a velocity vector, spacing of trace dots, and movement of image across the screen. The systematic covariance of these properties helps students to counter inappropriate ideas about speed, velocity, and acceleration. In general, students progress by seeking to reduce the differences between the motions that they can control in the Newtonian world and the motion they are trying to simulate and understand in the object world.

ThinkerTool is another computer-generated representational system designed to engender Christopherian thinking. Students are asked to attend to the relationships between different representations of the same physical events. For example, a ball representing a rocket moves diagonally along a docking ramp displayed on the screen. The student's job is to dock the rocket at a specific point on the bay without crashing the rocket against the walls of the docking ramp. While executing the task, the student has the opportunity to observe a graphic representation of the components that constitute the velocity of the rocket. It is also possible to represent the motion of the rocket along the docking ramp, the spacing of traces left in its wake, and the sound of rocket bursts that can provide acceleration bursts in any of four directions. Exercises challenge students to navigate the rocket, drawing on the graphic information provided about velocity and position.

In the world of daily experience, we rarely have the opportunity to encounter the world described by Newton, in which, for example, there is no friction; nor do we have the opportunity to examine what actually happens when we strike something that is already in motion. ThinkerTool provides a Newtonian world in which one can actually play with relevant parameters—for example, turning friction on and off or adjusting gravity. The learner thus has the opportunity to contrast her own conception, or model, of the universe with that put forth by Newton and to attempt to mediate between the two. Moreover, the learner comes to see directly the need for more complex representations and calculations—for instance, the need to use a vector (rather than a simpler scalar) representation in order to understand and answer questions involving force and motion.

In computer-based educational systems like the Envisioning Machine and ThinkerTool, we encounter a use of technology that is especially suited for handling challenging concepts in physics. Many students of physics are confused because the ideal world of the physicist's mind differs (by definition) from the often messier world of the laboratory and, even more so, from the unlabeled world of everyday experience. Technologies allow the student to re-create the physicist's ideal conditions and to compare them directly with observations and phenomena of a more real-world sort. Also, given the versatility of the computer, one can readily contrive a whole set of miniature experiments, arranging and rearranging parameters as frequently as one desires, thus developing an intuitive sense of the meaning of such initially confusing and difficult-to-isolate concepts as force, velocity, and acceleration.

A fair amount of experimentation has been done with systems like the Envisioning Machine and ThinkerTool. Even when students are afforded ample opportunity to use these devices, some confusions and misconceptions remain. In general, however, students do become aware of certain of the mismatches between their own intuitions and formal physics, and they make some progress toward mastering Newtonian principles and procedures. Performances on standard tests improve accordingly. James Minstrell and his colleagues have even devised a computer Hypercard system where students are asked to choose directly among misconceptions and conceptions, to indicate their confidence in their selection, and to identify the instance that best characterizes their reasoning. Used in conjunction with a well-taught course in physics, this technological assessment reveals far better informed students.

Other Christopherian variations also hold promise for conveying lessons in the physical sciences. Consider, for example, the *Visual Almanac*™, a multimedia videodisk with Macintosh computer and Hypercard software. In a section called "Playground Physics," students see videos of children just like themselves riding on merry-go-rounds. The merry-go-rounds turn around at different speeds, and the children place themselves at different loci around the edge or roll a ball back and forth to one another. Students viewing the video in their classroom then have the opportunity to predict what will happen under various conditions—for example, if a merry-go-round proceeds more quickly, with more people on it; if people are grouped closer to the center or spread out along the rim; if one attempts to roll a ball straight or in a curved arc.

Before or after viewing the video segments, students can carry out similar experiments with an actual merry-go-round or lazy Susan in the classroom. In addition to having the opportunity to watch the outcomes on videodisk and to observe them in their own classroom, students may also choose to graph the results in numerical or spatial terms. The technology makes it easy to view changes in slow motion and to track them as they are actually happening. Here lies the crucial bridge from an experiential or sensorimotor understanding of motion on a revolving platform to the manner in which this knowledge can be summarized in terms of numerical arrays and algebraic or geometric principles.

Learning with the *Visual Almanac*™ has not to my knowledge been formally tested, but I have little doubt that a student who learns the principles governing motion in this way is far less likely to remain in the grip of a misconception than one who is never confronted with the disjunction between intuition and demonstration or who has to make these connections without any pedagogical support. Consider, for example, the child's reaction of surprise when he notes that a ball that has apparently been directed absolutely straight leaves a decidedly curved track on the moving surface. Such experiences help the students to notice the Christopherian disjunctions among experiential, graphic, and formal notational renderings of the same phenomenon and encourage them to search for an explanatory principle, such as the conservation of angular momentum.

At the middle and secondary school levels, Christopherian confrontations seem a highly appropriate way to engage students' misconceptions and to seek to realign them with more appropriate representations and analyses. Such encounters do not offer a magical solution, however, any more than other educational interventions do. Sometimes the contradictions are not apparent to students, and even if they are, students are not necessarily overly concerned about them. Moreover, if they do register concern, they may not arrive at or retain a more appropriate conception of the situation. Changing one's initial, entrenched conceptions is no easy task; to be effective, Christopherian encounters must be recurrent, and they require repeated contemplation and analysis along many different lines. It is perhaps well to remember the limitations of Christopher Columbus' own example: Columbus thought that he had reached the Indian subcontinent and never understood that he had discovered a new world. Moreover, although educated people of his time had already come to appreciate that the world was spherical, many people even today still act as though our planet were flat or concoct a strange hybrid, according to which the earth as a whole is round, but we are located on a flat plane bisecting it.

Exploring the Relevant Semantic Worlds in Mathematics

In the traditional sciences, a major goal is to remove earlier misconceptions and replace them with discipline-based understandings of the concepts and bodies of knowledge in question. In mathematics, the problem exhibited by students is better described as a rigid adherence to a single algorithm or formula that has been learned in one situation but that may well need to be adapted or replaced in other circumstances. Effective pedagogy often centers around the opportunity to try out principles or formulas in a variety of circumstances, in an effort to determine where they remain appropriate; in an exploration of the domains of real life to which the formalisms pertain; and in a consideration of how best to yoke intuitive and experiential understandings to the formal algorithm. Asking students to make predictions or to consider extreme or limited cases often engages their interest and helps them to see the power and limits of the procedures in question. Technological adjuncts are not necessary; paper, pencil, and thought can suffice. But, once again, new inventions can be helpful handmaidens in the process.

A number of inviting multimedia means of exploring principles have been devised for high-school mathematics. In a geometric approach called the Geometric Supposer, students are given the opportunity to make arbitrarily complex Euclidean constructions on a primitive shape. For example, having proved a mathematical relationship between sides and base on one exemplar of a triangle, they can produce triangles of every conceivable size and determine to what extent the generalization in question holds. The Geometric Supposer allows students to achieve something that would, at best, have been tremendously time-consuming in a precomputer age: to transcend the particulars of a given instance or two and explore regularities across as wide a range of examples as one desires. In using it the student has the opportunity to become intimately acquainted with all conceivable possibilities within the domain in question—whether it be figures like triangles or parallelograms or constructions like bisected angles or dropped altitudes. These possibilities can then be related to the actual axioms and inferences used in proofs.

Similarly, in a prototype instrument developed at the Technology Education Research Centers, students are shown curves that capture a variety of relationships among distance, time, acceleration, velocity, and other variables handled by the calculus. Then, situated in front of a lens that has a sensor, the students are free to move around and see whether they can, in their movements, duplicate the curves that they are witnessing. In this way they have the opportunity to effect a link between motion as experienced phenomenally, and motion as it has been studied and notated in expressions of the calculus. In this case the goal is not to master the notation of the calculus but rather to explore how experimental situations can embody the phenomena and knowledge that actually motivate the notational expressions of calculus.

Note what has happened here. The student is first asked to explore a domain he may know intuitively but about which he may well never have thought systematically: the way in which his body moves through space at varying speeds over different time intervals. He is asked to make predictions about how this motion might be represented in some kind of notational system. He is then introduced to graphic representations and eventually to more formal approaches that have been developed to deal with the principles of motions of physical bodies. Over the course of a curriculum unit, he then has the opportunity to investigate the ways in which formal procedures or algorithms actually capture critical features of the phenomena about which he has presumably developed some reflective understanding. Such a procedure makes it far less likely that the student will in the future simply apply an algorithm rigidly, without considering the nature of the phenomena that it is seeking to explain; it becomes far more likely that, in the future, even after he has forgotten the precise algorithm, he may still understand the general approach that is taken in the calculus.

This same procedure can be applied to other demonstrations in which the student can manipulate crucial variables and observe the results "live" and dynamically. For instance, students can vary levels of water height and flow in different receptacles as a means of studying rates of change, accumulation, conditions of overflow, or steady state; or they can experiment with motions of their own bodies and motions of toy cars, making predictions of how distances and rates will be graphed. Building on such instances, students also can create their own patterns motorically, hazard predictions of what the curves will look like, and then check their intuitions against the actual graphic representations. Giving students the opportunities to collect data about issues of concern—like acid rain or waste disposal—and then to create methods for analyzing those data is also a useful way to develop an appreciation of various mathematical and statistical principles that might otherwise appear disembodied. Such "anchoring experiences" help students appreciate and flesh out the concepts and principles that a formal notation is designed to capture, such as functions or limits. In both the geometric and the calculus cases, the chances for fundamental misconceptions, biases, or rigid overextensions of a principle should be significantly reduced.

Reduced, but not eliminated. Even when misapprehensions are directly confronted, they are not necessarily vitiated; they sometimes prove incredibly robust. Recall the college engineering students who were unable to capture in a proper equation the fact that there were six times as many students as there were professors. Perplexed by this recurring difficulty with what seems to be an easy kind of problem, Jack Lochhead and his colleagues devised computer software that allowed students to create graphic versions of the problems on which they had faltered. Even a semester's work, however, did not succeed in converting students into expert algebraicists. Moreover, once the graphic tools were removed, most of the students reverted to the precise formulaic approach that yields the documented error.

The news is not all bad, however. Sometimes even in the absence of formal tutelage, erroneous conceptions or approaches are corrected. We know that such recovery occurs in the case of the Piagetian demonstrations. In the classical conservations, six- or seven-year-olds come to understand that an amount of water remains the same irrespective of its liquid configuration, and they acquire this enhanced understanding seemingly in the absence of formal tutelage. (Indeed, tutelage does not seem to help, at least not until the point where students are just about ready to acquire the knowledge on their own.) Also, as Susan Carey has shown, children in our culture supplant their person-centered, intentional view of biological organisms with a more appropriate view, one that acknowledges the genetic constitution of the organism, its different functioning systems, and the taxonomic classifications favored by biologists. While this reconceptualization takes place in a schooled context, little explicit pedagogy seems to be required; socialization within a biologically sophisticated culture seems to suffice.

What causes some misconceptions and rigidly applied algorithms to dissolve, while others endure? So far, there has been insufficient research on the phenomenon to allow a reliable answer to the question. It does seem likely that in cases where lay science has advanced (as in biology), students are more likely to abandon their earliest intuitions and at least move somewhat towards more sophisticated conceptualizations. Having parents, teachers, or friends who exhibit better understandings, or engaging in exploratory activities that lead to better-articulated intuitions, may also ease the way to deeper understandings. The apprenticeship approach, focus on projects, and emergence of self-assessment endorsed here ought all to make a positive contribution.

My own belief is that the kinds of direct Christopherian confrontations just described need to become a regular part of teachers' thinking and students' curricula; moreover, rather than simply appearing once or twice, they need to be revisited over and over again, until the simpler theory yields fully to the more comprehensive and more veridical one. By the same token, the habits of mind entailed in exploration of relevant domains and in the habitual testing of cases, to determine their applications and limitations, should guard against the stereotypical and inappropriate deployment of mathematical principles. On such an analysis, materials like ThinkerTool, the Envisioning Machine, the Geometric Supposer, and the Hypercard physics-assessing technique are no longer occasional curiosities or adjuncts to a researcher's project; rather, they become part of students' daily regimen, helping them to develop intuitions and to map them appropriately onto the formal knowledge structures of the disciplines.

Multiple Stances in the Arts and Humanities

In the area of science, one encounters the classical misconceptions most directly; in mathematics there is a rigidity in the application of principles. But in other areas of the curriculum, similar kinds of problems must be confronted as well. We have already noted that students often come to history, literature, art, or social studies classes with deeply held prejudices, stereotypes, and simplifications. As in the case of the sciences and mathematics, one cannot expect that these biases will simply dissipate after a single counterexample. It is important that these prejudicial views be regularly and repeatedly recognized as such and that the students have ample opportunities to develop richer and more rounded views of the subject.

While less research has been conducted in these curricular areas, the general approach to be followed seems clear enough. Three steps are involved. The first is to involve students as deeply as possible in the central problems of a discipline, so that they can acquire a fully rounded view of the data and the evidence. A month or even an entire term devoted to a particular topic proves effective. One third-grade class in Pennsylvania studied a single painting, Velasquez's "Las Meninas," for a year. The *Immigrant* unit can comfortably accommodate many weeks of work. Such immersion can help to counter the notion that works like paintings or events like social movements are simple entities that can be readily summarized and dismissed in a single characterization or phrase.

In a second step, students must come to understand that the materials they encounter in a humanities, social studies, or art course are not drawn from a world apart. Just as the demonstrations in a physics class are clearly related to daily experience, these latter materials concern human beings, with their own perspectives, biases, and aspirations. The people who are written about or depicted in a work of art are individuals like themselves, caught in their own historical circumstances, and the scholars doing the writing or carrying out the research are also human beings, for all their specialized training in the discipline.

The third step is perhaps the most crucial one. Given that the key problem in these curricular areas is a tendency toward stereotyping, the major compensatory procedure needs to address this problem directly and over time. Students must have the frequent opportunities to adopt multiple perspectives and stances with reference to the material in question. In the absence of such opportunities, students seem fated to maintain a one-dimensional view of the topic or material. When students are given numerous chances to approach the materials through a variety of disciplinary and personal stances, however, the limits of the stereotype should become increasingly clear to them and the complexity entailed in any human phenomenon should become increasingly apparent. The images of Hamlet or of Proteus must come to replace the one-dimensional messages of a sound-bite age.

Toward this end, it is effective to use subject matter that can be related to the students' own lives and to engage students in activities affording them the opportunity to take a hand at various roles, such as that of historian, novelist, or geographer. Historian Tom Holt has his pupils of different races and ethnicities study the establishment of the Freedman's Bureau during Reconstruction; they examine the very different stories told and conclusions drawn by contemporaries and historians about this controversial institution. Two contrasting accounts of the "same facts" are a most effective way to challenge the widely held notion that history is just an objective record of what happened. Historian Bernard Bailyn poses puzzles to his students: Why did the Founding Fathers hate and fear democracy? Why did so many Germans leave their homeland to cross the Atlantic in 1750, rather than simply moving to a more fertile region 150 miles away from their home? And many history teachers have asked their students to carry out oral histories with relatives or elderly people in their community or to investigate the origins of a local event that has caused controversy. Such activities give students the opportunity to assume the roles of fledgling reporter, investigator, demographer, and historian.

Arts PROPEL: Integrated Curricula and Assessment

Our own research group has developed an educational approach that seeks to enhance student understanding, this time in the arts and humanities at the middle and high school level.

Arts PROPEL is a five-year collaborative project with the Educational Testing Service and the Pittsburgh Public Schools. The name signals that it focuses on the arts, particularly music, the visual arts, and imaginative writing; and the acronym signals the ensemble of roles that we are seeking to inculcate: the producer of art (the writer of music or plays), the perceiver (one capable of making sensitive discriminations in an art form), and the reflector (one who can step back from his own activities, or from the artistry of someone else, and evaluate it—in a word, the critic).

Like several of the other projects with which I have been involved, Arts PROPEL began with a focus on assessment. We wanted to assess potential and achievement in the arts, and we hoped to move beyond the often wooden standardized instruments that have been used even in domains where they are manifestly inappropriate. But as in other projects, we soon came to the realization that it is pointless to conduct any assessment unless students have acquired knowledge, skills, and understandings that are worth assessing. In rather short order, Arts PROPEL became a project in curriculum and in teacher education, as well as a set of assessment tools.

A word about understanding in the arts is in order. If the notion of understanding is introduced in too literal a fashion in the arts, it may be taken as cognate to the mastery of certain concepts like "style" or "rhythm" or "the Renaissance." As I have noted throughout this book, however, any notion of understanding ought to center on the capacities exhibited and the operations carried out by masters of a domain, and each domain features its own characteristic constraints and opportunities.

Such a perspective reveals that, in the arts, production ought to lie at the center of any artistic experience. Understanding involves a mastery of the productive practices in a domain or discipline, coupled with the capacity to adopt different stances toward the work, among them the stances of audience member, critic, performer, and maker. The "understander" in the arts is one who can comfortably move among these various stances, just as the understander in the sciences can with suppleness alternate among several modes of knowing or representation, assuming the roles of experimenter, theorist, and critic of investigations carried out personally and by others.

This view of understanding is remote from the conception of the artist held by the young child and by many adults as well. In a more stereotypical version, the artist is a special person, born with unique talents, who sits alone in a garret waiting for inspiration. Great works either emerge or fail to emerge; there is no discernible relation between the processes engaged in and the product that results. Nor, in this view, is there any relationship between the artist and others; the creative artist is seen as remote from the audience, the critic, perhaps even the performer. Effective arts education must confront these stereotypes, ultimately replacing them with an appreciation of the complexity of the artistic process and the ensemble of roles it entails.

In Arts PROPEL we have developed two distinct forms of instrumentation that deliberately straddle the usually separate arenas of assessment and curriculum. *Domain projects* are extended curricular sequences based upon a concept or practice that is central to a discipline; examples include composition in the visual arts, rehearsal in music, writing an opening scene in imaginative writing. In a domain project, which can run from a few days to a few weeks, students encounter this central practice in a number of different ways and have ample opportunities to assume the stances of producing, perceiving, and reflection. Students also encounter many opportunities for assessment—self-assessment and assessment by peers, as well as assessment by teachers and even by outside experts, including some who are remote from the site of teaching.

Domain projects are evaluated on a number of domain-appropriate dimensions, with developmental scales employed as a means of assessing the student's emerging competence. Thus, in the fashion of a reflective apprentice, a student can determine how sophisticated is her concept of graphic composition, how expert a listener she is when rehearsing, how effective is the opening of her play in terms of choice of language, development of characters, and the like. In each of these areas, more sophisticated performances will transcend stereotypical conceptions and behaviors, giving rise to a more complex view of the artistic dimension in question. Over time students should attain higher levels of competence on these developmental scales; at the same time, it is anticipated that most students will exhibit uneven profiles, displaying greater strength on certain dimensions of production, perception, or reflection than on others.

Our other vehicle, sometimes called a portfolio, is more accurately described as a "process-folio." In the typical art portfolio, a student or artist assembles her best works, in the hope of gaining admission to a select art school, winning a prize, or securing a showing at a gallery or a staging at the playhouse. The emphasis falls squarely on the final product. In contrast, as the name suggests, our process-folios represent an effort to capture the steps and phases through which students pass in the course of developing a project, product, or work of art. A complete student process-folio contains initial brainstorming ideas, early drafts, and first critiques; journal entries on "pivotal moments" when ideas jelled; collections of works by others that proved influential or suggestive, in a positive or a negative sense; interim and final drafts; self-critiques and critiques by peers, informed mentors, and, again, outside experts; and finally some suggestion of how one might build upon the current project in future endeavors.

I contend that creation and maintenance of a process-folio is an important, perhaps even essential phase in the development of a mature artistic practitioner in our culture. In a culture where one simply follows the models of others, as in most traditional societies and as in China today, such reflective endeavors may be of limited importance; one is literally surrounded by master models that serve as support for one's learning activity and ultimately for one's finished products. In a culture where some degree of creativity or individuality or "ownership" is sought, however, it is important for the aspiring creator to be able to assume some distance from his work—to be able to see where he is headed, which leads are promising, which lines of work ought to be pursued, and which ones abandoned, and to have the opportunity to submit drafts to other sympathetic but critical colleagues for feedback, suggestions, and even, on occasion, praise!

Possibly there exist a few geniuses who can achieve mastery in isolation; possibly there are a few artists with sufficiently faithful memories that they can retain the traces of their earliest works and their gradual progress completely in their heads. But for most people, the opportunity of keeping a process-folio and the potential of returning to it to reflect upon progress as well as on regressions and plateaus proves invaluable.

A "Process-Folio Culture"

It is bracing to wax enthusiastical about process-folios, and it is wonderful to behold a talented student who displays finished works along with the process-folio that gave rise to them. But it would be highly misleading to suggest that such well-stocked collections are easy to come by.

Probably the most important factor in building up a "process-folio culture" is the belief on the part of teachers and students that such an atmosphere is useful and generative. If students observe their own teachers involved in projects, reflecting upon them, and keeping track of their own progress, such a model constitutes the most important lesson of all. Here, again, we encounter the power of the apprenticeship, because the master is engaged in genuine productive activity, in whose genesis and progress she is deeply involved and about which she will be appropriately reflective. A master's interest in the student's work is equally important. Even if the teacher lacks the time to consult the student's process-folio on a daily basis, it is extremely important for her to pore over it with the student from time to time and to offer strategic feedback. Once such a structure has been set up, older students can aid younger ones; peers can provide considerable help for one another; the teacher can sometimes carry out a "demonstration review" with a single student in front of her peers or have a discussion with a group of students; and gradually a student herself can assume responsibility for much of the early assessment-in-progress.

Another important ingredient in establishing such a process-folio culture is the articulation and maintenance of standards. No educational vehicle is good or bad in and of itself, and even though

TOWARD EDUCATION FOR UNDERSTANDING

process-folios call attention to items that students might in the past have thrown away, mere attention does not suffice. Teachers need to embody a concern with high standards; even as they support the efforts of their students, they must help these students bear in mind the importance of care, revision, reflection, discipline, regular self-examination, and sharing reactions with others. (Such a message assumes special importance in our mass media–suffused culture, where products are assumed to coalesce instantaneously and where slovenly performances or arguments are tolerated and even featured.) Taken together, such practices can help to bring about a community in which every member cares about quality and standards—the most important catalyst in bringing about such standards.

As we noted in the last chapter in discussing writing in the younger years, it is difficult to set up a literate culture unless teachers embody compatible beliefs and practices in their daily lives. Arts and humanities teachers have the potential to be practitioners and to maintain their own process-folios in a meaningful way, but more often than not they themselves need support as they ease into this more active and more vulnerable role. Our own experiences at the pilot Arts PROPEL site in Pittsburgh suggest that it takes at least two years, and often as many as four or five years, for teachers to become comfortable participants in a process-folio culture. Nor should this be surprising—after all, traditional apprenticeships often lasted at least that long!

Such assessment and curricular materials as the domain projects are, one hopes, of merit in themselves. But all are designed in part to change the nature of learning and education, not only in the school but in the daily hours outside of school and in the years after formal schooling has been completed. Of their various purposes, I consider especially crucial the notion of building up the student's own sense of responsibility—for learning, for maintaining progress, for devising and carrying out a meaningful network of projects or enterprises, and for making it a natural habit of mind to reflect on her progress. Note that, in this respect, the use of process-folios is not restricted to aesthetic or humanistic study; indeed, many teachers of science, social science, and mathematics have discovered the utility of journals, process-folios, and other self-monitoring devices.

This model of student activities and materials represents a significant departure from the ways in which children typically think of school and in many ways from parental, teacher, and community attitudes as well. In the stereotypic image of school, teachers impart knowledge and factual information to students in as efficient a way as possible. Students differ in how well they learn, but there is little that can be done about that. The drillwork and drafts that go into the learning are of little interest in themselves. By contrast, the Arts PROPEL approach makes what used to be background into foreground; the focus is on process rather than on product. The student is asked to bring about change in herself rather than to wait for change to be imposed from the outside (or to believe that change cannot occur at all) and to accept the possibility that assessment may be the burden not of the teacher primarily but of the learner herself. We have moved far from an educational milieu in which the correct-answer compromise dominates, and we have set into motion the creation of an environment in which students are willing to undertake risks for understanding.

Children attending a traditional school, when asked what they have done in school that day, are often heard to answer "Nothing." This response communicates a deep truth, as well as a flip reaction, because typically school is *done to* students—and, not infrequently, to teachers themselves. If responsible learning is to take place, if dynamic and generative understandings are to be achieved, it is crucial for students and teachers to take responsibility for education, to allow themselves to become vulnerable, and then to exploit that vulnerability in order to acquire knowledge and skills that may be mobilized in the acquisition of understanding.

Bringing about such an environment is no easy matter. Individual students have a variety of needs, fears, and aspirations, and in a world where many of the traditional supports have weakened, much of the burden for providing support falls on the schools. Only if schools are concerned with civility, with fair treatment of all students from all groups, with feelings, interests, motivations, and values as well as with cognitive goals, can such an environment be constructed and sustained.

In this chapter I have reviewed some of the efforts that can be undertaken with older children to help ensure a greater level of understanding. Many of these are integrally related to those undertaken with younger children as well: the fostering of a rich, project-centered environment, the involvement in an apprenticeship relation, the emphasis on cooperative learning. Some are efforts to deal directly with the misconceptions and biases of students: Christopherian confrontations of misconceptions in the domain of science; an exploration of domains in order to determine the powers and limits of mathematical principles; an attempt to encourage the adoption of multiple perspectives, in an effort to confront stereotypes and simplifications about the subject matter and the learner in the humanities and the arts. I have also stressed the importance of exposing students to a range of adult models and providing opportunities for students to engage in these complementary stances. Understanding is most likely to come about through a fusion of more appropriate conceptions, on the one hand, and an intuitive familiarity with competent adult roles, on the other. And it is most likely to come about in an effective manner if it has been sculpted to the particular intellectual strengths and ways of knowing of the young child.

THE NURTURING OF INDIVIDUAL
UNDERSTANDING: FIVE ENTRY POINTS

Recent advances in our understanding of individual learning can help in revitalizing the educational process. While educators have always noted differences among learners, they have been strongly inclined to believe that all students can learn in similar ways. This assumption works out well in practice for those students who are flexible learners, for those whose background and learning styles happen to be compatible with the teaching styles of their teachers, and for those who can learn in the way in which materials have traditionally been taught (say, from lecturing or from textbooks). But there are also casualties: students who are motivated to learn but whose own learning styles or profiles of intelligence are not in tune with prevailing instructional practices.

So long as the classroom contains one teacher with thirty or forty students and a single textbook, it may be necessary to teach all students in the same way. (Only a teacher of great talent and formidable energy can afford to individualize instruction at so unfavorable a teacher-student ratio.) But we need no longer work under such constraints. Through the use of some of the methods outlined in the previous chapter, a student as well as his parents can learn something about his own learning styles and can use this knowledge to find a preferred way into a mandated curriculum. Schools can exert efforts to match teaching and learning styles. Most important, schools can deliberately collect and make available resources—human and technological—that fit comfortably with the disparate learning styles and cultural backgrounds that exist in any student body.

My own belief is that any rich, nourishing topic—any concept worth teaching—can be approached in at least five different ways that, roughly speaking, map onto the multiple intelligences. We might think of the topic as a room with at least five doors or entry points into it. Students vary as to which entry point is most appropriate for them and which routes are most comfortable to follow once they have gained initial access to the room. Awareness of these entry points can help the teacher introduce new materials in ways in which they can be easily grasped by a range of students; then, as students explore other entry points, they have the chance to develop those multiple perspectives that are the best antidote to stereotypical thinking.

Let us look at these five entry points one by one, considering how each one might be used in approaching topics or concepts, one in the natural sciences (evolution) and one in the social sciences (democracy).

In using a *narrational entry point,* one presents a story or narrative about the concept in question. In the case of evolution, one might trace the course of a single branch of the evolutionary tree, or perhaps even the generations of a specific organism. In the case of democracy, one would tell the story of its beginnings in ancient Greece or, perhaps, of the origins of constitutional government in the United States.

In using a *logical-quantitative entry point,* one approaches the concept by invoking numerical considerations or deductive reasoning processes. Evolution could be approached by studying the incidence of different species in different parts of the world or in different geophysical epochs; or one might review the arguments for and against a particular claim about evolutionary processes. In the case of democracy, one could look at congressional voting patterns over time or the arguments used for and against democracy by the Founding Fathers.

A *foundational entry point* examines the philosophical and terminological facets of the concept. This tack proves appropriate for people who like to pose fundamental questions, of the sort that one associates with young children and with philosophers rather than with more practical (or more "middle-aged") spirits. A foundational approach to evolution might consider the difference between evolution and revolution, the reasons that we look for origins and changes, the epistemological status of teleology and finality. A foundational approach to democracy would ponder the root meaning of the word, the relationship of democracy to other forms of decision making and government, and the reasons why one might adopt a democratic rather than an oligarchic approach. The philosopher Matthew Lipman has developed engaging materials for introducing such a foundational approach to youngsters in middle childhood.

We shift gears quite sharply in considering an *esthetic approach*. Here the emphasis falls on sensory or surface features that will appeal to—or at least capture the attention of—students who favor an artistic stance to the experiences of living. In the case of evolution the examination of the structure of different evolutionary trees, or the study of the shifting morphology of organisms over time, might activate the esthetic sensitivity. With reference to democracy, one intriguing approach would be to listen to musical ensembles that are characterized either by group playing or by playing under the control of a single individual—the string quartet versus the orchestra. Another, less exotic tack might be to consider various forms of balance or imbalance as they are epitomized in different voting blocs.

The final entry point is an *experiential approach*. Some students—old as well as young—learn best with a hands-on approach, dealing directly with the materials that embody or convey the concept. Those bent on mastering concepts of evolution might breed numerous generations of Drosophila and observe the mutations that take place. Those in the social studies class might actually constitute groups that have to make decisions in accordance with various governmental processes, observing the pros and cons of democracy as compared with other, more "top-down" forms of government.

In one definition, a skilled teacher is a person who can open a number of different windows on the same concept. In our example, rather than presenting evolution and democracy only by definition, or only by example, or only in terms of quantitative considerations, such a teacher would make available several entry points over time. An effective teacher functions as a "student-curriculum broker," ever vigilant for educational prosthetics—texts, films, software—that can help convey the relevant contents, in as engaging and effective a way as possible, to students who exhibit a characteristic learning mode.

It should be evident that use of multiple entry points can be a powerful means of dealing with student misconceptions, biases, and stereotypes. So long as one takes only a single perspective or tack on a concept or problem, it is virtually certain that students will understand that concept in only the most limited and rigid fashion. Conversely, the adoption of a family of stances toward a phenomenon encourages the student to come to know that phenomenon in more than one way, to develop multiple representations and seek to relate these representations to one another. Christopherian encounters of the sort encouraged by the Envisioning Machine; explorations of the domain of one's own motion as a preparation for mastering the calculus; assumption of the Arts PROPEL stances of perception, production, and reflection vis-à-vis one's own work of art; learning about a topic though a combination of reading, discussion, and experimenting approaches—all these move in a direction away from the correct-answer compromise and encourage the risks necessary for a more complete understanding to be approached.

Ultimately, a full understanding of any concept of any complexity cannot be restricted to a single mode of knowing or way of representation. Indeed, I expect that the knowledgeable biologist or political scientist is characterized *precisely* by his capacity to access the critical concepts through a variety of routes and to apply them to a diversity of situations. Thus the person who has a command of evolutionary concepts can move readily among issues of definition, questions of morphology, and experimental demonstrations that embody important principles. Analogously, the person with a developed understanding of democracy, when confronted with the need to explain a recent event in Eastern Europe, can draw upon historical precedents, conceptual distinctions, and examples of political decision-making situations in which he has himself been involved.

Perhaps, indeed, the consummate thinker also exemplifies this flexibility of perspectives. As Philipp Frank wrote of Albert Einstein:

> When Einstein had thought through a problem, he always found it necessary to formulate this subject in as many different ways as possible and to present it so that it would be comprehensible to people accustomed to different modes of thought and with different educational preparations. He liked to formulate his ideas for mathematicians, for experimental physicists, for philosophers, and even for people without much scientific thinking, if they were at all inclined to think independently.

Taken together, the list of entry points just reviewed might help to suggest the different components that contribute to a full understanding on the part of students, teachers, and innovative thinkers. One can see that there is great distance to be traversed between initial conceptions (or misconceptions), early scripts and stereotypes, and initial understandings, on the one hand, and the rounded understandings of the disciplinary experts, on the other hand. Even under favorable circumstances, this distance cannot be traveled quickly; it requires the implementation of the kinds of educational procedures I have described in settings ranging from preschool classes through secondary school, and perhaps into college and graduate school classrooms as well.

Throughout our discussion, one point has emerged with special clarity: Education that takes seriously the ideas and intuitions of the young child is far more likely to achieve success than education that ignores these views, either considering them to be unimportant or assuming that they will disappear on their own. The ideas of the young child—the youthful theorist—are powerful and are likely to remain alive throughout life. Only if these ideas are taken seriously, engaged, and eventually trimmed or transformed so that more developed and comprehensive conceptions can come to the fore—only then does an education for understanding become possible.

Assuming that they take into consideration the young mind and treat it with the respect that it merits, educators possess concepts, materials, and techniques that can engender far greater degrees of understanding across the full range of students and the full spectrum of disciplinary topics. It is not easy to effect such an educational revolution; there will be setbacks, and certain kinds of misconceptions, rigidities, and biases may prove particularly difficult to dislodge. Development cannot occur in a day, or even in a year. But we cannot fall back on the assertion that these understandings are impossible to achieve, nor on the faith that they will come about strictly on their own. Good teachers, good materials, and the right educational atmosphere can make an enormous difference. Whether we will choose to follow this route, to educate for understanding, is a political issue rather than a scientific or pedagogical one.

CHAPTER
13

Toward National and Global
Understandings

With apologies to Charles Dickens and a nod to cultural literacy, this book might be thought of as *A Tale of Two Schools*. I have argued that, in one sense, we live in the "worst of times." Not only have most schools experienced difficulties in achieving their avowed goals, but even those deemed a success yield students who, by and large, do not display deep understandings. Lamenting the situation in the schools, I have tried not to place the blame in any quarter. After all, the failures to achieve understanding became manifest only when researchers began to search actively for evidence of them. The deficiencies with the schools reflect deficiencies in the wider society: in our grasp of learning and development and in ourselves—and our value systems—as teachers and citizens.

Yet I trust that the book's message is not seen as totally negative. Signs abound that this could become the "best of times," complete with the best of schools. We are coming to understand our situation, a necessary first step in any reform. Human beings have tremendous capacities to learn and develop, as can easily be seen if one watches a child actively exploring his environment during the first years of life. And at least some children continue to demonstrate ready assimilation and impressive mastery after they enter school or other educational milieus. The problem is less a difficulty in school learning per se and more a problem in integrating the notational and conceptual knowledge featured in school with the robust forms of intuitive knowledge that have evolved spontaneously during the opening years of life. If we can find ways in which to help students synthesize their several forms of knowing, we should be in a position to educate students for understanding.

THE TALE SO FAR

In the first part of this book, I described the course of development as it can be expected to occur in normal children throughout the world. Using their sensorimotor capacities and their abilities to master first-order symbol systems, young children develop a vast array of intuitive understandings even before they enter school. Specifically, they develop robust and functional theories of matter, life, the minds of other individuals, and their own minds and selves. They are aided in this task of theory construction by various constraints, some built into the genome, others a function of the particular circumstances of their culture, and still others a reflection of their own, more idiosyncratic styles and inclinations.

Of course, not all these conceptions are adequate, and the potent theories of early childhood are complemented by a large collection of stereotypes and simplifications. Still, from a practical angle, the child of five, six, or seven has a surprisingly serviceable grasp of relevant worlds. More crucially, the five-year-old is in many ways an energetic, imaginative, and integrating kind of learner; educators should exploit the cognitive and affective powers of the five-year-old mind and attempt to keep it alive in all of us.

In the second part of the book, I turned attention to the procedures whereby children are educated throughout the world. In traditional societies, much education takes place informally, through the use of simple processes of observation and imitation. This approach has been formalized in the apprenticeship system, in many ways a very powerful form of learning, in which the utility of various skills and approaches can be readily appreciated by the young apprentice. Schools evolved initially in order to aid in the acquisition of reading, writing, and other basic literacies; with time, they have come to acquire additional burdens, among them the formidable challenge of conveying the concepts and epistemic forms associated with specific disciplines. Like people, schools themselves are subject to various constraints that make it difficult for them to serve diverse clientele and to undergo smooth changes. When the constraints governing the human learner and the constraints governing school are both brought to bear, the difficult challenge facing educators becomes manifest.

While some of the problems associated with schools have become all too well known, it is only in recent years that researchers and educators have become aware of a new set of difficulties. There is now ample documentation that schoolchildren have difficulties in acquiring a deep understanding of the disciplinary materials presented to them. In the sciences, the difficulties take the form of misconceptions: disjunctions between intuitive theories whose inception can be traced to early childhood and the formal concepts and theories worked out by scientific researchers. In mathematics, the difficulties are manifested in the rigid application of algorithms: Rather than appreciating how a formalism captures objects and events in a domain, students simply treat the expression as a string of symbols into which values are to be "plugged." In the arts and humanities, the difficulties are more accurately described as stereotypes and simplifications that prevent students from appreciating the complexity and subtlety of social, historical, and esthetic phenomena. Oversimplified views of the learning and developing process per se also hamper the evolution of processes of thinking and reflection in schoolchildren.

In the third part of the book, I have zeroed in on our current educational dilemma. Having introduced this "worst of times" scenario, I have considered a number of ameliorating approaches. Neither approaches rooted in basic skills nor those based on cultural literacy or an approved Western canon seem adequate in themselves. More promising clues are available if we look to examples hewn in the American progressive tradition, certain traditional educational forms such as the apprenticeship, newer educational institutions such as children's museums, and various technological innovations such as videodisk-based learning environments.

In the previous chapters, proceeding from preschool through secondary school and surveying the sciences as well as the arts and humanities, I have introduced several programmatic approaches that appear to work. When properly implemented, programs embodying these approaches should excite teachers, engage students, and effect precisely those connections between intuitive and formal knowledge that hold the best promise of dissolving misconceptions, countering stereotypical thinking, and yielding a deep and lasting understanding.

Individual programs show that an effective education can be achieved. But if one wants to remake education, it is crucial to create environments in which the formation of links between forms of knowing is the governing principle, rather than an accidental occurrence or the product of a well-funded (but impractical to replicate) experiment. In classical apprenticeships, a person can routinely discern the connections among his activities, the ends toward which they are being directed, and the kinds of tools that can aid in the achievement of an effective product. In hands-on museums, youngsters have the opportunity to explore rich environments and to play out their emerging understandings in meaningful contexts. On-the-job training, mentoring relations, and the involvement of professionals in the schools are all mechanisms for reducing the gap between the "agenda of school" and the "agenda for life." And introduction into the classroom of meaningful projects, cooperative forms of interaction, and process-folios that document student progress can all sensitize students to their own thought processes and to the ways in which their conceptions mesh or collide with disciplinary knowledge.

One challenge facing educators is how best to fuse institutions—how to inject the apprentice method into schools, to introduce schools into community work settings, and to find ways to bridge the geographic and psychological distances between the school and the museum. Another challenge is to prepare a cadre of educators, be they termed masters, teachers, brokers, or curators, who feel comfortable in exhibiting the links among different forms of knowing and in drawing children and families into a fuller approach to learning and understanding.

If we are to achieve a milieu in which understanding is prized, it is necessary for us all to be humble about what we know and to move away from our present, invariably inadequate perspectives. Even under ideal circumstances, an education rooted in understanding takes time and effort to attain. We all suffer from misconceptions and stereotypes and risk wallowing in them unless we remain vigilant. It is necessary both to respect the conceptions that students of all ages bring to the schools and to be aware of our own predilections toward strongly held but unfounded beliefs.

Let me bring this perspective to bear on the content of this book. Most readers doubtless came to the book with a belief that understanding is important, and most educators probably felt that they were already taking the steps appropriate for such an achievement. I trust that their faith has been shaken by the evidence provided in the preceding chapters. I have sought to challenge the conception that one can get students to understand simply by presenting them with good models or with compelling demonstrations, as well as the idea that students who do not understand must simply work harder or adhere to the correct-answer compromise.

In contrast to these straightforward views, I have presented a far more complex and vexed picture. I have proposed that we must place ourselves inside the heads of our students and try to understand as far as possible the sources and strengths of their conceptions. I have proposed that we examine our own educational assumptions and practices, noting where they rest upon hope rather than upon demonstrated effectiveness. At the same time, I have tried to avoid the presentation of recipes for understanding. The various examples and models presented have reflected an effort to describe the kinds of procedures that may prod education in a positive direction. It is never the models per se that are important, however, but the thinking and the reflective facets thus captured that will determine whether students gain from their use—whether students will be stimulated to assume "risks for understanding."

If my analysis is correct, it may have relevance beyond the circle of students and teacher in the classroom. In every encounter in which learning is possible—and few of us spend appreciable time in any other kind of encounter—there are always misconceptions and biases, as well as opportunities for better communication and understanding. Relations at work, at home, on the street, between employees, families, lovers—all are touched by problems of egocentric assumptions about what others believe, understand, and desire. Only if we think deeply and sympathetically about these preconceived notions in ourselves and in others, and only if we strive to engage them fully, is it reasonable to expect that they can be transformed in productive ways.

THE FOUR NODES OF SCHOOL REFORM

Whatever the broader implications of this study may be, its current focus remains within the schoolhouse. When I first became involved in efforts at educational reform, I believed that the key lay in assessment. Altering the kinds of assessment that are to be done, I reasoned, would send a powerful and effective message throughout the educational landscape. I looked longingly at examples from England, where students assemble portfolios or "records of achievement," which are carefully reviewed by teachers in their own school, "moderated" by teachers from neighboring schools, and shared with prospective employers. I looked enviously at continental Europe, where students are examined at length on the full curriculum of school, rather than being tested on shards of knowledge or tokens of "scholastic aptitude" that they are expected to garner irrespective of the particular curricula used in their school system.

And so, with dedicated colleagues, I began to work on the creation of new assessment measures that could be employed throughout the educational system. Some of these instruments were described briefly in the previous chapters. We soon learned that the conundrum of educational reform is far more complicated, that reform in fact depends equally upon four different nodes: assessment, curriculum, teacher education, and community support.

One can have the best assessment imaginable, but unless the accompanying curriculum is of quality, the assessment has no use. It will simply sit on a shelf, unused and unusable. In fact, one praiseworthy aspect of several European educational systems is that the lengthy examination process seeks to ascertain students' mastery of carefully worked out, high-quality syllabi and curricula.

The presence of a curriculum that is worth assessing is a step in the right direction. Unless teachers accept the curriculum, however, and not only believe in it but embody its precepts in their teaching, the best curriculum and ways of assessing it are of little value. Thus teacher training and development become intrinsic to any educational reform. To the extent that master teachers believe in what they are teaching and know how to assess progress in understanding, they become excellent, indispensable leaders of the educational process.

Here one might note a possibly crucial difference between the teaching-and-assessment situations in America and in Western Europe. Alternative forms of assessment in Europe generally seek to document the practices that have long been carried out in classroom—for example, the careful review with students of their projects and accompanying notebooks. In contrast, alternative forms of assessment in the United States have recently been prescribed as a way of helping teachers alter classroom practice in certain desirable ways.

Obviously, it is more time-consuming to alter teacher practice than it is simply to codify a practice that is already standard.

Even a combination of fine teachers, exemplary curricula, and powerful, authentic assessments does not in itself suffice. Schools do not operate—and probably never have operated—in a vacuum. An essential partner in any kind of educational regimen is the community, represented by many individuals ranging from respected elders to powerful businesspeople and officials elected at the local and the national levels. In the United States today, probably the most important agents of change in the community are the parents, in their dual roles as advocates for their children and citizens of the society.

The fact that a community calls for a certain kind of education, of course, does not mean that it will be achieved. But if the community fails to support the desires and standards of school people, the educators are destined to fail. Such community involvement presupposes "stretch" on both ends; educators must share their vision with members of the community, and these citizens in turn must be willing to consider alternative classroom practices and assessment procedures.

COMMUNITY VERSUS NATIONAL CONTROL OF EDUCATION

The issue of community standards raises a question that has proved especially sensitive within the American context. In most other countries in the world, it is simply assumed that there will be a national curriculum, which will be implemented in every school in the country. Not all national curricula are as entrenched as the legendary curriculum of the "French empire," where fifth-grade children from Normandy to Nice, and possibly from Quebec to Tahiti, are all reciting the same mathematics lessons at 10 A.M. on Monday morning. But the contrasting American situation, in which over fifteen thousand school districts have the right—and some would claim the duty—to select their own curriculum, has no equivalent elsewhere; indeed, educators in most other countries are incredulous when our system is first described to them.

Of late, the national and educational media have reported numerous signs that we Americans have been rethinking the traditional local control of school systems. Most of us exhibit at least some ambivalence on this score. We value the role of local interest in and support of the educational system, and we worry about the imposition on "our" schools of values and content determined hundreds or even thousands of miles away, and yet we appreciate the confusion—and possibly the untenability—of having hundreds of different educational programs and approaches in practice at any given time.

In the wake of reports by many governmental and private commissions, I have reached the conclusion that national standards in education are likely to emerge in some form and that a complementary curriculum—either an implicit or an explicit one—will follow. From my perspective and that of many other observers, efforts to reform the system are essential; at such a time, and with decidedly limited resources, it simply makes no sense for every municipality, every discipline, every interest group to promulgate its favored approach. Indeed, the question is no longer whether there will be national standards and curricula but, rather, what those standards and curricula will be and who will determine them.

Still, any effort to bring about national standards in America must build upon the current situation of community attitudes toward education. In the past, there was a tendency to support the schools and to give them the benefit of the doubt. By the latter part of the twentieth century, however, such support has waned. With the accelerating disintegration of family life and the loss of many social supports in the community, children arrive at school far less prepared to deal with the unfamiliar demands that will be made on them. At the same time, the community looks to the school as the institution that is most likely to be able to compensate for its own lacks—to provide training in civility; to inculcate desired moral and social behaviors; to demonstrate how to complete homework and how to study for a test; to care for children from early morning through the early evening; and to counter the use of drugs, the resort to violence, and the racial tension that so often dominate the school environment, even as they pervade much of the wider society.

To compound these already overwhelming demands upon any institution, our society conveys decided ambivalence about the role of schools and the value of education. On the rhetorical level, of course, there is little disagreement. Education is vital; schools are central. Presidents wrap themselves in the mantle (and the argot) of education. As if to endorse this viewpoint, the well-to-do spend huge sums of money on private schools and universities, in order to purchase a margin of advantage for their children in later life.

And yet the extent to which education is genuinely valued in our

256

society can be doubted, and in fact it has been called into question for many decades. America is a country where one can achieve virtually unlimited success without formal education. It is also a country where it has long been prudent to hide the extent of one's education and to honor those who embrace an anti-intellectual or even an anti-educational stance. Lessons on the street and in the media are decidedly nonscholastic: "Street smarts" are more important than "school smarts," professors are absentminded, students are spoiled, book-learning won't get you anywhere. At the very least, those growing up in our culture receive decidedly mixed messages about education. In contrast, most of the cultures that have achieved educational successes—Japan, China, Israel, Western Europe—embrace educational goals wholeheartedly, obsess about the contents of their national examinations, and find ways to honor those who are knowledgeable.

Given our longtime ambivalence toward education and the sizable social problems facing our country, those who wish to change the educational climate have a huge task ahead of them. The search for national educational standards occurs at the very time when schools are receiving level funding at best and are being asked to fulfill roles in which the community and the nation have failed. Unless the public is aware of the enormity of this demand and strong efforts are made to help the schools to deal with these diverse challenges, schools will once again be seen as failing and simply sink deeper into despair. Far from having a national educational system, we will lack a system altogether.

Efforts to bring about change sometimes encounter a paradox. It is a curious fact that Americans, while critical of schools in general, usually feel that their own local schools are of good quality. And they believe that if students are not doing well, it is because these students lack academic talent. This viewpoint differs dramatically from that encountered in Japan, where poor performances are customarily attributed to lack of effort and work; where schools are considered of tremendous importance; and where criticism of the national scholastic effort is as constant as are efforts to improve the education of all students. Again, unless we as a nation are convinced of the scale of our educational problem and the need for cooperative efforts to solve it, reform initiatives will founder.

Certainly the infusion of additional resources into our schools—and particularly a sizable increase in the salaries of teachers—would be a boon to our system. Yet, as I have suggested, the problems in our educational system are due at least as much to values and priorities as to the provision of resources. Put differently, if we wished to have education of higher quality and more rigorous standards, education that took seriously the need to address individual differences and achieve widespread understandings, we could make enormous strides even with the present resources. As a nation, we must decide that we *desire* to have high-quality education and that we *are willing* to work for it, with the same dedication that we draw upon in placing a man on the moon, defending our values in wartime, or pursuing the pleasures of a commercial, consumer society.

THE DEFINITION AND ACHIEVEMENT OF NATIONAL UNDERSTANDINGS

I believe that we will not be able to improve our educational system materially in the next decade; fulfilling that assignment will take several decades. All that we can determine by the year 2000 is whether we are serious about bringing about major changes. If we are—and I think that we can be—then we have as good a chance at achieving a superior educational system as any country in the world. Indeed, I believe that the United States could lead the world in achieving an entirely new educational aim: the design and implementation of an education that yields understanding.

While schools in other lands have been much more successful in inculcating scholastic knowledge—in conveying notations, lists of facts, and disciplinary concepts—I am not convinced that the resultant understanding is necessarily much greater. The transfer from the scholastic setting to contexts in which such knowledge can be readily applied is not easy to achieve in any society. What is needed is the creation of a climate in which students come naturally to link their intuitive ways of knowing with scholastic and disciplinary forms of knowing. Needed as well as an educational milieu in which they use the resultant integrated knowledge to illuminate new problems and puzzles with which they are presented or which they happen upon themselves. American pragmatism, progressive values, institutions like children's museums, and ingenious interactive technologies can readily and appropriately be mobilized in order to bring about such an educational environment and to produce individuals who are prepared to take risks for understanding.

One hopeful sign has been the creation in recent years of collections of teachers and scholars who have set forth the knowledge and competences that students ought to achieve in the twenty-first century. Perhaps not surprisingly, the first published efforts have come in mathematics, with the statements of the National Council of Teachers of Mathematics and the Mathematical Sciences Education Board, and in science and technology, with the conclusions of Project 2061, undertaken by the American Association for the Advancement of Science. Similar efforts are under way in other areas of the curriculum, ranging from social studies to the arts. While one can certainly quibble with details of each program, the general validity of the goals and the degree of cooperation that has gone into their formulation are impressive. If we are going to move to a national curriculum in the United States, that curriculum should be based upon *understandings* and not upon thinly veiled ideology, isolated bits of knowledge, or rote, ritualized, or conventional performances.

Complementing this process of curricular definition, a number of states have moved well "beyond the bubble" in their assessments. Questioning the hegemony of standardized tests, Vermont is mandating the assembling of portfolios, while California and Connecticut are implementing performance-based examinations. Students in these and some other states are being asked to carry out extended projects, often cooperatively, in which they demonstrate "in practical situations" their understandings of concepts in mathematics, science, and other disciplines. As instances, they are asked to argue both sides of a controversial issue; to design a fiscally sound program for a financially troubled organization; to assess the toxicity of the local water supply; to determine which of several local media presents the most accurate weather forecasts. It is not possible to fake or commit such knowledge to memory. Rather, performance-based assessment requires sufficient mastery of concepts and principles so that students are able to bring them to bear appropriately on large multifaceted problems of the sort for which learnings ought to be mobilized.

In view of the fact that teacher education remains a linchpin of such reform efforts, it is encouraging to witness the emergence of the new National Board of Professional Teaching Standards. This independent group is articulating the standards a teacher must embody in order to merit certification—a statement that he or she now exhibits a high level of professional accomplishment. As presently envisioned, these assessments will bear little resemblance to paper-and-pencil instruments like the deservedly criticized National Teachers Examination. Instead, candidates for certification will visit performance assessment centers where, in front of knowledgeable master teachers, they will demonstrate their abilities to create curricula, analyze texts, and reflect on their own teaching. A crucial feature of such assessments will be the presentation of portfolios, in which teachers document what they have already accomplished in their teaching, how they conceptualize their achievements and their challenges, and how they assess the learning of their students in a comprehensive way.

Finally, a number of cities, states, and private not-for-profit institutions have recently joined efforts to create a national examination *system.* The notion of a system is important here. Rather than mandating a single paper-and-pencil test, the architects of the New Standards approach are calling for a three-part enterprise consisting of performance-based examinations, the execution of large-scale projects, and the maintenance and submission of a portfolio. While the system would initially be voluntary, the hope is that eventually all students in the nation would participate in the system and that the option of leaving school would be linked to successful completion of these requirements. Curricula and syllabi would remain flexible, so long as they yielded students who could cope with the system successfully.

Even to state the design requirements of such a system is to suggest how remote it is from current American practices, where students graduate upon the completion of a certain number of Carnegie units, from which it is impossible to determine what they know or what they can do. Again, it is sobering to realize that such a situation of national (and, possibly, student) ignorance does not obtain in other industrialized countries. Yet in mandating projects and portfolios, the new American effort goes well beyond other national examining systems, and if such a program, with its emphasis on understandings, can be implemented successfully here, it might well serve as a model for systems in other lands as well.

Putting into place curricula, assessment instruments, and teacher certification programs of high quality will not in itself ensure an outstanding educational system. Achieving such a system will take time and effort, and many pitfalls are likely to be encountered en route. Individuals who go through the motions or the jargon of reform will fool others—and perhaps themselves—into thinking that genuine reforms have been achieved. Competent performance on standard instruments has led us to believe that certain current educational systems have in fact been more successful than they have actually been; so, too, we may delude ourselves into thinking that new reforms have achieved their stated goals when in fact they have not. Nonetheless, it is important to begin to move in this direction, and partial successes are well worth achieving and documenting.

Recognizing all the problems, I still believe that the recommended course for the future emerges clearly. Progress is needed on two separate but related fronts. On the one hand, it is important to identify those educational structural reforms that appear to be working in various American settings and to determine which of them could be implemented on a broader scale. Important experiments are being carried out by James Comer, who has pioneered with parental involvement in inner-city elementary schools; Theodore Sizer, who has set up a coalition of "essential" high schools; Stanley Pogrow, who seeks to develop higher-order thinking skills in disadvantaged children; and Henry Levin, who attempts to accelerate learning for all children. It is vital to determine which of these approaches has demonstrated success, which can be more widely disseminated, and how they might best be integrated conceptually and pragmatically.

At the same time I call for a coordinated effort to identify those conceptions and practices that, taken together, constitute stages and forms of understanding in each of the major disciplinary areas. The delineation of such understandings cannot—and should not—be the burden of any particular interest group. Rather, they should emerge from sustained dialogue among the interested parties, in particular among disciplinary experts, subject matter teachers, psychologists knowledgeable about cognition and child development, and educational experts in curriculum, pedagogy, and assessment. Once such understandings have been identified, it should then prove possible to design curricula and assessments to support their cultivation. My own belief is that such national understandings, when well defined, could be useful around the world and might even help to bring the countries of the world, and their peoples, closer together.

If we can identify valued national understandings on the one hand and effective educational organizational structures on the other, we will have taken two crucial steps toward the improvement of our schools. Bringing the pedagogical means and the educational goals together will be a time-consuming process, and there will be many mistakes and miscalculations along the way. But the effort is a critical one, one worth undertaking, and one worth doing right.

In these efforts, there is an important partner that has not yet been mentioned. I refer here to American colleges and universities. While our primary and secondary institutions have been much criticized, our institutions of higher education remain admired throughout much of the world. The signals sent by colleges concerning the kind of learning they value and the kind of students they welcome are enormously important. While the College Board has delineated reasonable curricular goals for high school graduates, it has not captured these goals in its Scholastic Aptitude Tests. Were the College Board to look for student understandings and to recommend admissions policies based on students' performances and portfolios, this message could have enormous salutary effects on precollegiate education. Such a focus would also make it less likely that colleges would have to serve as institutions of remediation.

CONSTRAINTS AND POSSIBILITIES: A DEVELOPMENTALLY ATTUNED EDUCATION

A theme pervading this book has been the recognition of constraints in human life—constraints on what humans can readily learn, constraints concerning the mastery of knowledge and its application in new directions, and constraints governing the operation of complex human institutions, among them schools, communities, and nations. The connotation of the word *constraint* is often taken negatively as a set of factors that limit or channel human possibilities. I would argue, however, that the constraints that govern human cognition are potentially constructive. It is only because of deep constraints built into our cognitive system that we are able to master the initial symbol systems of our culture, and only parallel kinds of constraints allow us to develop those initial theories of life and matter, mind and self, that usher in a productive life in our world.

Constraints can assume an even more positive connotation in later life. In my view, it is constraints that make possible genuine achievements, including human innovation and creativity. In the absence of constraints, where all is theoretically possible, it would not be possible to make and recognize advances. But the existence of constraints in human thought make possible not only the early milestones of development but also the subsequent breakthroughs—the cherished moments when humans overcome a prejudice, a bias, an entrenched way of thinking and move on to a fuller and apparently more veridical conceptualization.

By the same token, it is at those moments in human history when individuals or groups confront what had been thought to be a limit or a constraint—a fear of falling off the end of the earth, a belief that each species is sacrosanct, a conviction that parallel lines never meet—and cast it aside that horizons open up, or perhaps that they are altogether redesigned or redefined. Disciplines are organized sets of constraints, but the fact that disciplines advance and are transformed proves that these constraints can be freeing as well as limiting. Genuine human creativity necessarily honors the deepest constraints in development, but at the same time such creativity alerts our consciousness to those chains that are not inexorably linked, permitting them to break or reconfiguring them into new arrangements.

This essay began with a survey of human cognitive development, particularly a consideration of the ways in which development constrains and guides human knowledge and learning. In the past, some of our greatest minds have denied that development in any way constrains education—for them, cultures may write what they like on the blank slate of our species membership. Other seminal thinkers have seen all knowledge as immanent in our genome; from such a perspective, education is chiefly a preventive operation, where—through inaction—cultures attempt to minimize the damage that they might otherwise wreak. The classical struggles between Locke on the one hand and Rousseau on the other have reflected these profoundly contrasting views of human nature.

In more recent times, other stances have developed with respect to the relation between development and education. Among the more compelling ones, those of an anthropological or cultural frame of mind have shown how much development in fact occurs courtesy of the knowledge already encoded in the rest of the culture. In following the leads put forth by Lev Vygotsky, Jerome Bruner, and Clifford Geertz, we gain a fresh appreciation of how learning has already been codified by past generations. Younger people have the opportunity to enter into the conversation of their culture by internalizing and then building upon the insights that have already been attained.

A fourth, Deweyan perspective, as realized most recently by Lawrence Kohlberg, discerns an almost preordained harmony between development and education. In this view, education is seen as a means of fostering human development, or, indeed, development is seen as the goal of education. To the extent that development entails a deeper understanding of the physical, social, and moral universe, I strongly endorse this vision.

To these already classical visions, I propose to add a new page from the developmental sciences. We now appreciate, in a far deeper way than did previous generations, how finely our growth is constrained, both by epigenetic factors and by the operations of institutions. Such an understanding of limits need not signal despair, however. Rather, this emerging understanding of our own nature can serve as a secure guide toward the planning and implementation of an educationally more effective society. Our constraints not only make possible our vital initial learnings; they also allow the occasional creative breakthroughs of human individuals, groups, and culture, as well as the capacity to recognize these breakthroughs as such. We might even say that a delineation of the precise constraints upon the human mind may be the greatest ally in coping with, and perhaps even dissolving, some of these constraints within and across disciplines. The great twentieth-century composer Igor Stravinsky once declared, "The more constraints one imposes, the more one frees one's self of the chains that shackle the spirit." Perhaps it is time to exploit this principle in our attempts to educate the human mind.

Notes

[The numbers in brackets following a short title refer to the page number of its original, complete citation in that chapter.]

Chapter 1. Introduction: The Central Puzzles of Learning

Page
3   The coin-tossing study is described in J. Clement, "Students' Pre-conceptions in Introductory Mechanics," *American Journal of Physics* 50 (1 [1982]): 66–71; J. Clement, "A Conceptual Model Discussed by Galileo and Used Intuitively by Physics Students," in D. Gentner and A. Stevens, eds., *Mental Models* (Hillsdale, N.J.: Erlbaum, 1983). See other physics references cited in chap. 8, p. 152–59. Examples from other domains are found in chaps. 8 and 9.
4   The occurrence of these misconceptions internationally has been confirmed by my colleagues Lauren Resnick (for Europe) and Giyoo Hatano (for Japan).
11   Different kinds of minds are discussed more fully in H. Gardner, *Frames of Mind* (New York: Basic Books, 1983).

Page

Chapter 2. Conceptualizing the Development of the Mind

23   C. Darwin, "A Biographical Sketch of an Infant," *Mind* 2 (1877): 286–94.

24   B. Spock, *Baby and Child Care* (New York: Pocket Books, 1968).

24   A. Gesell, *The First Five Years of Life*, 9th ed. (New York: Harper and Row, 1940).

24   On behaviorism, see J. B. Watson, *Psychology from the Standpoint of a Behaviorist* (Philadelphia: Lippincott, 1919); B. F. Skinner, *The Behavior of Organisms: An Experimental Analysis* (New York: Appleton-Century-Crofts, 1938).

25   T. Kuhn, *The Structure of Scientific Revolutions*, 2d ed. (Chicago: University of Chicago Press, 1970).

26   For overviews of Piaget, see J. Piaget, "Piaget's Theory," in P. Mussen, ed., *Manual of Child Psychology*, vol. 1 (New York: Wiley, 1970); J. Piaget and B. Inhelder, *The Psychology of the Child* (New York: Basic Books, 1968); and the selected writings in H. Gruber and J. Voneche, eds., *The Essential Piaget* (New York: Basic Books, 1977). For secondary accounts, see J. Flavell, *The Developmental Psychology of Jean Piaget* (Princeton: Van Nostrand, 1973); H. Furth, *Piaget and Knowledge*, 2d ed. (Chicago: University of Chicago Press, 1981); H. Gardner, *The Quest for Mind: Piaget, Levi-Strauss, and the Structuralist Movement*, 2d ed. (Chicago: University of Chicago Press, 1981).

28   For critiques of Piaget, see C. Brainerd, "The Stage Question in Cognitive-Developmental Theory," *The Behavioral and Brain Sciences* 2 (1978): 173–213; P. Bryant, *Perception and Understanding in Young Children* (New York: Basic Books, 1974); H. Gardner, *Frames of Mind* (New York: Basic Books, 1983); R. Gelman, "Cognitive Development," *Annual Review of Psychology* 28 (1978): 297–332.

30   On the neo-Piagetians, see R. Case, *Intellectual Development: Birth to Adulthood* (New York: Academic Press, 1985); K. Fischer, "A Theory of Cognitive Development: The Control and Construction of Hierarchies of Skills," *Psychological Review* 97 (1980): 477–531.

31   On information-processing researchers, see D. Klahr and J. G. Wallace, *Cognitive Development: An Information-Processing View* (Hillsdale, N.J.: Erlbaum, 1976); R. Siegler, "Information-Processing Approaches to Development," in P. Mussen, ed., *Handbook of Child Psychology*, vol. 1 (New York: Wiley, 1983); R. Sternberg, ed., *Mechanisms of Cognitive Development* (New York: Freeman, 1984).

33   For Chomsky's views, see N. Chomsky, *Rules and Representation* (New York: Columbia University Press, 1980); M. Piattelli-Palmarini, ed., *Language and Learning: The Debate between Jean Piaget and Noam*

Page

        Chomsky (Cambridge: Harvard University Press, 1980); N. Chomsky, "A Review of B. F. Skinner's *Verbal Behavior*," *Language* 35 (1959): 26–58.

33   For Peirce's views, see C. Hookway, *Peirce* (London: Routledge and Kegan Paul, 1985).

33   N. Chomsky, "A Review" [33].

34   For Goodman's comments on Chomsky, see N. Goodman, "The Emperor's New Ideas," in S. Hook, ed., *Language and Philosophy* (New York: New York University Press, 1969), 138–42.

35   The biological approaches to language are described in J. Fodor, *The Modularity of Mind* (Cambridge: MIT Press, 1983); N. Geschwind, *Selected Papers on Language and the Brain* (Dodrecht-Boston: Reidel, 1974); E. Lenneberg, *Biological Foundations of Language* (New York: Wiley, 1967; A. R. Luria, *The Higher Cortical Functions in Man* (New York: Basic Books, 1966); P. Rozin, "The Evolution of Intelligence and Access to the Cognitive Unconscious," *Progress in Psychobiology and Physiological Psychology* 6 (1976): 245–80. Roman Jakobson's remarks were made in Lennenberg's presence at a lecture at Harvard 1970.

38   C. Geertz, *The Interpretation of Cultures* (New York: Basic Books, 1973). The quotation is from pp. 76, 68.

39   Cultural perspectives are discussed in J. S. Bruner, R. Olver, and P. Greenfield, *Studies in Cognitive Growth* (New York: Wiley, 1966); M. Cole and S. Cole, *The Development of Children* (New York: Freeman, 1989); M. Cole and S. Scribner, *Culture and Thought* (New York: Wiley, 1980); R. Shweder and R. LeVine, eds., *Culture Theory* (New York: Cambridge University Press, 1984); L. S. Vygotksy, *Mind in Society* (Cambridge: Harvard University Press, 1978).

Chapter 3. Initial Learnings: Constraints and Possibilities

42   On the philosophical agenda, see H. Gardner, *The Mind's New Science* (New York: Basic Books, 1985), chaps. 1, 4.

43   W. James, *The Principles of Psychology* (New York: Henry Holt, 1890).

44   On the infant repertoire and infant study, see T. G. R. Bower, *Development in Human Infancy* (New York: Freeman, 1982); W. Kessen, M. Haith, and P. Salapatek, "Infancy," in P. Mussen, ed., *Manual of Child Psychology*, vol. 1 (New York: Wiley, 1970).

45   Infant color vision is discussed in M. Bornstein, "Perceptual Development across the Life Cycle," in M. Bornstein and M. Lamb, eds., *Developmental Psychology: An Advanced Textbook*, 2d ed. (Hillsdale, N.J.: Erlbaum, 1988); M. Bornstein, W. Kessen, and S. Weiskopf,

Page

"Color Vision and Hue Categorization in Young Human Infants," *Journal of Experimental Psychology: Human Perception and Performance* 2 (1976): 115–29.

46   On infant linguistic discriminations, see P. Eimas et al., "Speech Perception in Infants," *Science* 171 (1971): 303–6; see also M. Bornstein, "Perceptual Development" [45].

46   Aspects of early musical discrimination are discussed in M. W. Chang and S. Trehub, "Auditory Processing of Relational Information by Young Infants," *Journal of Experimental Child Psychology* 24 (1977): 324–31; L. Demany, B. McKenzie, and E. Vurpillot, "Rhythm Perception in Early Infancy," *Nature* 266 (1977): 718–19; W. Kessen, J. Levine, and K. A. Wendrich, "The Imitation of Pitch in Infants," *Infant Behavior and Development* 2 (1978): 93–99; S. E. Trehub, D. Bull, and B. Schneider, "Infant Speech and Nonspeech Perception: A Review and Reevaluation" (Unpublished paper, Centre for Research in Human Development, Erindale College, University of Toronto, 1979).

47   Intermodal associations in infancy are described in T. Bower, *A Primer of Infant Development* (San Francisco: Freeman, 1977); E. Spelke, "The Development of Intermodal Perception," in L. B. Cohen and P. Salapatek, eds., *Handbook of Infant Perception* (New York: Academic Press, 1984).

47   Piaget's view of infancy is described in his *The Construction of Reality in the Child* (New York: Basic Books, 1954).

48   Revisions of the Piagetian view of infancy are found in T. Bower, *Development in Human Infancy* (New York: Freeman, 1982); C. Raymond, "Pioneering Research Challenges Accepted Notions Concerning the Cognitive Abilities of Infants," *The Chronicle of Higher Education* (January 23, 1991), A5–7; R. Baillargeon, E. Spelke, and S. Wasserman, "Object Permanence in Five-Month-Old Infants," *Cognition* 20 (1985):191–208; R. Gelman and A. Brown, "Changing Views of Cognitive Competence in the Young," in N. J. Smelser and D. R. Gerstein, eds., *Behavioral and Social Science: Fifty Years of Discovery* (Washington, D.C.: National Academy Press, 1986), 175–207; A. Leslie and S. Keeble, "Do Six-Month-Old Infants Perceive Causality?" *Cognition* 25 (1987): 265–88; A. Michotte, G. Thines, and G. Crabbe, *Les compléments amodaux des structures perceptives* (Louvain, Belgium: Publications U. Louvain, 1964); E. Spelke, "Perceptual Knowledge of Objects in Infancy," in J. Mehler, E. Walker, and M. Garrett, eds., *Perspectives on Mental Representation* (Hillsdale, N.J.: Erlbaum, 1982), 409–30; P. Starkey, E. S. Spelke, and R. Gelman, "Numerical Abstraction by Human Infants," *Cognition* 36 (1990): 97–127.

Page
49   Early social communication of the infant is discussed in B. Rogoff, *Apprenticeship in Thinking* (New York: Oxford University Press, 1990); D. Stern, *The Interpersonal World of the Infant: A View from Psychoanalysis and Developmental Psychology* (New York: Basic Books, 1985); C. Trevarthen, "Descriptive Analyses of Infant Communicative Behavior," in H. R. Schaffer, ed., *Studies in Mother-Infant Interaction* (New York: Academic Press, 1977); C. Trevarthen, "Communication and Cooperation in Early Infancy: A Description of Primary Intersubjectivity," in M. Bullowa, ed., *Before Speech: The Beginning of Interpersonal Communication* (New York: Cambridge University Press, 1979).

52   On language development in blind children, see B. Landau and L. Gleitman, *Language and Experience: Evidence from the Young Child* (Cambridge: Harvard University Press, 1985).

52   On cognitive development in thalidomide babies, see T. Gouin Décarie, "A Study of the Mental and Emotional Development of the Thalidomide Child," in B. Foss, ed., *Determinants of Infant Behavior* (London: Tavistock Clinic, 1969): 167–87.

53   Individual differences among infants are discussed in S. K. Escalona, *The Roots of Individuality: Normal Patterns of Development in Infancy* (Chicago: Aldine, 1968); J. Kagan, *The Nature of the Child* (New York: Basic Books, 1984).

53   Kaluli child-rearing is described in E. Ochs and B. Schieffelin, "Language Acquisition and Socialization: Three Developmental Stories and Their Implications," in R. Shweder and R. LeVine, eds., *Culture Theory* (New York: Cambridge University Press, 1984).

53   Gusii parental behaviors are described in R. LeVine, "Infant Environments in Psychoanalysis: A Cross-Cultural View," in J. W. Stigler, R. A. Shweder, and G. Herdt, eds., *Cultural Psychology: Essays on Comparative Human Development* (New York: Cambridge University Press, 1990).

53   On environments that "depend" and "expect," see W. T. Greenough, J. T. Black, and C. S. Wallace, "Experience and Brain Development," *Child Development* 58 (1987): 555–67.

54   On infantile amnesia, see E. Schachtel, *Metamorphosis* (New York: Basic Books, 1959).

Chapter 4. Knowing The World Through Symbols

56   Major works by scholars of semiotics include E. Cassirer, *The Philosophy of Symbolic Forms* (New Haven: Yale University Press, 1953–59); N. Goodman, *Languages of Art* (Indianapolis:

Page

Hackett, 1976); S. Langer, *Philosophy in a New Key* (Cambridge: Harvard University Press, 1942); C. S. Peirce, *Philosophical Writings*, ed. J. Buchler (London: Routledge and Kegan Paul, 1940). See also H. Gardner, *Art, Mind, and Brain* (New York: Basic Books, 1982).

56 The period of symbolic mastery is described in J. S. Bruner, R. Olver, and P. Greenfield, eds., *Studies in Cognitive Growth* (New York: Wiley, 1966); A. R. Luria, *The Making of Mind* (Cambridge: Harvard University Press, 1979); J. Piaget, *Play, Dreams, and Imitation* (New York: Norton, 1962); H. Werner and B. Kaplan, *Symbol Formation* (New York: Wiley, 1963).

58 For a discussion of language in terms of phonology, syntax, and semantics, see H. Clark and E. Clark, *Psychology and Language* (New York: Harcourt Brace Jovanovich, 1977); R. Jakobson, *Essais de linguistique generale* (Paris: Editions de minuit, 1963).

59 S. Pinker discusses language learnability in *Language Learnability and Language Development* (Cambridge: Harvard University Press, 1984); *Learnability and Cognition* (Cambridge: MIT Press, 1989); and "Language Acquisition," in M. Posner, ed., *Fundamentals of Cognitive Science* (Cambridge: MIT Press, 1989).

59 Basic proofs of learnability are discussed in E. Gold, "Language Identification in the Limit," *Information and Control* 10 (1967): 447–74; K. Wexler and P. Culicover, *Formal Principles of Language Acquisition* (Cambridge: MIT Press, 1980).

59 Gordon's study is described in P. Gordon, "Level Ordering in Lexical Development," *Cognition* 21 (1985): 73–93.

61 Doubts about learnability are expressed in J. N. Bohannon, B. MacWhinney, and C. Snow, "No Negative Evidence Revisited: Beyond Learnability, or Who Has to Prove What to Whom?" *Developmental Psychology* 26 (1990): 221–26.

62 Ellen Markman describes mutual exclusivity in "How Children Constrain the Possible Meanings of Words," in U. Neisser, ed., *Concepts and Conceptual Development* (Cambridge: Cambridge University Press, 1987), 255–87; in "Two Different Principles of Conceptual Organization," in M. E. Lamb and A. L. Brown, eds., *Advances in Developmental Psychology*, vol. 1 (Hillsdale, N.J.: Erlbaum, 1981); and in *Categories and Naming in Childhood* (Cambridge: MIT Press, 1989).

63 Critiques of mutual exclusivity are found in W. E. Merriman and L. L. Bowman, "The Mutual Exclusivity Bias in Children's Word Learning," *Monographs of the Society for Research in Child Development* 54 (1989, 3–4 Whole).

63   J. S. Bruner describes the language acquisition support system in *Child's Talk* (New York: Norton, 1983).

63   For the two sides of the controversy over "motherese," see C. E. Snow, "Mothers' Speech Research: From Input to Interaction," in C. E. Snow and C. A. Ferguson, eds., *Talking to Children: Language Input and Acquisition* (New York: Cambridge University Press, 1979); and E. Wanner and L. R. Gleitman, eds., *Language Acquisition: State of the Art* (Cambridge: Cambridge University Press, 1982).

65   W. V. O. Quine's discussion of the word *gavagai* is in his *Word and Object* (Cambridge: MIT Press, 1960). The quotation is from p. 52.

65   On prototypes, see E. Rosch et al., "Basic Objects in Natural Categories," *Cognitive Psychology* 8 (1976): 382–439.

66   The onset of naming is discussed by W. Stern in *The Psychology of Early Childhood up to the Sixth Year of Age* (New York: Henry Holt, 1926); Helen Keller's description of her own experience is in *The Story of My Life* (New York: Doubleday, 1903).

66   Features that are noted and exploited are discussed in S. A. Gelman and J. D. Coley, "The Importance of Knowing a Dodo Is a Bird: Categories and Inferences in Two-Year-Old Children," *Developmental Psychology* 26 (1990): 796–804; D. Gentner and M. R. Ratterman, "Language and the Career of Similarity," in S. A. Gelman and J. P. Byrnes, eds., *Perspectives on Thought and Language: Interrelations in Development* (London: Cambridge University Press, in press); F. Keil, *Concepts, Kinds, and Cognitive Development* (Cambridge: MIT Press, 1989); L. Smith and D. Heise, "Perceptual Similarity and Conceptual Similarity" (*Indiana Cognitive Science Report*, Indiana University, 1990).

67   On scripts, see R. Fivush, "Scripts and Categories: Interrelationships in Development," in U. Neisser, ed., *Concepts and Conceptual Development* (New York: Cambridge University Press, 1987); K. Nelson, *Event Knowledge: Structure and Function in Development* (Hillsdale, N.J.: Erlbaum, 1986).

68   Language use in different communities is described by S. B. Heath in *Ways with Words: Language, Life, and Work in Communities and Classrooms* (New York: Cambridge University Press, 1983). See also E. Ochs, "Indexicality and Socialization," in J. A. Stigler, R. A. Shweder, and G. Herdt, eds., *Cultural Psychology: Essays on Comparative Human Development* (New York: Cambridge University Press, 1990); K. Watson-Gegeo and D. Gegeo, "Calling Out and Repeating Routines in Ka ara'ae Children's Language Socialization," in B. Schieffelin and E. Ochs, eds., *Language Socialization across Cultures* (New York: Cambridge University Press, 1986).

68   Use of scripts after damage to the brain is discussed in S. Weylman, H. Brownell, and H. Gardner, " 'It's What You Mean, Not What You Say': Pragmatic Language Use in Brain-Damaged Patients," in F. Plum, ed., *Language, Communication, and the Brain* (New York: Raven Press, 1988).

69   On the birth of play, see G. Bateson, "A Theory of Play and Fantasy," *Psychiatric Research Reports* 2 (1955): 39–51.

69   A. Leslie, "Pretense and Representation: The Origins of 'Theory of Mind,' " *Psychological Review* 94 (1987): 412–26; J. A. Fodor, *The Language of Thought* (New York: Crowell, 1975).

72   The study of early symbolization is described in H. Gardner and D. Wolf, "Waves and Streams of Symbolization," in D. R. Rogers and J. A. Sloboda, eds., *The Acquisition of Symbolic Skills* (London: Plenum Press, 1983) and in H. Gardner, "The Development of Symbolic Literacy," in M. Wrolstad and D. Fisher, eds., *Toward a Greater Understanding of Literacy* (New York: Praeger, 1986). Major colleagues on this study include Lyle Davidson, Martha Davis, George Forman, Patricia McKernon, Eric Phelps, Shelley Rubin, George Scarlett, Jennifer Shotwell, and Joseph Walters.

77   The correspondence of waves of symbolization with other schemes of cognitive development can be seen in J. S. Bruner, R. R. Olver, and P. M. Greenfield, eds., *Studies in Cognitive Growth* (New York: Wiley, 1966). It was also mentioned by R. Case in a personal communication, November 1990. For correspondence of specific crests, see E. Bates, *Emergence of Symbols: Cognition and Communication in Infancy* (New York: Academic Press, 1979); M. W. Watson and K. W. Fischer, "Development of Social Roles in Elicited and Spontaneous Behavior during the Preschool Years," *Developmental Psychology* 16 (1980): 483–94; J. DeLoache, "Rapid Change in the Symbolic Functioning of Very Young Children," *Science* 238 (1987): 1556–57.

78   For recent studies of simple counting procedures, see R. Case, *Intellectual Development: Birth to Adulthood* (New York: Academic Press, 1985); K. Fuson, *Children's Counting and Concepts of Number* (New York: Springer-Verlag, 1988).

78   Incipient sensitivity to genre is discussed in D. Wolf et al., "Beyond A, B, and C: A Broader and Deeper View of Literacy," in A. Pelligrini, ed., *Psychological Bases of Early Education* (Chichester, England: Wiley, 1988), 123–52.

80   On the theory of multiple intelligences, see H. Gardner, *Frames of Mind* (New York: Basic Books, 1983). For work building on the theory of multiple intelligences, see H. Gardner, "Intelligence in Seven Phases," *Proceedings of the Symposium in Honor of 100 Years*

of Education at Harvard University (in press); H. Gardner, "Balancing Specialized and Comprehensive Knowledge: The Growing Educational Challenge," in T. Sergiovanni, ed., *Schooling for Tomorrow: Directing Reforms to Issues That Count* (Boston: Allyn and Bacon, 1989); H. Gardner, "The School of the Future," *The Reality Club* 3 (1991): 199–218; H. Gardner and T. Hatch, "Multiple Intelligences Go to School," *Educational Researcher* 18 (1989): 4–10; J. Walters and H. Gardner, "The Development and Education of Multiple Intelligences," in F. Link, ed., *Essays on the Intellect* (Washington, D.C.: Curriculum Development Associates, 1985).

82 The period from age two to age seven is discussed in H. Gardner, *The Arts and Human Development* (New York: Wiley, 1983).

Chapter 5. The Worlds of the Preschooler: The Emergence of Intuitive Understandings

84 Instruction in China is described in H. Gardner, *To Open Minds: Chinese Clues to the Dilemma of Contemporary Education* (New York: Basic Books, 1989).

87 Frank Keil discusses children's ontology in *Semantic and Conceptual Development* (Cambridge: Harvard University Press, 1979); in "Constraints on Knowledge and Cognitive Development," *Psychological Review* 88 (1981): 197–227; and in "Mechanisms in Cognitive Development and the Structure of Knowledge," in R. J. Sternberg, ed., *Mechanisms of Cognitive Development* (New York: Freeman, 1984).

88 On the child's sense of number, see R. Case and S. Griffin, "Child Cognitive Development: The Role of Central Conceptual Structures in the Development of Scientific and Social Thought," in C. A. Hauert, ed., *Advances in Psychology* (Amsterdam: North Holland Press, 1990); R. Gelman and E. Meck, "Early Principles Aid Early But Not Later Conceptions of Number," in J. Bideaud and C. Meljac, eds., *Les Chemins du Nombre* (in press); R. Gelman and C. R. Gallistel, *The Child's Understanding of Number* (Cambridge: Harvard University Press, 1979); R. Gelman, "First Principles Organize Attention to and Learning About Relevant Data: Number and the Animate-Inanimate Distinction as Examples" (Unpublished paper, University of Pennsylvania, 1989); R. Gelman and A. Brown, "Changing Views of Cognitive Competence in the Young," in N. J. Smelser and D. R. Gerstein, eds., *Behavioral and Social Science: Fifty Years of Discovery* (Washington, D.C.: National Academy Press, 1986); R. Gelman and J. Greeno, "On the Nature of Competence:

Principles for Understanding in a Domain," in L. B. Resnick, ed., *Knowing, Learning, and Instruction: Essays in Honor of Robert Glaser* (Hillsdale, N.J.: Erlbaum, 1989); J. Greeno, "Some Conjectures About Number Sense" (Unpublished paper, Institute for Research in Learning, Palo Alto, Calif., 1989).

88   Problems in mastering number lines were discussed by R. Siegler and R. Case in a presentation of their research on number lines in disadvantaged populations (McDonnell Foundation Workshop on Cognitive Studies in Education, Pittsburgh, December 1990).

89   The child's theories about mechanics are discussed in A. DiSessa, "Unlearning Aristotelian Physics: A Study of Knowledge-Based Learning," *Cognitive Science* 6 (1 [1982]): 37–76; A. DiSessa, "Phenomenology and the Evolution of Intuition," in D. Gentner and A. Stevens, eds., *Mental Models* (Hillsdale, N.J.: Erlbaum, 1983), 15–34; C. Massey and R. Gelman, "Preschoolers Decide Whether Pictured Unfamiliar Objects Can Move Themselves," *Developmental Psychology* 24 (1988): 307–17.

90   A. Brown, "Domain-Specific Principles Affect Learning and Transfer in Children," *Cognitive Science* 14 (1990): 107–33.

91   S. Carey, *Conceptual Change in Childhood* (Cambridge: MIT Press, 1985).

92   On the child's theories of matter and theories of life, see R. Gelman and A. Brown, "Changing Views" [88]; S. A. Gelman and J. D. Coley, "Language and Categorization: The Acquisition of Natural Kind Terms," in S. A. Gelman and J. P. Byrnes, eds., *Perspectives on Language and Thought: Interrelations in Development* (New York: Cambridge University Press, in press).

92   Bertrand Russell's remark is quoted in R. Clark, *Einstein: The Life and Times* (New York: Avon, 1972), 124.

92   On theory of mind, see J. Astington, P. Harris, and D. Olson, eds., *Developing Theories of Mind* (New York: Cambridge University Press, 1988), especially J. Perner, "Developing Semantics for Theories of Mind" (pp. 141–72), and H. Wimmer, J. Hofgrete, and B. Sodian, "A Second Stage in Children's Conception of Mental Life: Understanding Informational Accesses as Origins of Knowledge and Belief" (pp. 173–92). See also Flavell et al., "Young Children's Understanding of Fact Beliefs versus Value Beliefs," *Child Development* 61 (1990): 915–28; C. Pratt and P. Bryant, "Young Children Understand That Looking Leads to Knowing (So Long as They Are Looking into a Single Barrel)," *Child Development* 61 (1990): 973–82; H. Wellman, *The Child's Theory of Mind* (Cambridge: MIT/Bradford Press, 1990); H. Wimmer and J. Perner, "Beliefs About Beliefs: Representation and Constraining Function of Wrong Beliefs in

Young Children's Understanding of Deception," *Cognition* 13 (1983): 103–28.

93   Queen Elizabeth's comment is quoted in S. Wells, ed., *The New Penguin Shakespeare: Richard II* (London: Penguin, 1969), 13.

94   On views of self, see C. Dweck and E. Elliot, "Achievement Motivation," in P. Mussen, ed., *Handbook of Child Psychology*, vol. 4 (New York: Wiley, 1983); J. Ogbu, *Minority Education and Caste: The American System in Cross-Cultural Perspective* (New York: Academic Press, 1978).

96   On the stages of development of a theory of mind, see D. Olson, "Making Up Your Mind," *Canadian Psychology* 30 (1989): 617–27; D. R. Olson, "Representation and Misrepresentation: On the Beginnings of Symbolization in Young Children," in D. Tirosh, ed., *Implicit and Explicit Knowledge: An Educational Approach* (Norwood, N.J.: Ablex, in press).

97   On the child's understanding of irony, see E. Winner, *The Point of Words* (Cambridge: Harvard University Press, 1988); E. Winner and S. Leekam, "Distinguishing Irony from Deception: Understanding the Speaker's Second-Order Intention," *British Journal of Developmental Psychology*, Special Issue on Theory of Mind (in press).

99   On script knowledge, see K. Nelson, *Event Knowledge: Structure and Function in Development* (Hillsdale, N.J.: Erlbaum, 1986).

99   Stereotypes are discussed by E. Maccoby in "Children Are Ruthless Stereotypers" (Address to the American Psychological Society, reported in *The American Psychological Society Observer*, July 1990, 5–7).

100   On performances of understanding in young children, see R. Coles, *The Spiritual Life of Children* (Boston: Little, Brown, 1990).

100   On esthetic standards, see H. Gardner, *Artful Scribbles* (New York: Basic Books, 1980); M. Parsons, *How We Understand Art* (New York: Cambridge University Press, 1987).

100   Esthetic conceptions are discussed in H. Gardner, E. Winner, and M. Kircher, "Children's Conceptions of the Arts," *Journal of Aesthetic Education* 9 (1975): 60–77; A. K. Rosenstiel, et al., "Critical Judgment: A Developmental Study," *Journal of Aesthetic Education* 12 (1978): 95–107.

101   On early moral values, see R. A. Shweder, M. Mahaptara, and J. G. Miller, "Culture and Moral Development," in J. W. Stigler et al., eds., *Cultural Psychology: Essays on Comparative Human Development* (New York: Cambridge University Press, 1990).

101   On taste, see P. Bourdieu, *In Other Words: Essays Toward a Reflective Sociology*, trans. Matthew Adamson (Stanford: Stanford University Press, 1990).

102   Temperament and personality are discussed in W. Damon, *Social and Personality Development: Infancy Through Adolescence* (New York: Norton, 1983); S. Escalona, *The Roots of Individuality* (Chicago: Aldine, 1969); J. Kagan, *The Nature of the Child* (New York: Basic Books, 1984).

102   On constraints, see S. Carey and R. Gelman, eds., *Structural Constraints in Cognitive Development* (Hillsdale, N.J.: Erlbaum, in press).

103   Basic cognitive capacities are discussed in J. Kagan and R. Klein, "Cross-Cultural Perspectives on Early Development," *American Psychologist* 28 (1973): 947–61.

105   On schooled and unschooled children, see P. R. Dasen, *Piagetian Psychology: Cross-Cultural Contributions* (New York: Gardner, 1977); A. R. Luria, *Cognitive Development* (Cambridge: Harvard University Press, 1976); S. Scribner and M. Cole, "Cognitive Consequences of Formal and Informal Education," *Science* 182 (1973): 553–59; S. Scribner and M. Cole, *The Psychology of Literacy* (Cambridge: Harvard University Press, 1981).

107   Metamemory and metacognition are discussed in A. L. Brown, "Knowing When, Where, and How to Remember: A Problem of Metacognition," in R. Glaser, ed., *Advances in Instructional Psychology*, vol. 1 (Hillsdale, N.J.: Erlbaum, 1978); J. H. Flavell, "Metacognition and Cognitive Monitoring: A New Area of Cognitive-Developmental Inquiry," *American Psychologist* 34 (1979): 906–11; D. Kuhn, ed., *Developmental Perspectives on Teaching and Learning Thinking Skills* (Basel: Karger, 1990).

107   For discussions of U-shaped curves, see S. Strauss, ed., *U*-Shaped Behavioral Growth (New York: Academic Press, 1982); see especially H. Gardner and E. Winner, "First Intimations of Artistry," in the Strauss volume just cited; and A. Karmiloff-Smith, "From Meta-Processes to Conscious Access: Evidence from Children's Metalinguistic and Repair Data," *Cognition* 23 (1986): 95–147.

110   On the strengths and weaknesses of the five-year-old's mind, see M. Chi and R. D. Koeske, "Network Representation of a Child's Dinosaur Knowledge," *Developmental Psychology* 19 (1983): 29–39; D. Feldman, *Nature's Gambit* (New York: Basic Books, 1986); H. Gardner, *The Arts and Human Development* (New York: Wiley, 1973). For a general discussion, see S. J. Gould, *Ontogeny and Phylogeny* (Cambridge: Harvard University Press, 1977). The quotation from Nietzsche is courtesy of Rudolf Arnheim in a personal communication, November 1990. The Freud quotation is from his *Moses and Monotheism* (New York: Random House, 1939), 161.

112   The lines by Lepicié are quoted on the label for the painting at the National Gallery in London.

Chapter 6. The Values and Traditions of Education

119   On mimetic and transformative approaches to teaching, see P. Jackson, *The Practice of Teaching* (New York: Teachers College Press, 1986).

119   On creativity versus basic skills, see H. Gardner, *To Open Minds: Chinese Clues to the Dilemma of Contemporary Education* (New York: Basic Books, 1989).

121   Apprenticeships, in the past and the present, are discussed in J. Bowen, *A History of Western Education*, vol. I (London: Methuen, 1982); A. Collins, J. S. Brown, and S. E. Newman, "Cognitive Apprenticeship: Teaching the Crafts of Reading, Writing, and Mathematics," in L. Resnick, ed., *Knowing, Learning and Instruction* (Hillsdale, N.J.: Erlbaum, 1989); S. Hamilton, *Apprenticeship for Adulthood: Preparing Youth for the Future* (New York: Free Press, 1990); D. Hawkins, *The Informed Vision* (New York: Agathon Press, 1974); J. Lave, *Cognition in Practice: Mind, Mathematics, and Culture in Everyday Life* (New York: Cambridge University Press, 1989); L. Resnick, "Learning in School and Out," *Educational Researcher* 16 (9 [1987]): 13–20; B. Rogoff, *Apprenticeship in Thinking* (New York: Oxford University Press, 1990).

122   M. Polanyi, *Personal Knowledge* (Chicago: University of Chicago Press, 1958), 53.

123   On training in weaving, see C. P. Childs and P. M. Greenfield, "Informal Modes of Learning and Teaching: The Case of Zinacanteco Learning," in N. Warren, ed., *Studies in Cross-Cultural Psychology*, vol. 2 (New York: Academic Press, 1980); P. M. Greenfield and J. Lave, "Cognitive Aspects of Informal Education," in D. A. Wagner and H. E. Stevenson, eds., *Cultural Perspectives on Child Development* (New York: Freeman, 1982); B. Rogoff and J. Lave, eds., *Everyday Cognition* (Cambridge: Harvard University Press, 1984).

Chapter 7. The Institution Called School

126   On paleolithic notations, see A. Marshack, "Hierarchical Evolution of the Human Capacity: The Paleolithic Evidence" (Fifty-fourth James Arthur lecture on the evolution of the human brain, American Museum of National History, New York, 1985); A. Marshack, "Some Implications of the Paleolithic Symbolic Evidence for the Origin of Language," *Current Anthropology* 17 (2 [1976]): 274–82.

126   The invention of notations is discussed in A. Aveni, "Non-Western Notational Frameworks and the Role of Anthropology in Our Understanding of Literacy," in M. E. Wrolstad and D. F. Fisher, eds.,

Toward a New Understanding of Literacy (New York: Praeger, 1986); I. Gelb, *A Study of Writing* (Chicago: University of Chicago Press, 1963).

127   On the history of schools in different cultures, see M. J. Fischer, *Iran: From Religious Dispute to Revolution* (Cambridge: Harvard University Press, 1980); J. Henry, "A Cross-Cultural Outline of Education," *Current Anthropology* 1 (4 [1960]): 267–305.

129   Bush schools are described in M. H. Watkins, "The West African 'Bush' School," *American Journal of Sociology* 48 (1943): 666–77.

129   On South Seas navigation, see T. Gladwin, *East Is a Big Bird: Navigation and Logic on Puluwat Atoll* (Cambridge: Harvard University Press, 1970).

129   On schooling in Sweden, see H. Graff, "Whither the History of Literacy: The Future of the Past," *Communication* 11 (1988): 5–22.

131   The material on modern secular schools is largely drawn from H. Gardner, *Frames of Mind* (New York: Basic Books, 1983) and the references cited in that book.

132   Epistemic forms were discussed by D. Perkins and A. Collins in a workshop sponsored by The MacArthur Foundation, Harvard University, January 1990.

132   On the history of testing, see D. P. Resnick and L. B. Resnick, "Standards, Curriculum, and Performance: A Historical and Comparative Perspective," *Educational Researcher* 14 (April 1985): 5–20 and the references cited there.

133   On the arbitrariness of knowledge measured on standardized tests, see U. Neisser, *Cognition and Reality* (San Francisco: Freeman, 1976).

134   On school as a context in itself, see M. Solomon, "Decontextualization: Does It Really Explain the Cognitive Effects of Schooling?" (Unpublished paper, Harvard Graduate School of Education, 1990); C. Strauss, "Beyond 'Formal' versus 'Informal Education': Use of Psychological Theory in Anthropological Research," *Ethos* 12 (3 [1984]): 195–222.

134   On talk in school, see H. Mehan, *Learning Lessons: Social Organization in the Classroom* (Cambridge: Harvard University Press, 1979); D. Olson, "From Utterance to Text: The Bias of Language in Speech and Writing," *Harvard Educational Review* 47 (1977): 257–82; D. Olson and J. W. Astington, "Talking about Text: How Literacy Contributes to Thought," *Journal of Pragmatics* (in press).

135   L. Vygotsky, *Thought and Language* (Cambridge: MIT Press, 1981).

136   Distributed knowledge is discussed in R. Pea, "Distributed Intelligence and Education," in D. N. Perkins et al., eds., *Teaching for Understanding in the Age of Technology* (in press); D. Perkins, "Person Plus: A Distributed View of Thinking and Learning" (Paper

presented at the American Educational Research Association meetings, Boston, April 1990).

136   On the general effects of school, see M. Cole and S. Scribner, *Culture and Thought* (New York: Wiley, 1974); B. Rogoff, *Apprenticeships in Thinking* (New York: Oxford University Press, 1990).

136   On the effects of literacy per se, see D. Olson, "Literacy Is Metalinguistic Activity," in D. R. Olson and N. Torrance, eds., *Literacy and Orality* (New York: Cambridge University Press, in press); S. Scribner and M. Cole, *The Psychology of Literacy* (Cambridge: Harvard University Press, 1981).

137   Constraints within scholastic institutions are discussed in R. Callahan, *Education and the Cult of Efficiency* (Chicago: University of Chicago Press, 1962); C. Handy and R. Aitken, *Understanding Schools as Organizations* (Harmondsworth, Middlesex, England: Penguin, 1986); L. McNeil, *The Contradictions of Control: School Structure and School Nature* (New York: Methuen, 1986); S. Sarason, *The Culture of the School and the Problem of Change* (Boston: Allyn and Bacon, 1971); T. B. Timar and D. L. Kirp, *Managing Educational Excellence* (New York: Falmer Press, 1988); A. T. Wise, *Legislated Learning: The Bureaucratization of the American Classroom* (Los Angeles: University of California Press, 1978). I am grateful to Mindy Kornhaber for bringing several of these references to my attention.

138   T. Kidder, *Among Schoolchildren* (New York: Avon Books, 1989). The quotation is from p. 115.

140   On the protective devices of school, see D. Cohen, "Educational Technology and Social Organization," in R. Nickerson and P. Zodhiates, *Technology in Education: Looking Toward 2020* (Hillsdale, N.J.: Erlbaum, 1988), 231–64; L. Cuban, "Restructuring Again, Again, and Again," *Educational Researcher* 19 (1 [1990]): 3–13; S. M. Johnson, *Teacher at Work* (New York: Basic Books, 1990); S. Sarason, *Schooling in America: Scapegoat and Salvation* (New York: Free Press, 1983).

141   L. McNeil, *Contradictions* [137]. The quotation is from p. xviii.

Chapter 8. The Difficulties Posed by School: Misconceptions in the Sciences

144   The advent of universal schooling is discussed in L. Cremin, *American Education: The Metropolitan Experience* (New York: Harper and Row, 1988); D. Tyack, *The One Best System* (Cambridge: Harvard University Press, 1974).

144   On the Committee of Ten, see E. Boyer, *High School* (New York: Harper and Row, 1983); D. Ravitch, *The Schools We Deserve* (New

York: Basic Books, 1985). The Committee's pronouncement is quoted in the Ravitch book, p. 138.

146   Conservation studies and conflict are discussed in J. S. Bruner, R. Olver, and P. M. Greenfield, *Studies in Cognitive Growth* (New York: Wiley, 1966).

148   Literacy in colonial America is discussed in B. Bailyn, *Education in the Forming of American Society* (Chapel Hill, N.C.: University of North Carolina Press, 1960); R. Butts and L. Cremin, *A History of Education in American Culture* (New York: Holt, 1953); D. Tyack, *One Best System* [144].

148   P. Freire, *Pedagogy of the Oppressed* (New York: Seabury Press, 1971).

152   A. DiSessa, "Unlearning Aristotelian Physics: A Study of Knowledge-Based Learning," *Cognitive Science* 6 (1 [1982]): 37–75. The quotation is from pp. 58–59.

154   Misconceptions in physics are discussed in A. Arons, "Toward Wider Public Understanding of Science," *American Journal of Physics* 41 (1973): 769–76; B. Bruce, J. Gee, and J. Whitla, "Report of the Literacies Institute" (Educational Development Center, Newton, Mass., 1989); A. Caramazza, M. McCloskey, and B. Green, "Naive Beliefs in 'Sophisticated' Subjects: Misconceptions about Trajectories of Objects," *Cognition* 9 (2 [1981]): 117–23; J. Clement, "Student Preconceptions of Introductory Mechanics," *American Journal of Physics* 50 (1982): 66–71; A. DiSessa, "Phenomonology and the Evolution of Intuition," in D. Gentner and A. Stevens, eds., *Mental Models* (Hillsdale, N.J.: Erlbaum, 1983); J. Larkin, "The Role of Problem Representation in Physics," in D. Gentner and A. L. Stevens, eds., *Mental Models* (Hillsdale, N.J.: Erlbaum, 1983); M. McCloskey, A. Caramazza, and B. Green, "Curvilinear Motion in the Absence of External Forces: Naive Beliefs about the Motion of Objects," *Science* 210 (1980): 1139–41; R. Osborne, "Children's Dynamics," *The Physics Teacher* (November 1984), 504–8; G. Posner et al., "Accommodation of a Scientific Conception: Toward a Theory of Conceptual Change," *Science Education* 66 (2 [1982]): 211–27; E. Smith and R. Tyler, *Appraising and Recording Student Progress* (New York: Harper, 1942).

155   The commitment to a Newtonian view is described in G. Posner et al., "Accommodation" [154]; the quotation is from p. 219.

158   On biological misconceptions, see B. Bishop and C. Anderson, "Student Conceptions of Natural Selection and Its Role in Evolution," *Journal of Research in Science Teaching* 27 (1990): 415–27; S. Carey, *Conceptual Change in Childhood* (Cambridge: MIT Press, 1985); E. Gellert, "Children's Conceptions of the Content and Function of the Human Body," *Genetic Psychology Monographs* 65 (1962): 291–411; G. Hatano and K. Inagaki, "Everyday Biology and School Biology:

How Do They Interact?" *Quarterly Newsletter of the Laboratory of Comparative Human Cognition* 9 (October 1987): 120–28; A. C. Hildebrand, "Confusing Chromosome Number and Structure: A Common Student Error" (Unpublished paper, University of California at Berkeley, 1990); J. Kinnear, "Identification of Misconceptions in Genetics and the Use of Computer Simulation in Their Correction," in H. Helm and J. Novak, eds., *Proceedings of the International Seminar on Misconceptions in Science and Mathematics* (Ithaca: Cornell University, Department of Education, 1983), 84–92; D. Perkins et al., "Inside Understanding," in D. Perkins et al., eds., *Teaching for Understanding in the Age of Technology* (in press); J. Stewart, "Student Problem Solving in High School Genetics," *Science Education* 67 (1983): 523–40; J. H. Wandersee, "Students' Misconceptions about Photosynthesis: A Cross-Age Study," in Helm and Novak, just cited, 441–65; J. P. Mestre and J. Lochhead, *Academic Preparation in Science*, 2d ed. (New York: The College Board, 1990).

160   Problems in algebra are discussed in J. Lochhead and J. Mestre, "From Words to Algebra: Mending Misconceptions," in A. Coxford and A. Schulte, eds., *The Ideas of Algebra K–12* (Reston, Va.: National Council of Teachers of Mathematics, 1988), 127–35; P. Rosnick, "Some Misconceptions Concerning the Concept of Variable," *Mathematics Teacher* 74 (1981): 418–20.

162   Problems in the decimal system are discussed in J. Hiebert, "Mathematical, Cognitive, and Instructional Analyses of Decimal Fractions," in G. Leinhardt and R. T. Putnam, *Cognitive Research: Mathematics Learning and Instruction* (in press); T. Kieren, "Rational and Fractional Numbers as Mathematical and Personal Knowledge: Implications for Curriculum and Instruction," also in Leinhardt and Putnam, *Cognitive Research*, just cited.

162   On the word *is*, see P. Nesher, "Microworlds in Mathematical Education: A Pedagogical Realism," in L. Resnick, ed., *Knowing, Learning, and Instruction* (Hillsdale, N.J.: Erlbaum, 1989), 197–216. See also P. Rosnick, "Some Misconceptions Concerning the Concept of Variable," *The Mathematics Teacher* 74 (September 1981): 418–520; P. Rosnick, "The Uses of Letters in Precalculus Algebra" (Unpublished doctoral dissertation, University of Massachusetts, 1982).

162   E. W. Orr, *Twice as Less* (New York: Norton, 1987).

163   On programming problems, see D. Perkins et al., "Conditions of Learning in Novice Programmers," *Journal of Educational Computing Research* 2 (1 [1986]): 37–56; D. Perkins and R. Simmons, "Patterns of Misunderstanding: An Integrative Model for Science, Math, and Programming," *Review of Educational Research* 58 (1988): 303–26.

164   P. Cobb, "The Tension between Theories of Learning and Instruction in Mathematics Education," *Educational Psychologist* 23 (1988): 87–103; the quotation is from p. 98. See also L. Resnick and S. F. Omanson, "Learning to Understand Arithmetic," in R. Glaser, ed., *Advances in Instructional Psychology* (Hillsdale, N.J.: Erlbaum, 1987), 41–95; J. T. Sowder, "Making Sense of Numbers in School Mathematics," in G. Leinhardt and R. P. Putnam, *Cognitive Research: Mathematics Learning and Instruction* (in press).

164   R. Lawler, "The Progressive Construction of Mind," *Cognitive Science* 5 (1981): 1–39.

165   Problems in solving arithmetical problems are discussed in G. Hatano and K. Inagaki, "Sharing Cognition through Collective Comprehension Activity," in L. Resnick and J. Levine, eds., *Socially Shared Cognition* (Washington, D.C.: American Psychological Association, in press); M. Lampert, "Teaching Mathematics," *Journal of Mathematical Behavior* 5 (1986): 241–80; M. Lampert, "Knowing, Doing, and Teaching Multiplication," *Cognition and Instruction* 3 (1986): 305–42; N. Minick, "Comments on the Problematic Relationship between Task/Goal and Cognitive Technologies in Classroom Discourse and Practice" (Paper presented at the American Educational Research Association, Boston, April 1990).

165   On the divergence of school math and "real" math, see A. Schonfield, "When Good Teaching Leads to Bad Results: The Disasters of 'Well-Taught' Mathematics Courses," *Educational Psychologist* 23 (2 [1988]): 145–66.

Chapter 9. More Difficulties Posed by School: Stereotypes in the Social Sciences and the Humanities

168   J. Voss et al., "Informal Reasoning and Subject Matter Knowledge in the Solving of Economics Problems by Naive and Novice Individuals," in L. Resnick, ed., *Knowing, Learning, and Instruction* (Hillsdale, N.J.: Erlbaum, 1989), 217–50; J. Voss et al., "Problem Solving Skill in the Social Sciences," in G. H. Bower, *The Psychology of Learning and Motivation: Advances in Research Theory*, vol. 17 (New York: Academic Press, 1983), 165–213.

168   D. Perkins, *Knowledge as Design* (Hillsdale, N.J.: Erlbaum, 1986); D. Perkins, "Postprimary Education Has Little Impact on Informal Reasoning," *Journal of Educational Psychology* 77 (1985): 562–71.

169   On statistical misjudgments, see D. Kahneman, P. Slovic, and A. Tversky, eds., *Judgment and Uncertainty: Heuristics and Biases* (New York: Cambridge University Press, 1972); A. Tversky and D. Kahneman, "Extentional vs. Intuitive Reasoning: The Conjunc-

tion Fallacy in Probability Judgment," *Psychological Review* 90 (1983): 237–304; A. Tversky and D. Kahneman, "The Framing of Decisions and the Psychology of Choice," *Science* 211 (1981): 453–58.

171   On the fundamental attribution error, see L. Ross, "The Intuitive Psychologist and His Shortcomings: Distortions in the Attribution Process," in L. Berkowitz, ed., *Advances in Experimental Social Psychology*, vol. 10 (New York: Academic Press, 1977), 173–220.

171   J. Baron, "Harmful Heuristics and the Improvement of Thinking," in D. Kuhn, ed., *Developmental Perspectives on Teaching and Learning Thinking Skills* (Basel: Karger, 1990).

172   Problems in reading expository writing are discussed in I. Beck and M. G. McKeown, "Expository Text for Young Readers: The Issue of Coherence," in L. Resnick, ed., *Knowing, Learning, and Instruction* (Hillsdale, N.J.: Erlbaum, 1989), 47–66.

173   Stereotypes in the humanities and social sciences are discussed in R. Anderson, "The Notion of Schemata and the Educational Enterprise," in R. C. Anderson, R. S. Spiro, and W. E. Montagu, eds., *Schooling and the Acquisition of Knowledge* (Hillsdale, N.J.: Erlbaum, 1979), 415–31; I. Beck, M. McKeown, and E. Gromoll, "Learning from Social Studies Texts," *Cognition and Instruction* 6 (2 [1989]): 99–158; W. Kintsch, "Learning from Text," in L. Resnick, ed., *Knowing, Learning, and Instruction* (Hillsdale, N.J.: Erlbaum, 1989), 1–24; B. Tuchman, S. M. Wilson, and S. S. Wineburg, "Peering at History Through Different Lenses: The Role of Disciplinary Perspectives in Teaching History," *Teachers College Record* 89 (1988): 525–39.

174   T. Holt, *Thinking Historically* (New York: The College Entrance Examination Board [D. P. Wolf, Coordinating Editor], 1990); on student involvement in the use of historical sources, see also P. Boyer and S. Nissenbaum, *Salem Possessed: The Social Origins of Witchcraft* (Cambridge: Harvard University Press, 1974).

174   On conversational postulates, see H. P. Grice, "Logic and Conversation," in P. Cole and J. L. Morgan, eds., *Syntax and Semantics*, vol. 3, *Speech Acts* (New York: Seminar Press, 1975), 41–58.

174   G. Leinhardt, "Weaving Instructional Explanations in History" (*Learning Research and Development Center Technical Report*, Pittsburgh, August 1990).

175   J. Bamberger, "Intuitive and Formal Musical Knowledge," in S. Madeja, ed., *The Arts, Cognition, and Basic Skills* (St. Louis: CEMREL, 1982); "Revisiting Children's Descriptions of Simple Rhythms," in S. Strauss, ed., *U-Shaped Behavioral Growth* (New York: Academic Press, 1982).

177   I. A. Richards, *Practical Criticism* (New York: Harcourt Brace, 1929);
       the quotation is from p. 12. See also J. A. Zaharias, "Literature
       Anthologies in the United States: Impediments to Good Teaching
       Practice," *English Journal* (October 1989): 22–27.
          On good argumentation, see A. Lesgold, "Facilitating dialectical
       interaction in school subject matters" (Presentation to the Mc-
       Donnell Foundation Workshop on Cognitive Studies and Educa-
       tion, University of Pittsburgh, December 1990).

178   Conceptions about art are discussed in H. Gardner, *Art Education
       and Human Development* (Los Angeles: Getty Center for Education
       in the Arts, 1990); M. Parsons, *How We Understand Art* (New York:
       Cambridge University Press, 1987). For conceptions in other art
       forms, see H. Gardner, *The Arts and Human Development* (New York:
       Wiley, 1973), chap. 5.

Chapter 10. The Search for Solutions: Dead Ends and Promising Means

186   D. Perkins et al., "Inside Understanding," in D. Perkins et al., *Teaching
       for Understanding in the Age of Technology* (in press).

186   The most widely cited call for basic skills is *A Nation at Risk: The
       Imperative for Educational Reform* (Washington, D.C.: National
       Commission on Excellence in Education, 1983).

187   Saving students time was discussed in J. Rush, "Conceptual Con-
       sistency and Problem Solving: Tools to Evaluate Learning in Studio
       Art" (Paper presented at the Workshop on Evaluation in Art Ed-
       ucation, Boosenhooft, The Netherlands, December 1990); the quo-
       tation is from p. 18.

187   Changes in school population and practices are discussed in A. Powell,
       E. Ferrar, and D. Cohen, *The Shopping Mall High School: Winners
       and Losers in the Educational Marketplace* (Boston: Houghton Mif-
       flin, 1985).

188   On teachers' reading habits, see C. E. Feistritzer, *Profiles of Teachers
       in the United States* (Washington, D.C.: National Center for Edu-
       cation Information, 1986), 61.

188   E. D. Hirsch, *Cultural Literacy* (Boston: Houghton Mifflin, 1987).

188   A. Bloom, *The Closing of the American Mind* (New York: Simon and
       Schuster, 1987).

191   The contrasting pulls on education are discussed in O. Handlin, *The
       Uprooted* (Boston: Little, Brown, 1952).

192   On the common schools, see R. Butts and L. Cremin, *A History of
       Education in American Culture* (New York: Holt, 1953); L. Cremin,
       The American Common School (New York: Teachers College Press,

1951); L. Cremin, *American Education: The National Experience 1783–1876* (New York: Harper and Row, 1982); D. Tyack, *The One Best System* (Cambridge: Harvard University Press, 1974). Horace Mann's comment is quoted in L. Cremin, *American Education: The Metropolitan Experience 1876–1980* (New York: Harper and Row, 1988), 137.

193   Progressive education is discussed in L. Cremin, *The Transformation of the School* (New York: Knopf, 1961); L. Cremin, *Traditions of American Education* (New York: Basic Books, 1977); N. Wilson, "Remembering a Progressive Education," *Pathways* 6 (2 [1990]): 10–13.

193   On progressive education, see L. Cremin, *Transformation*, just cited; J. Dewey, *The School and Society* (Chicago: University of Chicago Press, 1967 [original publication 1899]); *Democracy and Education* (New York: Macmillan, 1916); F. Parker, *Notes on Teaching* (New York: E. L. Kellogg, 1883).

194   On the Eight-Year Study, see W. Aiken, *The Story of the Eight-Year Study* (New York: Harper, 1942); P. Minuchin, *The Psychological Impact of School Experience: A Comparison Study of Nine-Year-Old Children in Contrasting Schools* (New York: Basic Books, 1969).

194   L. Cremin, *Transformation* [193].

195   On the limits of progressive education, see P. Graham, *Progressive Education from Arcady to Academe* (New York: Teachers College Press, 1967).

196   E. C. Lagemann, "The Plural Worlds of Educational Research," *History of Education Quarterly* 29 (1989): 185–213; the quotation is from p. 185.

Chapter 11. Education for Understanding During the Early Years

200   Children's museums are discussed in F. Oppenheimer, "Everyone Is You . . . or Me," *Technology Review* 78 (7 [1976]); R. Gelman, "Constructivism and Supporting Environments," in D. Tirosh, ed., *Implicit and Explicit Knowledge: An Educational Approach* (New York: Ablex, in press).

205   On Project Spectrum, see U. Malkus, D. H. Feldman, and H. Gardner, "Dimensions of Mind in Early Childhood," in A. Pelligrini, ed., *The Psychological Bases of Early Childhood* (Chichester, England: Wiley, 1988), 25–38; M. Krechevsky and H. Gardner, "The Emergence and Nurturance of Multiple Intelligences," in M. Howe, ed., *Encouraging the Development of Exceptional Abilities and Talents* (in press).

210   Exemplary preschool education programs are described in J. Bauch, ed., *Early Childhood Education in the Schools* (Washington, D.C.: National Education Association, 1988).

211   On the whole-language approach, see N. Atwell, *In the Middle* (Portsmouth, N.H.: Heinemann, 1987); G. Bissex, *GNYS AT WRK: A Child Learns to Write and Read* (Cambridge: Harvard University Press, 1980); L. M. Calkins, *Living between the Lines* (Portsmouth, N.H.: Heinemann, 1990); D. Graves, *Balance the Basics: Let Them Write* (New York: Ford Foundation, 1978); J. Harste, V. Woodward, and C. Burke, *Language Stories and Literary Lessons* (Portsmouth, N.H.: Heinemann, 1984); D. Taylor, ed., Special Issue on Assessment in Whole Language Teaching, *English Education* 22 (1 [February 1990]).

212   On incorporating mathematics in the atmosphere of the primary school, see O. de la Rocha, "Problems of Sense and Problems of Scale: An Ethnographic Study of Arithmetic in Everyday Life" (Unpublished doctoral dissertation, University of California at Irvine, 1986); J. Easley and E. Easley, *Math Can Be Natural: Kitameno Priorities Introduced to American Teachers* (Urbana, Ill.: Committee on Culture and Cognition, University of Illinois, 1982, publication #23); M. Lampert, "When the Problem Is Not the Question and the Solution Is Not the Answer: Mathematical Knowing and Teaching," *American Educational Research Journal* 27 (1990): 29–64; R. Lawler, "The Progressive Construction of Mind," *Cognitive Science* 5 (1981): 1039; D. Newman, M. Cole, and P. Griffin, *In the Construction Zone* (New York: Cambridge University Press, 1989); R. Pea and J. Greeno, Presentation at the American Educational Research Association, Boston, 1990; A. Schoenfeld, "Learning to Think Mathematically: Problem-Solving, Metacognition, and Sense-Making in Mathematics," in D. Gouws, ed., *Handbook for Research on Mathematics Teaching and Learning* (New York: Macmillan, 1990); J. A. Turner, "From Gerolamo Cardano to the Fighting Bernoulli Brothers, a Math Professor Brings the Great Mathematicians to Life," *Chronicle of Higher Education* (July 18, 1990), A13.

212   Early science education is discussed in E. Duckworth, *The Having of Wonderful Ideas and Other Essays* (New York: Teachers College Press, 1987); G. Forman and M. Kaden, "Research on Science Education for Young Children," in C. Seefelt, ed., *The Early Childhood Curriculum: A Review of Current Research* (New York: Teachers College Press, 1987), 141–42; B. Watson and R. Konicek, "Teaching for Conceptual Change: Confronting Children's Experience," *Phi Delta Kappan* (May 1990): 680–85.

215   On the Key School, see L. Olson, "Children Flourish Here: Eight Teachers and a Theory Changed a School," *Education Week* 7 (1 [1988]): 18–19; M. Winn, "New Views of Human Intelligence," *New York Times Magazine, Part 2: The Good Health Magazine* (April 29, 1990): 16–17, 28–29.

216   Assessment of projects is discussed in H. Gardner, "Assessment in Context: The Alternative to Standardized Testing," in B. Gifford and M. Connor, eds., *Future Assessment: Changing Views of Aptitude, Achievement, and Instruction* (Boston: Kluwer Press, in press).

217   The role of cooperation in learning is discussed in B. Rogoff, *Apprenticeship in Thinking* (New York: Oxford University Press, 1990); R. Slavin, *Cooperative Learning* (New York: Longman, 1983).

219   Other experimental programs are described in W. S. Hopfenberg et al., "Toward Accelerated Middle Schools" (Report submitted to the Edna McConnell Clark Foundation, New York City, August 1990); S. Pogrow, "Teaching Thinking to At-Risk Elementary Students," *Educational Leadership* 46 (April 1988): 79–85.

219   The after-school program in San Diego is described in D. Newman, M. Cole, and P. Griffin, *The Construction Zone* (New York: Cambridge University Press, 1989); see also C. Bereiter and M. Scardamalia, "Intentional Learning as a Goal of Instruction," in L. Resnick, ed., *Knowing, Learning, and Instruction* (Hillsdale, N.J.: Erlbaum, 1989).

220   On reciprocal teaching, see A. L. Brown and A. S. Palincsar, "Guided, Cooperative Learning and Individual Knowledge Acquisition," in L. Resnick, ed., *Knowing, Learning, and Instruction* (Hillsdale, N.J.: Erlbaum, 1989), 393–452; A. Palincsar and A. L. Brown, "Reciprocal Teaching of Comprehension-Fostering and Comprehension-Monitoring Activities," *Cognition and Instruction* 1 (1984): 117–76.

221   Japanese classroom procedures are described in V. L. Hamilton et. al., "Japanese and American Children's Reasons for the Things They Do in School," *American Educational Research Journal* 26 (4 [1989]): 545–71; G. Hatano, "Learning to Add and Subtract: A Japanese Perspective," in T. P. Carpenter, J. M. Moser, and T. A. Romberg, eds., *Addition and Subtraction: A Cognitive Perspective* (Hillsdale, N.J.: Erlbaum, 1982), 211–23; J. Stigler and M. Perry, "Mathematics Learning in Japanese, Chinese, and American Classrooms," in G. Saxe and M. Gearhart, eds., *Children's Mathematics: New Directions for Child Development* (San Francisco: Jossey Bass, 1988), 27–54; M. White, *The Japanese Educational Challenge: A Commitment to Children* (New York: Free Press, 1987).

221   M. Lampert, "When the Problem Is Not the Question and the Solution Is Not the Answer: Mathematical Knowing and Teaching," *American Educational Research Journal* 27 (1 [Spring 1990]): 29–63.

222   *Jasper* is described in J. D. Bransford et al., "New Approaches to Instruction: Because Wisdom Can't Be Told" (Paper presented at the Conference on Similarity and Analogy, University of Illinois, June 1986). Immigrant materials are available from Harvard Project Zero, Cambridge, Mass.

Chapter 12. Education for Understanding During the Adolescent Years

227   R. Osborne, "Children's Dynamics," *The Physics Teacher* (November 1984): 504–608.

229   Roschelle's Envisioning Machine is described in J. Greeno, "Situations, Mental Models, and Generative Knowledge" (Institute for Research in Learning, Technical Report No. 5, Palo Alto, Calif., 1988); J. Roschelle, "Designing for Conversations" (Paper presented at the AAAI Symposium on Knowledge-Based Environments for Learning and Teaching, Stanford University, March 1990).

230   ThinkerTools are described in B. White and P. Horwitz, "Thinker-Tools: Enabling Children to Understand Physical Laws" (Technical Report #6470, Bolt, Beranek, and Newman, Cambridge, Mass., 1987); B. White, "Sources of Difficulty in Understanding Newtonian Dynamics," *Cognitive Science* 7 (1 [1983]): 41–65.

231   The *Visual Almanac* has been demonstrated at several conferences and is on display at the Computer Museum in Boston.

233   The Geometric Supposer is described in J. Schwartz and M. Yerushalmy, "The Geometric Supposer: Using Microcomputers to Restore Invention to the Learning of Mathematics," in D. N. Perkins, J. Lochhead, and J. Bishop, eds., *Thinking: Proceedings of the Second International Conference* (Hillsdale, N.J.: Erlbaum, 1987), 525–36; J. Schwartz, "The Power and the Peril of the Particular: Thoughts on a Role for Microcomputers in Science and Mathematics Education," in V. A. Howard, ed., *Varieties of Thinking* (New York: Routledge, 1990), 76–83; see also C. M. Krohn, " 'There's a Mirror': Learners, Representations, and Comparing Decimals" (Unpublished paper, Stanford University School of Education, 1990).

234   Projects of the Technology Education Research Centers are described in "Microcomputers in Education—Innovations and Issues: Hands On" (Technical Education Research Centers, Cambridge, Mass., 1990); "Measuring and Modeling Projects" (First Year Annual Report, Technical Education Resources Center, Cambridge, Mass., July 1990).

235   On overcoming misconceptions in physics, see J. Clement, "Overcoming Students' Misconceptions in Physics: The Role of Anchoring Intuitions and Analogical Validity," in J. D. Novak, ed., *Proceedings of the Second International Seminar on Misconceptions and Educational Strategies in Science and Mathematics*, vol. 3 (Ithaca, N.Y.: Cornell University Department of Education, 1987), 84–97; J. Minstrell and E. Hunt, "Diagnoser: A Computer Program That Assists Students in Thinking about Their Own Thinking" (Presentation at the McDonnell Workshop on Cognitive Studies in Education, Pittsburgh, December 1990).

235   Overcoming misconceptions in algebra is discussed in E. Solloway, J. Lochhead, and J. Clement, "Does Computer Programming Enhance Problem-Solving Ability? Some Positive Evidence on Algebra Word Problems," in R. J. Seidel, R. Anderson, and B. Hunter, eds., *Computer Literacy: Issues and Directions for 1985* (New York: Academic Press, 1982); J. Lochhead, "Some Ways in Which Computer Technology May Be Used to Improve the Reasoning Capabilities of Students" (Unpublished paper, University of Massachusetts at Amherst, 1985).

235   Overcoming misconceptions in biology is discussed in S. Carey, *Conceptual Change in Childhood* (Cambridge: MIT Press, 1985); D. Perkins et al., "Inside Understanding," in D. Perkins et al., *Teaching for Understanding in the Age of Technology* (in press).

237   Long-time exposure to works of art has been studied by J. Pazienza, in unpublished research, Pennsylvania State University, 1988.

237   Dealing with stereotypes in arts and humanities was discussed by B. Bailyn in a seminar presented to the Spencer Workshop on Understanding (May 8, 1990); see also T. Holt, *Thinking Historically* (New York: College Board, 1990).

238   On Arts PROPEL, see H. Gardner, "Zero-Based Arts Education: An Introduction to Arts PROPEL," *Studies in Art Education* 30 (2 [1989]): 71–83; *Portfolio*, Issues 1–5 (Publication of Harvard Project Zero and Educational Testing Services, 1988–91); D. Wolf, "Portfolio Assessment: Sampling Student Work," *Educational Leadership* 46 (7 [1989]): 35–39.

241   On creating a culture with high standards, see R. Berger, "Building a School Culture Where Quality Is 'Cool,' " *Harvard Education Letter* (in press).

245   On foundational thinking, see M. Lipman, A. M. Sharp, and F. Oscanyan, *Philosophy in the Classroom* (Philadelphia: Temple University Press, 1980); G. Mathews, *Philosophy and the Young Child* (Cambridge: Harvard University Press, 1980).

246   On the esthetic stand, see M. Parson, *How We Understand Art* (New York: Cambridge University Press, 1987).

247   P. Frank, *Einstein: His Life and Times* (New York: Knopf, 1953), 9.

247   On the prospects for overcoming misconceptions, see R. Case, "Gearing the Demands of Instruction to the Developmental Capacities of the Learner, *Review of Educational Research* 45 (1 [1975]): 59–87.

Chapter 13. Toward National and Global Understandings

252   On restructuring the schools, see A. Shanker, "Restructuring Our Schools," *Peabody Journal of Education* 65 (3 [Spring 1988]): 88–100.

257   Pressures against changing schools are discussed in J. Cannell, *Nationally Normed Elementary Achievement Teaching in America's Public Schools: How All Fifty States Are Above the National Average* (Daniels, W.V.: Friends in Education, 1987); D. Cohen and P. Peterson, *Report on California Mathematics Curriculum* (Center for Research on Teaching, Michigan State University, 1990).

257   Explanations of students' poor performances are discussed in C. Dweck and J. Bempechat, "Children's Theories of Intelligence: Consequences for Learning," in S. G. Paris, G. M. Olson, and H. W. Stevenson, eds., *Learning and Motivation in the Classroom* (Hillsdale, N.J.: Erlbaum, 1983).

258   On national understandings, see H. Gardner, "The Academic Community Must Not Shun the Debate on How to Set National Educational Goals," *The Chronicle of Higher Education* (November 8, 1989), A52.

259   Performance-based assessments are described in *Assessment at Alverno*, 2d. (Milwaukee: Alverno College, 1985); J. B. Baron et al., "Toward a New Generation of Student Outcome Measures: Connecticut's Common Core of Learning Assessment" (Paper presented at the American Education Research Association, San Francisco, March 1989); J. R. Frederiksen and A. Collins, "A Systems Approach to Educational Testing," *Educational Researcher* (December 1989): 27–32; G. Wiggins, "A True Test: Toward More Authentic and Equitable Assessment," *Phi Delta Kappan* (May 1989): 703–13.

259   On national curriculum standards, see Project 2061, *Science for All Americans* (Washington, D.C.: American Association for the Advancement of Science, 1989); National Research Council, *Everybody Counts: A Report to the Nation on the Future of Mathematics Education* (Washington, D.C.: National Academy Press, 1989). See also E. Culotta, "Can Science Education Be Saved?" *Science* 250 (December 1990): 1327–30; M. Barinaga, "Bottom-Up Revolution in Science Teaching," *Science*, 249 (August 1990): 977–79; L. B. Resnick and L. E. Klopfer, eds., *Toward the Thinking Curriculum: Current Cognitive Research* (Washington, D.C.: Association for Supervision and Curriculum Development, 1989).

259   National Board of Professional Teaching Standards, *A Nation Prepared: The Report of the Task Force on Teaching as a Profession* (Washington, D.C.: Carnegie Forum on Education and the Econ-

omy, May 1986). See also G. Maeroff, *The Empowerment of Teachers* (New York: Teachers College Press, 1988).

261   On various promising experiments, see J. Comer, "Educating Poor Minority Students," *Scientific American* 259 (5 [1988]): 42–48; T. Sizer, *Horace's Compromise* (Boston: Houghton Mifflin, 1984); see also the regular publication *Horace*, issued by the Brown University–based Coalition of Essential Schools.

261   For references to the work of Levin and Pogrow, see note to page 219.

261   For other instances, see D. S. Ogle, W. T. Pink, and B. F. Jones, eds., *Restructuring to Promote Learning in America's Schools* (Elmhurst, Ill.: North Central Regional Educational Laboratory, 1990).

261   On going through the motions of reform, see D. Cohen and P. Peterson, *Report on California Mathematical Curriculum* (Unpublished report, Michigan State University, East Lansing, Mich., 1990).

263   L. Kohlberg and R. Mayer, "Development as the Aim of Education," *Harvard Educational Review* 42 (4 [1972]): 449–96; for an elaboration of my views, see H. Gardner, "The Tension between Education and Development" (The Lawrence Kohlberg Memorial Lecture, delivered at Notre Dame University, November 1990); see also D. Hawkins, *The Informed Vision: Essays on Learning and Human Nature* (New York: Agathon Press, 1974).

263   On the effects of culture on learning, see J. S. Bruner, *Acts of Meaning* (Cambridge: Harvard University Press, 1990); C. Geertz, *The Interpretation of Culture* (New York: Basic Books, 1973); L. Vygotsky, *Mind in Society* (Cambridge: Harvard University Press, 1978).

264   I. Stravinsky, *The Poetics of Music* (Cambridge: Harvard University Press, 1970 [originally published 1942]), 42.

Name Index

Aristotle, 190

Bailyn, Bernard, 238
Bamberger, Jeanne, 175–177
Baron, Jonathan, 171
Bates, Elizabeth, 77
Berkeley, George, 34
Bloom, Allan, 188, 189–191, 198
Bransford, John, 222
Brown, Ann, 90
Bruner, Jerome, xii, 39, 58, 63, 77, 263

Carey, Susan, 91, 158, 235
Case, Robbie, xi, 30, 88
Cassirer, Ernst, 56
Chardin, Jean-Baptiste-Simeon, 112

Chomsky, Noam, 32–35, 38, 39, 40, 58, 61, 62, 64, 72
Clement, John, 154, 160
Cobb, Paul, 164
Cole, Michael, 39, 136, 150
Coles, Robert, 100
Columbus, Christopher, 11, 229, 232
Comer, James, 261
Cremin, Lawrence, xii, 194

Darwin, Charles, 23, 26, 40, 41
DeLoache, Judy, 77
DeMan, Paul, 179
Derrida, Jacques, 178–179
Descartes, René, 42–43
Dewey, John, 193, 195, 196, 199, 210
Dickens, Charles, 249
DiSessa, Andrea, 89, 152–153
Donne, John, 177

Subject Index

algorithms, 151–152, 159–166, 226–227, 233–236; *see also* mathematics; misconceptions; stereotypes

apprenticeship, 13, 17–18, 19, 121–125, 127, 147, 181, 200– 201, 203, 252; in the arts, 241–242; in early childhood education, 206, 207–208; in middle childhood, 214–219, 225–226; *see also* educational and cultural institutions; museums; schools

arts and humanities, 117–118, 236–243; children's aesthetic values, 100–101, 178; multiple stances in, 236–238, 247; stereotypes and simplifications in, 4, 151–152, 166, 167, 172–179; U-shaped development in, 107–108, 109; *see also* history; literature; music; poetry; stereotypes

Arts PROPEL, 238–243

assessment, 132–134, 141–142, 145; in the arts, 239–241; in context, 204–205; in educational reform, 253–254, 259–260; and individual differences, 12–13, 14; new forms of, 145; in progresive education, 197–198, 210; of projects, 217–218; Spectrum Report, 207–209; *see also* national examinations; performances; portfolios; tests

basic skills, 119–120, 186, 190, 198, 201; limits of, 186–188; in progressive education, 196; reforms for mastery of, 203–304; *see also* educational approaches; literacy; mathematics; reading; writing

behaviorism, 24–25, 31, 38

bias, *see* constraints

biology, misconceptions in, 158–159, 235–236; *see also* science; intuitive theories, of life; evolution, theory of

297